D1571114

ALONG FOR THE RIDE

ALONG FOR THE RIDE

Navigating Through the Cold War, Vietnam, Laos & More

HENRY ZEYBEL

CASEMATE

Philadelphia & Oxford

Published in the United States of America and Great Britain in 2021 by
CASEMATE PUBLISHERS
1950 Lawrence Road, Havertown, PA 19083, USA
and
The Old Music Hall, 106–108 Cowley Road, Oxford OX4 1JE, UK

Copyright 2021 © Henry Zeybel

Hardback Edition: ISBN 978-1-63624-038-1
Digital Edition: ISBN 978-1-63624-039-8

A CIP record for this book is available from the British Library

Printed and bound in the United States of America by Sheridan

For a complete list of Casemate titles, please contact:

CASEMATE PUBLISHERS (US)
Telephone (610) 853-9131
Fax (610) 853-9146
Email: casemate@casematepublishers.com
www.casematepublishers.com

CASEMATE PUBLISHERS (UK)
Telephone (01865) 241249
Email: casemate-uk@casematepublishers.co.uk
www.casematepublishers.co.uk

To Janice Lea;
my mother and father;
and the many other people who allowed me to
choose my own path through life,
right and wrong, good and bad.

Contents

Preface: My Heroes Have Always Been Soldiers

The woman stared deeply into my green eyes. I was the only Westerner at a birthday party in a Bangkok nightclub. The year was 1970—the Vietnam War era. She took my hand, studied my palm, and spoke to me in Thai. Prawat Lojananont—who once had been my student at Squadron Officer School—translated her words: "She says you will have much health. Also, you will not die by accident." I said, "She's goddamn right. Those little bastards in Laos shoot at us deliberately." Prawat placed a hand on my shoulder and said, "Yes. And to die of thirst in the jungle or to die as the result of prolonged torture is no accident."

As it turned out, neither of Prawat's fates became mine, but they did happen to too many guys who were a lot better than me. So let me tell you what did happen to me and, along the way, relate the exploits of other Air Force officers I knew and worked with for more than 20 years. I promise stories that will deliver insight, controversy, thrills, and chills, along with laughs if you enjoy black humor. If the writing goes as planned, I might cleanse that sin-crusted lump that represents my heart.

Writing beats going to a "shrink." I've tried the two. Done properly, both take years of self-analysis and both reveal great wads of hidden knowledge. But writing differs from psychoanalysis in that strangers pay the patient (in other words: Please, buy this book) instead of the patient paying a stranger. But then, money is only money. What can it do beyond purchasing political power and capturing the attention of attractive women?

My aim as a writer has been to tell entertaining stories. Perhaps my goal evolved from the fact that my father wrote for *The Pittsburgh Press* for 45 years, working his way up from copy boy to financial editor. Like him, I merely want to be a good reporter. Cynics claim anyone who writes for any reason other than making as much money as possible is an idiot. If that's true, sit back and prepare to read the remembrances of a fool.

★ ★ ★

My father did not serve in the armed forces, being too young for World War I and too old for the Second. During World War II, however, he befriended dozens of GI Joes who visited *The Press* or came from Pittsburgh's North Side neighborhood where he grew up. Weekly, we hosted somebody in uniform. I listened spellbound to tales of adventure while my father poured Canadian whiskey and my mother served snacks on gold-trimmed Noritake china.

Soldiers who sat in our living room became my heroes—from trim Captain Ed Rittenbaugh, who piloted artillery-spotting Piper Cubs, to a pair of burly ANZAC infantrymen who wore their overseas caps at such a jaunty tilt that, I think, my mother fell in love with both of them. I can still picture Captain Ed's khaki green coat with the crossed golden muskets of the infantryman and his silver-tan pants. Jesus, I wanted to be him. Does the man make the uniform or does the uniform make the man? When a muscular submariner named Libencheck unfurled a tattered Japanese battle flag across our couch, my life felt complete.

My hero of heroes was Sergeant Leonard "Tex" Gilmore, an uncle by marriage. In a time when six-footers ranked as truly tall, at six-two and with blond hair and Newman-blue eyes, he walked through crowds like Gulliver among the Lilliputians. Having come from "way out west" in West Virginia, he perfectly fulfilled Pittsburghers' image of "Tex." He enlisted in the army before the Japanese attacked Pearl Harbor, went to England with the initial shipment of troops, and ended up in Germany. I wrote V-mail letters to him and, for his eyes alone, included my drawings of battle scenes of American forces slaughtering the Nazis, scenes he was likely living through on the advance across France.

The intensity of the war impacted me daily because I plotted its progress by pinning tiny battle flags to a map of the world on a wall beside my bed. In the evening I spread Pittsburgh's three newspapers—*Press*, *Post-Gazette*, and *Sun-Telegraph*—on the living room floor, culled the war news, good or bad, and translated my findings to the map. As the Japanese advanced across the Pacific, my replacing the Stars and Stripes with the Rising Sun struck me like a personal defeat. But after the United States took the offensive, removing a Japanese flag scored a personal triumph. Of course, the Pacific's island by island battles made any advance definitive. Meanwhile, plotting the war in North Africa and Italy proved more complex and involved tiny towns where American, British, German, and Italian flags shared the same pinhole. Following D-Day in Europe, American and German flags formed dense offensive and defensive lines pressed tightly against each other. Advancing an American flag a 16th of an inch made my day.

After the troops returned from overseas, I shook hands with Sergeant Charles "Commando" Kelly, the North Side's pride as the first enlisted man awarded the Medal of Honor on the European continent. My father and I met him on the sidewalk in front of Zeyfang and Thomas' saloon on Madison Avenue. He wore street clothes but grinned with the confidence of a military hero. He took my hand with both of his as if I were the important person and said, "Good luck to you, pal." I felt blessed.

And then, decades after that, I found myself sitting in our home, once filled with World War II heroes, telling tales of Southeast Asian adventures to my father. Without ceremony, I assumed the place of men I had worshipped. Yet my suit of knightly armor did not fit exactly right; in my mind, I could not radiate the pure and shining glow of my childhood heroes, the men from "The Good War" that saved the world.

CHAPTER I

Downtown Tchepone

"As of this moment, once you find a truck, you will stay with it until it is destroyed or damaged. You will not be driven off by antiaircraft fire," Lieutenant Colonel Ken "Grouchy Bear" Harris announced at a special meeting for only the officers of the 16th Special Operations Squadron—Spectre. "You will hang in there and live with the antiaircraft fire. Nobody ever told you it would be easy. Now let's kill trucks. And no more excuses." Scanning the hundred or so warm bodies in the briefing room, he asked, "Do I make myself clear? Are there any questions?"

Nobody in the audience spoke. The crewmen understood Harris's idea of a group discussion: You are the group and I will do the discussing. As my dear departed mother often said, "The boss is always a son of a bitch." But on my own, I learned to love SOBs that made the right calls.

As commander of the only AC-130 gunship squadron in the United States Air Force, Harris spoke within his jurisdiction and his attitude was justified. For a week, he had read After Battle Reports and had grown angry with aircraft commanders who explained they had searched out but failed to destroy trucks because of intense groundfire. In his eyes, they did nothing but waste time and resources. Such reports drove him wild.

In typical military fashion, Harris's blanket indictment accused every man of guilt, whereas only a small minority of aircraft commanders had broken off attacks. Therefore, his declaration created unanimous resentment: the guilty felt misunderstood, while the innocent saw themselves as unjustly convicted.

Harris's decision would have been easier to accept if the crews hadn't been doing their job of killing trucks along the Ho Chi Minh Trail in Laos in larger numbers than anyone had thought possible. In the dry season from November 1970 to May 1971, Spectre destroyed more than 10,000 and damaged nearly 3,000 vehicles. Now it was early April 1971 and Harris knew we had no more than a month before the southwestern monsoon pushed low clouds across the Laotian panhandle and vehicles of the North Vietnamese Army's 559th Transportation Group ground to a halt as heavy rains turned the region into a quagmire. Then, for Spectre, the war stopped until the trucks resumed rolling approximately six months hence when the monsoon reversed and weather over the Trail cleared.

Along with killing trucks, Spectre crewmen had already eaten enough flak to exist on an iron-free diet for the rest of their lives. As the dry season progressed, antiaircraft fire over the Trail grew thicker and thicker. The NVA moved in more and more 57-mm guns to support its extensive 37-mm network. Spectre's salvation was that none of the guns had radar control. But some of the six-pound 57-mm rounds were magnum and/ or tracerless. Our crew's rear scanner described them best: "Magnum rounds? Zing-bang! They're on you before you know it. Dodging them is pure knee jerk. And tracerless? Definitely something else. It goes off in your face with no warning, makes your heart just leap. There should be a rule in the Geneva Conventions against using scary shit like that." Worse than growing thicker, flak had become accurate. In the week before Harris's speech, two gunships had suffered major battle damage. The crews had a right for concern, perhaps caution.

Naturally, Grouchy Bear Harris knew that. He would win no medal for tact, however. His nickname proved his spirit, but he asked no more of his troops than what he produced. For a semi-old guy, he flew the AC-130 and shot better than the average bear. I liked Harris. He was congruent. When pleased, he showed it with big, honest smiles and left no doubt in anyone's mind as to when he was pissed off. He'd look daggers. He and our crew's pilot, Major Ed Holley, had similar personalities: hardnosed, single-minded, goal-oriented, and loyal beyond belief to men who were loyal to them. Harris and Holley were physically alike too: tall, husky, lumbering types—the Bear and the Elephant. With a little imagination they could have passed for father and son. About ten years older, Harris had developed deep lines in his face and neck that, when added to his thick black hair and heavy features, gave him a rugged handsomeness that Holley was only beginning to acquire. And they both loved gunships.

The AC-130 Spectre was the final product in a line of weapon systems that evolved from the AC-47 Spooky through the AC-119 Stinger. Converted from cargo planes, gunships were designed to orbit slowly at low altitudes and use side-firing weapons to destroy targets. Spectre was the ultimate truckbuster. F-4 Phantom pilots who escorted us called Spectre "The Fabulous Four-engine Fighter." Painted solid black on the outside and with the left side of its fuselage lined with gun ports and protruding weapons, a Spectre gunship was reminiscent of a pirate ship. Two 20-mm Vulcan cannons, six-barrel Gatling guns capable of firing 2500 rounds per minute, stuck out ahead of the left main wheel well. Above the well, a pair of 7.62-mm machinegun modules, also six-barrel, provided fire at the rate of either 3000 or 6000 rounds per minute. Aft, two 40-mm Bofors that could pump 100 two-pound shells a minute provided the primary punch for killing trucks.

Although the Trail bristled with antiaircraft artillery (triple-A), the NVA's primary defense was darkness. Few trucks moved in daylight. Therefore, Spectre carried an array of sensors that permitted crewmen to see in the dark. A high-resolution infrared detector (IR) and low-light-level television camera (TV), with wide angle and telephoto lenses, worked in conjunction with a Black Crow sensor (BC) that detected electro-magnetic radiation from internal combustion engines. The BC showed targets as green blips on an oscilloscope. The IR and TV provided black-and-white pictures. A video recorder taped battle action. A gunship's three-man sensor team could do everything but sniff out the enemy.

Following Harris' edict, Ed Holley made no comment because he had no need for concern: he had never backed off from a target. Strangely enough, however, somewhere in the brain of the bravest warrior lurked a single cell of self-doubt. The night after calling his special meeting, Harris showed up unannounced to fly with our crew. Holley's single cell of doubt erupted into a tumor. He whispered to me, "Did you know he was coming?"

I shook my head and said, "I didn't even hear him breathing hard."

In no mood for humor, Holley whispered, "Why do you think he's here? What's up? You have any idea?"

Harris said he wanted to fly as copilot and Holley's tumor turned malignant: The Man intended to sit and watch and take notes, he thought, and in some way make an example of perhaps the entire crew. Achievements that had gone before—his 103 missions, the 930 trucks damaged or destroyed—had no validity now, Holley concluded. He determined that once again he must prove, beyond the slightest suspicion, his crew's skill and courage under fire—but primarily courage. Holley quietly told Major Dick Kauffman, our navigator, "I want to go to Tchepone straight off. Downtown."

Major Jim Ballsmith, our BC operator, exhaled loudly.

Captain Lee Schuiten, IR, stared at me.

I shrugged. I manned the TV. I outranked Holley, but he was the pilot and the pilot was the aircraft commander. If he wanted to fly us to hell, it was okay with me. Less than a month before, his flying skill had saved all our lives. In my eyes, he could do no wrong.

Actually, I could have challenged his plan. The Spectre commander before Harris had declared the area within three miles of the center of Tchepone off-limits to gunships simply because the triple-A was too heavily concentrated there. That order hadn't stopped our crew from poaching along the edge of the area and, although we sucked up a lot of flak, the tactic proved worthwhile because we found and destroyed a lot of trucks.

After finishing with Kauffman, Holley said to Schuiten, Ballsmith, and me, "When we get there, find something right away." We nodded. It would be impossible not to find something, I thought. And our crew's gunners used to complain that they had no say in what we did. If only they knew.

A full Spectre crew numbered thirteen: seven officers (pilot, copilot, navigator, IR operator, TV operator, BC operator, and a frequently unmanned fire control officer FCO position) plus six enlisted men (flight engineer, three weapon mechanics/loaders called "gunners," and two scanners).

As ordered, Kauffman navigated us directly to Tchepone. On BC, Ballsmith picked up blips from miles out. Schuiten locked the IR onto a convoy of eight trucks about a mile from the center of town. Flying 9,500 feet above the terrain, Holley rolled into a 30-degree left bank and went to work with a Forty: "Ka-pung. Ka-pung, ka-pung, ka-pung. Ka-pung. Ka-pung, ka-pung, ka-pung." One. One-two-three. One. One-two-three. Over and over and over. Ed's firing rhythm was so perfect that we could have danced to it.

We completed three orbits before the antiaircraft artillery opened up: one moment we sailed along undisturbed and the next moment continuous streams of fire chased us. The scanners sounded like two auctioneers simultaneously trying to sell different items to the same audience. "Two o'clock, five rounds," said Sergeant Scotty Wolf, the right scanner, "no problem. One o'clock, three rounds, hold what ya—"

"Nine o'clock, four rounds, accurate, break right," rear scanner Staff Sergeant Bob Savage shouted. Like eyes in the back of the pilot's head, he provided a view of the vulnerable six o'clock low position—the pilot's blind spot.

"Got it. Thanks," Holley said. He rolled out level until rounds passed on both sides of the gunship, rolled back into a left bank, realigned the computer, and resumed firing.

"Six o'clock, three, six, nine rounds, hold what you have," Savage said.

"Two o'clock, four rounds. Three o'clock, three rounds. No sweat," Wolf called.

"Eight o'clock, four rounds, accurate, break right," Savage shouted. The rounds detonated below and behind the turning aircraft. "Damn, that watered my eyes," he said. "I won—"

"Three o'clock, three rounds accurate. Oh shit. Stop!" Wolf's call was late and the rounds exploded directly in front of the gunship, lighting up the cockpit.

"Close," said Harris from the copilot's seat. "Damn close."

I laughed out loud at the right scanner's advice. Hollering "Stop" did as much good as closing your eyes to halt the plummeting Cyclone ride at Astroworld. Never before had I heard so many triple-A calls made so rapidly. Warnings flowed continuously from the two scanners. Of course, never before had I been to downtown Tchepone.

Apart from following the scanners' directions, Holley added evasive maneuvers of his own. I pictured him, hell-bent for glory, hunched over the wheel, steering a course that only he saw, pumping the rudder pedals with the fury of the Phantom of the Opera before an antiquated, aerospace pipe organ. Holley's maneuvers expanded beyond any normal pattern. The gunship's movements and firing tempo would have better accompanied a dance to a symphony by a madman.

Conditions grew worse.

All of Savage's calls became breakaways. Gunners reeled helplessly back and forth across the cargo compartment. Airman Chuck Heigist passed clips of 40-mm shells from a kneeling position to lower his center of balance. "I'm going to be black and blue for a month," Sergeant Jim Riffo moaned. One breakaway flung him off his feet. He bounced against the side of the sensor booth, momentarily caught his balance, and then was tossed against the number one Forty as it commenced firing. "Goddamn it to hell," he shouted and leapt back in surprise only to be thrown against the firing, rapidly cycling gun again. "How in hell can he shoot in the middle of this? Let's go, hurry up, pass the ammo."

Unless a target exploded or burned, a gunship pilot did not see it. He aimed and fired the guns by aligning electronic symbols on an illuminated panel. In essence, a computer display allowed him to aim where the sensors looked. Undaunted, Holley intersected segments along the ideal circular flight path from where he shot off long strings of 40-mm rounds. But his rhythm had left him. He blasted away as if trying to keep time to an album titled *Jimi Hendrix Goes Completely Fucking Nuts*.

In 20 minutes, Holley set fire to four trucks. "Look at them burn," he said to no one in particular. Or was he talking to Harris?

The three sensor operators (and FCO if assigned) sat in a 16-foot long by 8-foot high and wide room, called "the booth," located off center to the right in the middle of the cargo compartment. Now the booth was bedlam. It took every bit of Schuiten and my skills to hold the IR and TV crosshairs on target throughout Holley's erratic maneuvers. The sensor platforms slammed from one extreme to the other, taking stresses beyond design limits. As usual, we communicated without using interphone. Ballsmith had the duty of recording the number of rounds called by the scanners and he shouted, "That's a thousand."

"In twenty minutes?" I said. On an average mission we logged around 300–400 rounds. But that was over three or four hours. I couldn't recall taking more than 800 on an entire mission. "You sure?" I asked.

The scanners continued to call a steady stream of advice while the gunship lurched left and then right, shuddered briefly, then lurched right again and then left before Holley fired another dozen rounds.

"One thousand fifty," Ballsmith shouted.

When I lined up the TV crosshairs on one gunpit, a pit next to it opened fire. I swung onto the new pit and still another opened fire. Usually we hammered triple-A gunners who gave us too much grief, hosed streams of forties down on them. We owned the high ground. If a gunpit became a pain and our F-4 Phantom escorts were carrying smart bombs, we put one of those 2,000-pound beauties on it, guided the bomb right down the gun barrel using a laser targeting designator aligned with the TV. Doing that was like being a god and throwing lightning bolts, but that was another story from another time.

Tonight we had no escorts and nothing could have helped us. The whole world was a gunpit. Tracers blurred the television screen as their flashes overdrove the camera beam current and left long dark streaks on the monitor picture.

The gunship lurched, shuddered in a partial stall, yawed.

"What the fuck's Ed doing?" Schuiten shouted. He had both hands wrapped around the IR tracking control and was out of his seat, swaying, throwing his body weight against the handle to gain greater leverage. He was attempting to overpower electrical impulses with sheer physical force. Watching him futilely strangle the tracking control handle made me laugh. "Fuck," Schuiten screamed.

Then Holley violently pushed the plane's nose down, a maneuver that, like going over the top of a roller coaster ride, negated gravity inside the airplane. We became weightless. Holley recovered from his dive by hauling back on the control wheel and, like hitting the bottom of a roller coaster dip after a steep drop, we were jammed into our seats by the force of extra gravity. Clutching the tracking control handle for support, Schuiten stayed on his feet. Holley regained the lost altitude and resumed firing.

My mind classified that type of maneuver as unsafe in our high-wing aircraft—as if it fucking mattered. I aimlessly stirred the TV crosshairs from one triple-A site to another. The situation had lost meaning, had turned into a dream that made no sense. I could only wait for it to end. A rumbling laugh beyond my control bubbled out of me.

Thus spoke Holley: "Listen up, men. That's it. Those gunners have zeroed in on us. We've got to move."

In the booth we slumped in relief. Schuiten dropped into his seat. Ballsmith gave a thumbs up. I recognized that I had been contracting the muscles of my upper body and they felt as if I had just finished 20 minutes of push-ups.

"That's it for up here," Holley said. "We're going down to seventy-five hundred and that stuff will be above us."

Schuiten leaned backward and stretched out his arms as if awaiting crucifixion.

Ballsmith turned his thumb down.

Holley dived the aircraft 2,000 feet. For moments we again felt weightless. Holley maneuvered back into orbit, confirmed Kauffman had corrected the ballistics in the gunfire computer, and that Schuiten had a target, and resumed firing. After a couple of minutes, he said, "It worked. That stuff is going off above us. The gunners have the fuses set for the wrong altitude."

The intensity of the antiaircraft fire had decreased, probably because the loaders had tired or ran out of ammo.

"Doesn't he know," Schuiten said, "that shit has to go through this altitude to get up there?"

Ballsmith said, "I wish we'd take a nice clean hit so we could go home."

We destroyed the remaining trucks. In 45 minutes of orbiting, Ballsmith recorded 1,684 rounds shot at us. He later admitted missing several calls. "That's a low ball figure," he said.

Kauffman guided us away from Tchepone. Over the next two hours we searched out and destroyed two trucks and damaged four before running out of ammunition. Holley had been prodigal at Tchepone. Reserved and methodical in our work, we encountered little opposition from the ground: Kauffman knew Laos. One of his credos said: "If you want to find trucks, you have to go where the guns are. The NVA doesn't position guns to protect trees and karst. Find guns, you find trucks. If you don't want to get shot at, you won't find batches of trucks." We didn't find many trucks and nobody complained. Tomorrow was another day, after Holley got us through this one.

Back home at Ubon, in Thailand, we deplaned and boarded the waiting bus, dragging our feet as if walking the last mile. Harris took Holley's arm and led him behind a revetment wall, out of sight of the rest of us. Master Sergeant Mel Bean, our flight engineer who sat between but slightly aft of the pilot and copilot in the plane, grinned broadly when he saw them walk away. "I'll bet I know what he's saying," Bean said. "Major Holley turned Colonel Harris a little white knuckled. Shit was lighting up the sky like Fourth-a-July, you could read a newspaper from the flashes. Major Holley was jukin' around it and Colonel Harris was shaking his head and looking at me. Hell, it wasn't my place to say anything. You know how Major Holley is. He wouldn't look at Colonel Harris. He'd just watch the flak and fly through it and be back in the gunsight and blaze away. I'll admit, a few times I didn't think we'd make it. That Major Holley is a flying fool."

Somber faced, Harris and Holley reappeared and boarded the bus. Nobody spoke throughout the ride to the squadron building.

The following afternoon Harris met with the Spectre aircraft commanders. He explained that he had reconsidered his previous day's decision and realized that in certain situations discretion was better than valor. He flatly stated that he did not expect anyone to commit suicide in order to destroy trucks. Harris concluded his talk with an afterthought: he removed the restriction from operating over Tchepone.

CHAPTER 2

You Get What You Ask For

I flew 775 combat support sorties in Vietnam—transporting the living, wounded, and dead; making resupply air drops at Khe Sanh and in the A Shau Valley; relocating villagers; and performing an endless list of mundane tasks that qualified C-130 Hercules crewmen to be called "Trash Haulers." We got shot at on the ground and in the air without returning fire. That experience factored big in my decision to volunteer for a second tour in Southeast Asia. I wanted to shoot back and so requested assignment to B-26 Invaders that flew low-level strafing and bombing night strikes in Laos where, according to our government, no war existed. With just a two-man crew in the B-26, the navigator flew in the copilot seat, which offered the opportunity for plenty of up-close aggressive excitement. The mission promised to satisfy the onset of my middle-age crazies.

When I named the Invader, an assignment officer said, "That's not a choice I'd make." Because I volunteered for a second tour, however, he was committed to give me what I wanted. I ended our discussion by telling him, "But you're not me." Some caring cosmic thunderer must have been looking out for me because a week or so later, the Air Force removed the B-26 from its inventory: the planes' loss quotient had outgrown their productivity level, a quotient that included the deaths of two of my friends—Captains Jerry Stout and Larry Lively. As a consolation prize, I accepted a Spectre gunships crew slot.

Spectre crews shot a lot of things but, as I've already explained, the gunfire traveled in both directions. Often bluntly put, "Non-Christian gomers who didn't speak English were shooting at us with communist guns." And yet 37- and 57-mm antiaircraft artillery (triple-A) wasn't the worst of the threats.

★ ★ ★

We slaughtered them. As the night's first AC-130 Spectre gunship into Laos, we found *beaucoup* trucks plus more. In less than three hours, our crew, piloted by Ed Holley, destroyed 21 and damaged 15. In the booth in the belly of the gunship, we sensor operators gloated as if we had free passes to a shooting gallery. Normally, I operated the TV sensor, but that night I was giving on-the-job combat training to Major Ed Coogan. He had no other place to learn the trade: the dozen Spectre gunships flying out of Ubon Royal Thai Air Force Base were the only ones in the world.

On his first mission, Coogan wildly guided the attack, practically tripped over targets and set fire to most of what he found. Having the time of his life, he asked, "Is it always like this?" I nodded. Soon, on his own, he'd learn there was no Santa Claus.

With an hour of on-target fuel and a couple hundred 40-mm rounds remaining, we broke into laughter when Jim Ballsmith used his BC's electronic magic to lead us to 16 more vehicles. We appeared certain to run up our highest one-night score of the 1970–71 dry season.

The sight of that many untouched trucks keyed Coogan to a higher pitch. He jerked the TV's electronic crosshairs toward a truck and called, "TV tracking." IR sensor operator Lee Schuiten looked at me, started to speak, but sucked on a tooth instead. I shrugged, then suggested to Coogan, "You ought to take a break."

"No," he said. "I'm fine." Tightening his grip on the TV joystick, he hunched his shoulders like a dog guarding a bone. Looking into his eyes, I saw nothing but flaming trucks. He was afloat in a world of pure adrenalin. "Schuiten's ready to track targets for a while," I said.

Unwritten booth etiquette demanded that the TV and IR operators, such as Schuiten and I, shared in tracking targets, when possible. That was the fun part of the mission. Perhaps I had failed to explain booth protocol adequately, I decided, and said, "Hey, Coogan, you've shot thirty-six fuckin' trucks in a row. How 'bout giving Schuiten his turn."

Less than a minute later, with Coogan apologizing and Schuiten happily tracking, Holley set fire to the convoy leader. Kauffman, our navigator seated behind the pilots on the flight deck, best described the situation: "*Lam Son 719* was in progress and we were not allowed to fly east of Tchepone at the time, where the South Vietnamese Army had invaded. A lot of NVA [North Vietnamese Army] truck traffic was heading west, trying to end run the push on the ground. The triple-A was pretty intense. The trucks Ballsmith found were five miles southwest of Tchepone. When we pounded the group, multiple triple-A guns started up."

Coogan later said, "I knew I was an FNG [fucking new guy] without reference points, but I still couldn't believe the intensity of the triple-A. I kept hoping it wasn't going to be like this on every mission."

About then, Our Lady of Loreto or Saint Therese of Lisieux or Saint Joseph of Cupertino, or whichever bony relic supposedly protected the living flesh of fliers, snoozed off at the switch. Working a new truck, Holley fired one 40-mm round—"Ka-pung"—as if clearing his throat. In that short pause before he followed with his usual lethal burst of three, Ballsmith said, "I have a SAM activity light."

Holley did not fire. Nobody spoke. SAM was Death.

"I have a SAM activity light," Ballsmith repeated with conviction, as if trying to convince himself as much as the rest of the crew. The scope display on his Radar Homing and Warning (RHAW) gear indicated a surface-to-air missile (SAM) launch site was tracking our slow-moving, high-winged, four-engine airplane—the worst imaginable mismatch of the war. "Turn to a heading of two-seven-zero," Ballsmith said and locked unblinking eyes on his RHAW-gear.

Holley turned to the heading, putting the radar tracking site behind us, and then rammed the airspeed up to 185 knots. He said, "Are you pos—"

"I have a SAM ready-to-launch light," Ballsmith announced.

On board the gunship, everyone froze.

The SAM employed in Southeast Asia was the Soviet-built SA-2 (NATO codenamed *Guideline*) that, once it got humming, reached twice the speed of sound. Ground radar (NATO codenamed *Fan Song*) guided the missile. An SA-2's 300-pound high-explosive warhead detonated upon impact or upon command of a *Fan Song* operator.

The SA-2 had been designed for use against high performance aircraft, fast movers. A lot of swift F-4 Phantoms had outmaneuvered SA-2s, but a lot of them had also watched the missile eat their lunch. Our turkey was no match for missiles. Our predicament appeared similar to drifting along in an old South Sea steamer and being attacked by a torpedo-firing nuclear submarine.

Fliers knew North Vietnam was stacked wall-to-wall with SAM sites. However, to that date—2 March 1971—no SA-2s had been detected in Laos. Air Force Intelligence publications declared the *Guideline* had "poor cross-country ability and would not be expected to be deployed in forward areas." Did North Vietnamese planners not read those pubs?

I pulled out all of the control buttons on my intercom box and heard the high-pitched rattle, similar to a continuous whine, of the ground radar that had homed on us.

In training I had listened to tape recordings of ground radar activity. First came the short mid-range squeaks, several seconds apart, of the normal 360-degree search scan of *Fan Song*; each time the radar beam passed over the airplane, the RHAW-gear picked up and converted its energy to light signals, for the BC to read, and to sounds for the other crewmen to hear. When radar tracked the airplane, its sweep narrowed to a few degrees as it painted back and forth across the target; in the airplane, the RHAW-gear squeaks became higher pitched and more frequent, like twice a second. When the ground radar scan narrowed to approximately one degree for aiming a missile, the RHAW-gear picked up a high-pitched rattle. Instructors had likened the sound to a rattlesnake about to strike.

"I have a SAM launch light," Ballsmith said loudly and clearly. The RHAW-gear signaled a missile had been fired at the gunship.

"Ohhhhh," somebody moaned over interphone.

Kauffman later told me: "I could hardly believe how fast the enemy radar got on us with sweep location and an altitude finder. They suddenly barrage fired. We started to dance around the fire and the SAM radar came up and transitioned from low to high rate within seconds. Then Ballsmith called launch."

Acting like a pair of eyes in the back of the pilot's head and prone on the open aft cargo ramp, Bob Savage searched the blackness of the night.

A moment after Ballsmith's "SAM launch" call, he reported, "I saw a flash, six o'clock. Eight to ten miles." Held by a thin steel safety line, Savage leaned far beyond the edge of the ramp until he hung partially airborne in the aircraft's slipstream. "I saw another flash," he shouted over interphone, "think it was separation." The SA-2 had two stages, a liquid propelled and a solid fuel booster.

Savage recognized the missile engine's fire. "I see it," he shouted. "It's climbing. Turn right, sir." Holley banked hard right, and a moment later Savage said, "It turned with us. Break left, sir." Holley rolled hard to the left and again the missile turned with him. "It's leveling off," Savage said.

I looked at Coogan and grinned. The fire in his eyes had flickered out: already Santa Claus was dead.

"It's coming straight at us," Savage said. He later stated he had read accounts by fighter pilots who had described *Guidelines* as "the size of telephone poles." Nose to nose with one of the big white bastards, he agreed, the missile was huge. "It's coming in the ramp," he said. "Dive. Dive."

"Hang on," Holley said, "we're going down."

There have been great moments in sports when the man transcended the moment by calling his shot. Remember? "The Babe" pointing to the stands before belting a World Series homer! Underdog "Broadway Joe" predicting Super Bowl victory and then delivering it! Time and time again, Ali naming the round for a knockout! Those feats birthed immortality, but no such feat ever related to cheating death, calling the shot with premeditated certainty. That was what Holley was about to try: he intended to snatch 14 souls—including his own—from the gates of hell, exactly as he had told us he would.

Based on my instrument readings in the booth, from an altitude of 9500 feet, Holley rolled the gunship into a 135 degree bank, practically upside down, and then arced the nose earthward in a 4000-foot-per-minute dive. The maneuver was like turning over a dump truck and still steering it. Our turkey wasn't designed for such a feat. Yet Holley did it. Maintaining a positive one-gravity load on the creaky, antiquated airframe, he plunged downward in open defiance of several laws of aerodynamics.

On the flight deck, Kauffman viewed the maneuver from a different perspective: "We had already turned away from the source. I had logged our position. When Sergeant Savage said, 'Dive,' Holley rolled to the right. I was staring at the attitude gyro and watched it flash through ninety degrees of bank. Seconds later we passed a hundred twenty degrees of bank and then the gyro failed. I was calling barometric altimeter readings. I had the radar altimeter on and noted the height above the terrain at the start of the descent. When the gyro failed, I looked at the radar altimeter and it had no pulse to indicate height. I assumed it was looking sideways or upward. We pulled out, according to the barometric altimeter, at between fifteen hundred and two thousand feet. The elevation of the ground was six hundred feet in the area. Our heading was approximately one hundred eighty degrees difference from when we started the roll."

Throughout the maneuver, Kauffman's soothing voice spoke only to Holley: "Maximum terrain elevation is thirty-one hundred feet," which meant that somewhere in the general area below us a chunk of karst jutted that high. Acting as if he knew there definitely was a tomorrow, Kauffman calmly read the altitudes as we vertically flashed through them: "Eighty-five hundred feet…eight thousand feet…seventy-five hundred feet…." Old Gert Stein once wrote something like, "A rose is a rose is a rose." Had she described Holley and Kauffman in tandem, she would have said, "Cool is cool is cool. And then some."

While Kauffman tolled the altitudes, I shouted at Coogan, "Don't give up yet." I didn't know what he thought, but I put little faith in my words. I found it difficult to believe what we were doing. I aimlessly tapped the altitude indicator. The airplane did not have ejection seats. The crew had no choice but to ride it out.

Holley's maneuver was termed a "split-S." He had explained its use one morning over breakfast when the crew had been playing "What If…?" Thinking the unthinkable, I had asked, "What if they launch a SAM at us?" Everyone at the table had laughed, except Holley. Without hesitation he had said, "I'll dive and turn into it. The maneuver works for fighters. No reason it can't work for us." He had been irritated when his answer had brought more laughter. "I can do anything with a one-thirty that you can do with a jet," he had claimed, "only I do it lower and slower and tighter. I can escape from a SAM." He had called his shot. Now he was doing it—maybe, I thought.

I also recalled a conversation with a pilot who had flown with Ed Holley in Alaska. He had said, "I've watched Ed land resupply flights in total whiteouts. In that situation, there's no sky or ground or horizon to see or guide by. It's nothing but a world of white. Flying in it is done strictly on confidence and instinct. Ed's the best Herky pilot in the business—on wheels or skis or anything you can name."

Now, fixated on the unwinding altimeter, I wondered how many men had sat in exactly the same manner, expecting to be hit by a missile— ground-to-air or air-to-air—and unable to do anything except wait it out. I decided a lot of guys had died that way. Right before it happened, they probably had thought exactly what I was thinking: "This could be the end." Seconds passed like minutes. I looked at Coogan and grinned again, but my guts growled. We hung suspended in an aerodynamic world of Holley's creation.

Involuntarily, I hunched my shoulders, contracted my neck, and lowered my head. After a long moment, I grew aware of my reactions and looked up. The three others in the booth had struck similar motionless poses. I realized I was holding my breath and wondered about the others. I expected death but, at the same time, held no fear of dying. I didn't hope or pray.

Then the plane leveled and, after a prolonged silence, Holley asked, "Bob? Anybody? You see it?" Anti-climactic beyond belief.

"No, sir," Bob Savage said softly. "I think it went over top of us."

Somewhere that big deadly son of a bitch was still chugging along in the dark, I thought.

Holley eased the gunship's nose above the horizon and started a climb back to 9500 feet. He had outflown the most fearsome threat: the sparrow had escaped the hawk. He said, "Nice work, Sergeant Savage. You too, Major Ballsmith. Great work." He spoke to Kauffman without calling him by name: "Think you can find that last convoy again?" Kauffman instantly gave him a heading. Holley said, "What do you think, gang, want to finish off those trucks?" It was a rhetorical question.

Coogan asked me, "Should we be working around out here anymore tonight?"

I shrugged: Why pass up a piece...?

"That had to be an SA-2," Ballsmith said.

"Affirmative, sir," Savage said. "It looked just like the pictures."

"How long did that take?" Kauffman asked.

I said, "About forty-five minutes."

Schuiten corrected me: "More like forty-five seconds."

"Seemed like an hour and a half to me," I shouted at Coogan off interphone, and I meant it.

He waved a hand irritably, as if dismissing me. "How come you were grinning like that? You think it was funny?"

"No," I said. "Except when we all hunched over—you know...."

"We should be coming up on that intersection," Kauffman said. "You see it, sensors?"

"IR has it."

"TV has the trucks. TV tracking."

"Put IR in the computer," Holley said. He rolled into a 30-degree left bank, intercepted the firing orbit, and opened up with a 40-mm. Rounds impacted near the last truck in line.

Schuiten said, "You hit—"

"Good God," Ballsmith shouted, "I have another SAM activity light. Turn to three-zero-zero."

I looked at Coogan and tried not to grin, but I couldn't control my face. "Here we go again," I said. Coogan said something I didn't hear and tightened the leg straps on his parachute.

The next part of the mission is impossible to comprehend—even today, even if I live to be a hundred. What made us go back? Gallantry? Arrogance? Ignorance? We later learned that simultaneous with the first missile launch against us, another missile made a head-on pass at another gunship. For some reason, that crew didn't detect *Fan Song* activity and had no inkling of being under attack until a SAM loomed in front of the cockpit. Before the pilots could react, the missile streaked over the gunship and disappeared back into the night. That crew broadcasted SAM launch warnings and—except for us—all aircraft evacuated *Steel Tiger*, the southern section of Laos. Meanwhile, occupied with our own missile, we failed to hear the message and remained oblivious to the other activity.

Holley turned to Ballsmith's new escape heading and we repeated the same sequence of actions as the first attack: "Ready-to-launch light," then "Launch light." Savage reported: "I have two flashes." He narrated the flight of the two missiles in a dull monotone, and I wondered if he was in shock or if practice made perfect. Holley executed the same evasive maneuver.

"You believe this shit?" I shouted at Coogan.

He said, "I don't like any of it." Under his eyes were bags that would have qualified as two-suiters. I couldn't guess what I looked like.

To me, events followed the same script but took place more rapidly, yet in finer detail. It was like sitting through a movie I'd seen before. Somehow, the action lacked reality. I couldn't believe we actually were doing it again. My mind tried to tell me I was seeing a replay of the first time, or that now was merely a continuation of the first time. I suppose I couldn't believe we had encountered—had stupidly walked into—the identical trap twice within such a short period. More than anything, I just wanted it to end. The outcome didn't matter. Yet I knew the outcome. I'd seen the movie before. My mind and central nervous system had short-circuited.

Both SA-2s missed—of course! Our copilot, Captain Mike Scott, believed he saw them detonate in the distance, far beyond us, out of range. Holley headed homeward to Ubon, flying at low level.

Kauffman couldn't resist the temptation to deliver a small barb: "Ed, what about those trucks? We just gonna leave them?"

The booth became a madhouse. The gunners and scanners piled in with the sensor operators and shouted and beat on Savage. He said, "I don't think those last two guided very well."

Coogan looked a little brighter. I fed him food for thought: "What do you think the odds are against doing what we did—against doing what we did twice?"

He frowned. "Is it like this every mission?"

"No," I said. "Sometimes it's a lot worse."

Of course, *Lam Son 719* (South Vietnamese offensive operations into Laos) was a perfect time for the NVA to sneak SA-2 *Guidelines* into *Steel Tiger*. Our intelligence experts had focused on the area east of Tchepone, thereby ignoring activity northward. Consequently, intelligence officers had provided aircrews with no warning of an NVA SAM deployment. In fact, one of Coogan's sharpest memories of the night concerned our crew debriefing. He told me, "I vividly remember the after-mission briefing when the so-called Intel people tried to talk us out of what we experienced. The tape the Black Crow had of the rattlesnake warning of the SAM radar helped to convince them that we were really attacked by SAMs. I remember how hard the Intel people worked to discredit us. Intel simply didn't want to admit that they had been outsmarted." Rumors later made the rounds that the North Vietnamese Air Force had planned to sneak a couple of MiGs into *Steel Tiger* to shoot down a Spectre gunship, but it never happened.

Dick Kauffman had the final word. Reassigned to Seventh Air Force at Tan Son Nhut in the dry season, he researched intelligence reports for the two months before 2 March 1971. He discovered one report that talked of SA-2s and their launchers being moved into the general area around Tchepone a week before we were attacked. As far as he could determine, nobody passed the information to aircrews. He also learned that, according to Seventh Air Force planners, a 50 percent loss rate for the AC-130 throughout the 1970–71 dry season had been calculated as acceptable. "No one ever asked me if that was acceptable," Kauffman said.

The morning after we escaped the SAMs, Kauffman, with whom I roomed, said, "I still can't believe any of it. Ed split-Sed. Twice. I don't know if he actually rolled exactly one-eighty to complete a perfect split-S, but what he did was good enough to have the missiles go over top of us. What amazed me was that I didn't have my seat belt on and I didn't come out of the chair. Ed held a positive one G throughout the whole thing. He is outstanding."

"Ed's the champ," I said. "Undefeated." We owed him our lives.

What more could anyone say?

★ ★ ★

When volunteering for a second tour in Southeast Asia, I was toting a semi-heavy death wish: nothing sounded better than being killed in action—a memorable way for a soldier to die, right? At the time, I was totally booze-free. A divorced major, I was sleeping with beautiful young women; dining at the finest restaurants; driving a Thunderbird a hundred miles an hour to wherever, whenever; and doing whatever else made me happy. I walked around like the crown prince of Montgomery, Alabama, so why not check out while on top and have everybody miss me? Well, maybe not everybody. One bird colonel angrily warned me not to date his daughter—that old, dirty minded devil. As television's Fast Eddy used to ask, "How do you like me so far?"

I had sped to a divorce from my first wife after choosing a post-Vietnam nine-to-five staff assignment at Air Command and Staff College intended to ensure a marital atmosphere of tranquillity and bliss. My wife saw through me from the start. I recognized no psychic changes in me even when she drove off in her brand-new car and left me stranded on an unfamiliar street corner far from our recently purchased house. I had deluded myself into believing that we had bought a home. I had deluded myself into thinking that I would enjoy a desk job. But I failed to delude her in any manner.

I went to war for a second time, unaware my best friend—Jon Mallard—was recording what I didn't. Jon died in 2009 and his sister—Cynthia Luck—sent me letters I had written to him from Thailand. As a combat control team leader, Jon had served in Nam early in the war. Combat controllers parachute into an area as spearheads for anything that happens after that. Jon had been a distinguished graduate and the student leader of a section I supervised at Squadron Officer School in 1964. He resigned his commission in the late sixties and attained meteoric success in real estate, much of it working for Jack Nicklaus.

Jon had more contacts than an electric chair. Thanks to him, Jan—my darling wife since 1976—and I had the pleasure of visiting and dining as guests of Marie Lombardi—Green Bay Packer Coach Vince's lady—in Palm Beach, Florida. Her sprawling top-floor condominium was white, light, and airy, and she dripped diamonds and gold jewelry—rings, bracelets, and a necklace reflecting National Football League triumphs—that she wore with utter ease. At dinner, the people who waited on us busted their humps to make her happy. They put on unashamed displays of ass-kissing that surpassed my wildest imagination. A maitre d' salaamed each step of the way as he led us to our table. For a moment, when he seated Marie, I thought he would kiss her feet. She had to ask for nothing because everything she wanted had been anticipated. The lady ruled like a queen.

I needed years to find enough fortitude to unpack my letters to Jon and examine my past. I recalled I had written straight off the top of my head and transparency should overflow. Here are my thoughts from long ago.

* * *

[No date or salutation.]
Life here is pretty good. Of course, it doesn't compare to our summer vacation. In one way, that is good—excellent.

The weather has been dog-shit. Therefore, we abort frequently. The crew that consorts together aborts together.

I have found a friend that I will play house with. The VD rate is so fucking (no pun) high that a steady is the safe solution (but no guarantee). It is groovy to do nothing but fuck and fly combat missions.

I was so excited on my first mission in the AC-130 that while we were "hunting" (I was on the low light television), I fell asleep. My instructor thought that was funny. Yeah! Soon I shall be permitted to go to West Vietnam without an instructor. Quite an accomplishment for a 37-year-old navigator with 3500 hours. Because our airplanes normally are so fucking sick, I play much handball, racquetball, and tennis.

It is fun to write letters to my friends in the United States who are so solidly behind the socio-political efforts that are being expended here.

I do not differentiate in regard to the military expenditures because this phase of operations is merely an extension of our detailed and well-planned political program.

I am not sorry I came here. It is fun. Ubon is a nice place.

Please write and tell me how your life is. Crewmembers are vital to mission success. I will write you again next month when I am given paper.

Your friend, Henry

* * *

[Undated]
Dear Jon,
PEACE TODAY
Bullshit! Not when I'm having so much fun.

This is a liberating exciting moment of life, to stand eye to eye with the world/all that is beautiful/and ugly/good/and evil/and say Here I Am! I have my shit together!

BDA [bomb damage assessment] for the week (my crew only)–15 trucks destroyed–7 trucks damaged–2 cargo boats damaged and beached–and three successful TICs [close air fire support for troops in contact with the enemy]. And we took only 996 rounds of 37-mm AAA for the week. We shoot off the low light level TV about 75 percent of the time—and I am the TV operator on our crew. I also FAC fighters but we do not get credit for their BDA.

The schedule is beautiful! This month I have flown on 1-3-4-5-6-8-9-10-11-12-13 and am scheduled for 14-15-16-17 but get 18 off. At times I am so happy and exhilarated that I trip out on my own mind. This is what it is all about and it is what I should have been doing all my life.

FUN CAN CHANGE PEOPLE
I shall write again soon.
Z

★ ★ ★

Christmas [1970]
Dear Jon,
Yesterday I had my first day off in I don't know how long and my girlfriend gets drunk and I get pissed off and now I am brooding.
Your pal, Z

★ ★ ★

29 January 71

Dear Jon,

JETS KO OVER 1,000 RED TRUCKS

You probably saw a story similar to this in your local paper. Believe me, this is Spectre. At one point, the squadron racked up over 100 damaged-or-destroyed per day for an entire week. What makes it more impressive is that we have a video tape recorder aboard the aircraft and manage to get perfect BDA photography of at least 50 per cent of the total. The video tapes also record the interphone conversation, which causes frequent concern because the language is particularly gross at times—for example, when you are trying to shoot a fast-mover who is attempting to outrun you at the same time you are being hosed by AAA. The tapes frequently go as far as the White House; therefore, believe it or not, Intelligence now "bleeps" our tapes.

One pilot says, "What do you want, good grammar or dead trucks?"

Sorry for the B.S. about work. However, I just returned from a squadron party saying farewell to eight great crewmembers. My esprit-level is way up. A few days ago I also logged my 50th mission of this tour. At times I am ready to sign up for a six-month extension over here.

Some expert in Psychology Today says: There doesn't seem to be many pleasant reasons left for getting up in the morning. The fifth mode of immortality...a psychic state of ecstasy or rapture to break the ordinary bounds of existence, or the senses, and of mortality itself...requires ecstatic experiences in...battle, sexual love....

From what this guy says, I have it all right here.

I am on this theme and may as well finish. The ecstasy is here—especially in the aircraft. There are times after we cross the river that I put on my survival vest, parachute, and flak helmet as if I am suiting up for a game. I used to get a similar rush before playing soccer—especially a game I wanted to win—which, I guess, was every game. One night while dressing in the dark (we work blacked out and I waited until we were in the target area ready for action), I thought about you. I have not jumped, but I unexpectedly recognized that the period prior to jumping must be as exciting as the jump itself. I wondered how often you hooked up and felt exactly the same.

You see, I am qualified in three sensors. Two are sophisticated enough to be located in a booth—a closed room in the center of the aircraft. The other sensor (NOD) [Night Observation Device, which is a telescope that sees in the dark and ties to the fire control system] is a sighting tube located in the opening that used to be the forward entrance door. The NOD is best because the operator is practically standing in the slipstream directing fire and seeing—almost feeling—all the shit thrown at him.

I get to fly the NOD about one out of five missions. I find I am damn near hanging out of the aircraft looking for AAA fire and especially AAA guns. Once a gun is located, we roll in and hose the bastard. It is a beautiful duel. It is a wild, powerful feeling to watch that shit come up and shout "Fuck you" into the face of it and then squirt 40-mm rounds down on the son-of-a-bitch.

What I am saying is that now that I know this is here—now that I know what it is about—I wonder if I will ever get my fill of it. I presently cannot imagine returning to the States and never doing this again. In some way, life would be ended.

[No signature]

★ ★ ★

6 March [1971]

Dear Jon,

You understand the idea that a group with common goals needs no appointed leader. A situation close to that now exists in the 16th SOS [Special Operations Squadron]. The squadron experience level is exceptionally high. I would estimate that the average rank of the officer crewmembers is major with between ten to 15 years rated. We have one war baby: Lieutenant Colonel Hutto was born in 1918—during World War I. Anyhow, we have experience in depth—and age. Both are assets because the individuals know what they can do and what they want to do. Individual goals and self-promotion are at a distinct minimum. The crew concept reigns—with the emphasis on killing trucks. And we are doing it!

Our BDA is so high that we are under close scrutiny. We photograph everything we do, but PI [photo intelligence] claims only 60 per cent of our BDA can be verified. However, using the 60 per cent figure, our 12 airmachines destroy more NVA vehicles than all other aircraft in SEA combined. Much of the unverified BDA is beyond our control. Give us half of it, however, and we double the combined efforts of the rest of the world.

Since the push into Laos [*Lam Son 719*] began, the NVA is hurting. As a result, the pressure is on us. It now is normal to take 500 rounds of AAA on a mission—and it gets more and more accurate. Before the push into Laos, we averaged about 100 rounds each mission. A few days ago, our crew had the distinction of having three missiles fired at the aircraft. If that wasn't the high point of the tour regarding excitement, I don't know if I can accept what is to come. Yesterday, our crew logged its 500th truck (destroyed 299, damaged 210). We are among the top three or four guns in the squadron.

I suppose all of the above has been background material in order to tell you that this is what it is all about. I said this before but you are the only person who probably understands. You see, we fly-fly-fly. I flew missions nine out of the last ten days. I get super-hyper and don't realize it. I am not at peace and cannot relax unless I am in the airplane. How is that for a hang-up? Nothing on the ground makes a rat's ass. I sun bathe in the nude about three hours a day, read, and wait until it is time to fly.

I got rid of my girlfriend.

You and I know that when it is all said and done, you can never do it over. I am about ready to make a pact with myself that when I am 50 I will voluntarily cash-in and, therefore, until then, will go stark fucking mad crazy wild. If I just had enough money to delay the court proceedings! Being a fugitive is no fun.

Z

★ ★ ★

Based on reading letters written more than half my life ago, I feel as if I performed like a mechanical man. My emotions appear ordained. Were the most meaningful events of my military career predicated on three facts?

The simplest fact is that Spectre did not lose a gunship that season.

The amazing fact is that during more than 800 days in-theater and 922 combat support sorties/interdiction missions, I never came face-to-face with an enemy soldier. Exactly who did I fight?

The sobering fact is that I would unhesitatingly do everything again.

★ ★ ★

I have yet to completely rid myself of the emotions I expressed to Jon Mallard. Evidently I strongly possessed them when I wrote a novel about my year with Spectre. A reviewer of that book said:

> *An Unusual Take on War.* This guy actually seemed to enjoy his war on some level. Probably this was because it was not physically (for sure mentally) demanding: he sat in an aircraft that operated from Thailand, so he could treat the war a little differently than men who lived in areas exposed to fire.
>
> Another reason for his apparent attitude is, aside from one or two incidents, the enemy had no real chance of actually damaging his aircraft with anything of matching technology: any large gun that fired from the ground risked being fired back at by massive firepower, according to the author. Meanwhile, ground combatants were genuinely concerned about the weaponry arrayed against them.
>
> There weren't many wars in the 20th century in which the chief protagonist had such a situation of out-matching the opponent in this way. He seems to view the whole war as a kind of game on some level, perhaps as a means of distancing himself from the carnage his gunship causes. His approach is a different take on a much-written-about war. It's kind of a rare book these days.

That reviewer's critique cued memories of a night when we discovered 16 tanker trucks in a shallow valley. Stretched along a narrow road, the trucks had slowed to ford a stream. Five had already crossed and waited on a hillside for the others. Two were in the water. The other nine formed a tight line along the valley floor. Guiding off my TV, we first shot the leading truck on the hillside and set it ablaze. We next quickly shot the last truck in line down the valley, also setting it afire. The flames were massive, exactly what one would expect from blowing up a 6000-gallon fuel-filled tanker. Our tactic blocked escape routes in both directions. We then methodically shot the trucks in the middle of the line and worked our way outward, creating an inferno along the valley floor and up the hillside. Not a single round of antiaircraft fire interrupted our work, our unforgettable victory.

Neil Renic, an up-to-date scholar of international relations, argues that "when assessing the humanity of war, we should look not only to the fate of civilians but also as to whether combatants have exposed themselves to risk on the battlefield." He questions the justness of a remote-control drone operator's ability to kill an enemy without stepping foot on the battlefield. Renic says that, in terms of a threat, the drone operator's victim is no different from a non-combatant civilian. To him, the crux of the matter is the type of danger someone in a battle zone presents. His "humane war" more than likely precludes harming an innocent truck, more so one in which a driver—as we had heard—might be chained to the steering wheel.

With greater certitude, many combat veterans argue only people who fight face to face on a battlefield are warriors. Any other participants in war are support personnel, rear echelon groups that include artillerymen and airplane crews. Hard core combat veterans claim that guys who bombed North Vietnam and took ridiculously high losses merely interdicted enemy supply lines in support of our grunts on the ground in South Vietnam.

★ ★ ★

Touché—thrice? You say I am not writing stories about honest-to-god warriors? Should I label what I write as history lessons, but not the kind you read in school? Or should we call such work a journal, and think of it as a Billy-Mitchell-type chronology, telling how a bunch of fliers took somebody else's invention and maximized its use.

A "history lesson" sounds satisfactory because, like many other writers' accounts of war, my gunship work is a small part of lengthy combat records, to wit, Spectre's 1970–1971 Dry Season that was the first year of operation for a full squadron of AC-130 gunships. I recorded an insider's view of the learning-to-run stage of a weapon system's development. Spectre is still at work where needed.

Today I no longer possess the unrestrained ego required to tell that story so transparently. But I am pleased that it is in print because it provides evidence for and against war.

CHAPTER 3

Killing Myself

At an airport gate in Pittsburgh, my father formed a welcoming committee of one. I kissed his lips, hugged him tightly. We had kissed hello and goodbye for as long as I could remember. Within the year my father would be dead, and the last thing I would do before the coffin lid closed was kiss his lips, lips that tasted like cold ashes.

Anyone who saw us embrace should have interpreted the situation at a glance: my father's grinning through his tears and my wearing a blue Air Force uniform set with rows of ribbons—red, yellow, and blue like the plumage of a male bird—a son returned home from the war. Perhaps the meeting wasn't so obvious to my father.

When I had last seen him, my father had looked like my twin, although born 30 years earlier. Now, for the first time, he appeared old.

As if stealing words from my mind, he surprised me by saying, "You look worn out. You're so thin. Are you all right?"

Lighter by a few pounds that hadn't been spare, my body felt gristly. Could he see that? "Maybe a little tired," I said, "but you look great."

Later, in the tiny bathroom of the home where I grew up, I studied myself in the medicine-chest mirror. My face was burnt to mahogany. A crimson cleft between the eyebrows looked as deep as a stigmata, ready to bleed. Tightly bunched pucker lines radiated down my chin in a network of visible nerves, as if etched by flame. Neck muscles bulged like cords. The jaws ached as if being squeezed by a powerful, invisible hand. I counted my pulse by the visible throb of a vein in my temple.

Like a metronome for universal time, it beat once a second. The sun had bleached my thinning blond hair with long platinum streaks that appeared frosted, theatrical, a confession of vanity I no longer possessed.

At the airport, my father had asked, "Were you burned?"

I had looked at him quizzically. Now I understood what he had meant.

Meshing youth and age, innocence and experience, I crawled onto my boyhood bed as if lying down for the final time on a slab of my tombstone. My rambling mind questioned my totalitarian self-confidence, my sureness of self. Recognizing my luck had been stretched to the limit, I unhappily concluded little remained to be done beyond what I had already experienced and that, in the future, I will have to be satisfied in simply adequate ways.

★ ★ ★

My father dragged me around town to visit my aunts and uncles, people overwhelmed by the insignificance of their lives, people who knew nothing about Vietnam, people for whom war had ended forever on the day the Nazis surrendered. I listened while they detailed illnesses and deaths among themselves and their friends. They reminded me of ghosts speaking of other ghosts, appeared to have already reached an afterlife and were simply waiting for Resurrection Day. When they actually died, would they recognize the difference?

They made me aware of how much I missed Spectre, living among the fit and strong, mocking the aspects of life these people took seriously.

The person I most enjoyed visiting was my Great Uncle Joe, a veteran of 50 years in the Jones and Laughlin steel mills. He came to America in his teens and went straight to feeding the open hearths. Now he was bed-ridden in a ward of Kane Hospital. When he saw me, he dropped his Polish newspaper and grasped my hand, pulled me down to kiss my forehead. "You're Henry's boy," he said. I returned his kiss.

He owned prototype models of the hooked nose and small ears that hung on my skull. Fine lines and creases covered his face, more detailed than any topographic map. His skin appeared translucent, shimmered as if it had been buffed. "My body's ruined, but my mind still works," he said. A year earlier, my father had bought him a wheelchair, but now Joe was too weak to crawl into it. "Even my hair feels tired," he said.

He asked to hear war stories, and I told him several that were black but funny. He laughed in the right places.

Disappointed that I didn't read Polish, he rattled his newspaper. "American papers don't tell the truth. Stalin was a bigger butcher than Hitler. He wanted to murder all the Poles and turn Poland into part of the Soviet Union. Communism is pure evil. Don't ever argue with anyone who's against democracy. Just kill the bastard."

He squeezed my hand when I kissed him goodbye and told him, "I probably won't see you for a while."

"Better in hell than in Russia," he said.

★ ★ ★

Dad and I ate out, at least two big meals a day, more than I had grown accustomed to. We skirmished for the check. "We could avoid a lot of hassle if you'd let me pay," I told him.

He stiffened his spine. "I have money."

One morning at Niedhurst's when my father had nothing but a $20 bill for a $5 tab, I let him pay and told the waitress, "Keep the change."

"What?" Dad said.

The waitress' eyes danced over me.

"Wait a minute," Dad said to her, "that's my money. Bring the change."

The waitress shook her head at me. While we waited for her to return, Dad watched me as if he didn't know me.

After he got his change, I dropped a fiver on top of his tip.

"I don't understand you," he said.

At another restaurant, I left half of my food on the plate and he asked, "Don't you like this place?"

"There's too much. Way too much of everything," I said. Southeast Asia had provided only the moment.

★ ★ ★

We were standing near the corner of North Avenue and East Street, waiting for a streetcar. My father had never owned an automobile, never learned to drive. Where we waited, the neighborhood was in rubble, awaiting the construction of an overpass. Across a four-lane street, an abandoned apartment house stared down at us with three stories of unbroken windows. I found a handball-size rock and threw it at a top story window, a tough shot. The rock bounced off the building's brick wall, clattered around on the sidewalk, and rolled out into sparse evening traffic.

"What're you doing?" my father said. A man without malice, he often had rescued drowning bugs—bees and wasps—from our backyard birdbath.

Finding more right-size rocks, I handed him a pair.

"We'll get arrested," he said.

"Second floor, window in the middle. I doubt you can reach it."

He threw with a funky underhand delivery that I didn't understand or appreciate until 25 years later when I caught myself throwing with the same limited motion.

By the time our ride came into view, we had our coats off and had broken windows, but not the one we wanted.

Seated beside me on the streetcar, Dad wiped the sweat band of his gray homburg with a handkerchief and said, "Don't tell anyone we did that."

I took a while to understand the rock tossing had violated my father's integrity. Caught in the act, he could have been classified as some sort of lesser vandal and damaged his reputation. He grew up along the Allegheny River on the North Side of Pittsburgh in a rough neighborhood. Among his contemporaries, he was the only one to become a white-collar worker. His friends had the best nicknames in the world. Mark Twain would have loved those guys: Sacky. Raggy. Plootney. Zip—the first guy in the neighborhood to wear pants with a zipper fly. Sixteen Bridges. Slam Bang Harry Taylor. They said his name like one word—Slambangharry. He was a middleweight boxer. Spin. Barney Google. Chinky. Tarzan. Russian Pete. My dad was Ducky because he was a champ at duckpin bowling. There wasn't a spare he wouldn't bet on, and he made damn near every one.

★ ★ ★

Unshaven and wearing an olive-drab T-shirt and faded jeans, I wandered through an automobile showroom on Baum Boulevard, trying on Cadillacs. My father trailed behind, suited up in his usual white shirt and tie.

The cars showed no price tags. A salesman gave me a quote on a model that interested me. The number was $2000 higher than the overseas Base Exchange listing.

"Way overpriced," I said.

The salesman, who had already looked me up and down, said, "Overpriced—or more than you can afford?"

I looked into his eyes and quietly said, "Fuck you very much."

Outside, my father gave me another lengthy stare.

★ ★ ★

On my first return from the Vietnam War, I arrived home at dusk on Halloween. Night's approaching coolness hunched my shoulders. I wore a short-sleeve uniform that I had put on two days earlier in overheated Saigon. In our unearthly quiet North Little Rock suburban neighborhood, two child-size ghosts provided the only sign of life. My attitude had been simmering ever since I had reached the civilian terminal in Frisco, and now I expected something evil to happen. I said to Jane, "What's wrong?" She frowned but said, "Nothing." Her kiss at the airport had been more like a welcome home following a day of work rather than after a year's separation.

I lugged my B-4 and A-3 bags into the house from the car, didn't have time to sit down before Karen asked to go trick or treating. Jane said, "Daddy's tired, Darling. Maybe later." Karen bowed her head. Her hair was redder, wavier, thicker than I remembered. I doubted that I would have recognized her if she hadn't been standing beside Jane at the airport. Like her, I knew that "later" equated to "never" because in an hour or two porch lights would be turned off and the goodies gone until next year.

I remembered the day my Uncle Tex had returned from World War II, months after the war's end. Our family had gathered at my grandmother's house on Suismon Street in Pittsburgh to greet him. As impossible as it sounds, nobody in my family owned a car. Tex would arrive by train, downtown at Penn Station, and find a way home from there. We expected that he would arrive that evening. Like a sentry, I had stood on the front stoop for hours, alert for the sight of him rounding the corner from Chestnut Street, a long block away. I was so anxious to see him that when his wife, Aunt Anne, came and stood beside me, I began to cry. "He isn't coming," I said. As if my tears were a signal, Tex appeared. Dressed in an Ike jacket and carrying a duffel bag hoisted over a shoulder, he marched with Gulliver strides. Anne ran toward him. I ran to the bathroom, too excited to control myself. By the time I finished, relatives had surrounded Tex. He was holding an Iron City beer and swapping hug and kisses. He looked as handsome as ever—tallest in the family. Rows of ribbons testified to his worthiness. I verged on crying again because he didn't see me. Then he reached out and lifted me off my feet, hugged and kissed me, called me pal, dug inside his shirt, slipped off his dog tags, and looped them around my neck. I didn't take them off for the next three years.

Now, I picked up Karen, hugged her, and said, "Hey, what're you waiting for? Put on your costume. Let's get the road on the show."

"Dad…?"

"Unless you don't want to."

"I want to," she said and ran to her room.

"You don't have to," Jane said. "I'll do it."

"No problem," I said.

I shivered and broke out in goose bumps before Karen and I had gone half a block. Kids in costumes appeared and disappeared around us. Shadows had lives of their own. I walked a little faster. Karen said, "Dad, it's not a race."

The houses on our block looked brand new—brightly painted, well lighted, secure, and aglow with life. I didn't follow to the door while Karen did her thing. A beefy man who greeted her at the first house wore a sleeveless undershirt. Behind him, a stereo blasted out Jefferson Airplane—"White Rabbit." He nodded at Karen when he dropped a handful of Hershey kisses into her bag, said, "Whatever," after she thanked him.

At the second house, two overweight people—man and woman, both eating Clark bars—answered the door. Each dropped a candy bar into Karen's bag. The woman said, "Who you dressed as, Sugar?" Karen said, "Snow White." The man said, "Tell Dopey I said hello." The woman laughed. The man handed Karen a third candy bar.

A man at the next house was shirtless, showing a hairy beer gut.

At each house, I grew a little more pissed off.

By the tenth house, I wanted to shoot the obese son of a bitch who opened the door.

Over the past year, I had grown accustomed to a world filled with hard, lean bodies. And I identified with them. To me, the stature of Southeast Asians reflected lifetimes of physical strife. For decades, the Vietnamese had fought the French and now fought each other—and us. The sight of self-indulgent, undisciplined neighbors made me understand why Americans lacked compassion for the South Vietnamese cause: they had no fucking idea what sacrifice included.

Karen filled her bag and I carried her home.

Jane took one look at me and asked, "What's wrong."

"Nothing," I said. I couldn't bring myself to tell her I wanted to go back to the war.

★ ★ ★

My last night home, my father and I had just finished dinner at the Wood Street Grill when a man and woman sat down at the next table. I leaned toward my father: "I know that guy. We went to high school together. I haven't seen him in what—twenty years?"

"You sure it's him?"

"Larry Raymond," I whispered.

My father slowly nodded as if the name meant something to him.

Raymond now had shoulder-length hair and a thick black moustache, becoming a paradox between age and aging. He'd added a few pounds but still looked fit. It was him for sure.

"Is that his wife?" my father said, forever disappointed for Karen's sake that Jane and I had divorced.

"You kidding?"

Barely out of her teens, the woman practically sat on Raymond's lap, eyes focused on his, awaiting his words. She hadn't quite finished filling out, but her enthusiasm said a lot about her potential.

Raymond intercepted my stare. Memory was on my side, blankness on his.

"How are you tonight, Mister Raymond?" I said.

The sound of his name erased the irritation in his face: "Fine. Thanks. Do I know you?" he said.

"Didn't you go to Perry? Graduate in fifty-one?"

We were beyond our neighborhood, far beyond our time together.

He squinted. "You go there?"

"Ever been back?"

"Yes. Twentieth reunion. Two months ago." He exhaled deeply. "I don't know you."

"Tell him who you are," my father said.

"How was the reunion," I asked.

Raymond's eyebrows did a little two-step. "Lots more people showed up than I expected. It was good. Fun."

I named several members of our class and Raymond told me what he knew about each. When he appeared to grow bored, I named myself.

"He wasn't there. Somebody said he was in Vietnam."

My father said, "This is—" but I touched his arm and stopped him.

"Anyone who would go there is a fool," I said.

Raymond's lips puckered. "You ask me, it's one big waste."

"Now you mention it, I think I remember hearing Zeybel was shot down over there." Although the idea wasn't new to me, I surprised myself with the words. "Killed in action."

Raymond's eyes widened.

I furrowed my brow as if struggling to retrieve memory: "In Laos, I think."

"If that's true...." Raymond's eyes drifted away from me. "I'm sorry to hear that. He wasn't a bad guy."

This was a form of death we all desired: to attend our own funeral, to hear how others judged us, and then to be reborn, as we willed.

"That's not funny," my father said. "Tell him who you are."

"Well, I'm not certain about any of this," I said.

"Tell him," said my father. "Stop playing games."

Raymond's face was blank.

Then his girlfriend whispered in his ear, and his face jitterbugged through a you-got-to-be-shitting-me routine. "You're him? Zeybel?" Now Raymond stared hard at me. "You were in Vietnam?"

"He just got back," my father said. "Tell him," he urged me, but didn't wait for me to speak. "It was his second time over there."

"I still don't recognize him," Raymond said.

"He's a lieutenant colonel."

Both Raymond and his girlfriend stared at me. I appreciated her more than before: as a disinterested observer, she had found the answer.

"He was in gunships," my father said.

"Helicopters?" Raymond said, trying to understand.

They talked about me as if I weren't there. I could have just as easily been dead and they would have gone on without me.

"Spectre," my father said, telling Raymond nothing. He nudged me. "Tell him how many missions you flew."

"Two," I said.

My father sat bolt upright and his hands jerked in a way that made me duck my head, expecting to be slapped, something he had never done to me.

The girlfriend opened her menu.

Raymond studied me. "Man, you've changed," he said. I thought he was going to pick up a candle off the table and shine it on me, get a better picture. "You look ripped, man—hard." He shook his head. "I would've never guessed it was you."

I tried to smile.

Raymond did it for me: "How does it feel to be alive again?"

★ ★ ★

My father's death involved no heroism, unless one credited him for calmly accepting the inevitable. I hadn't a clue that he was in trouble until Uncle Joe's daughter phoned me: "I don't want to upset you, but I saw Henry on Ohio Street yesterday and hardly recognized him. He's so thin, his clothes are falling off him. I asked if he's seeing a doctor, and he said his friends tell him to, but he won't. You should call him. He'll listen to you."

When I phoned, my father said, "I haven't been able to eat for a month. I get hungry, but after one or two bites, I gag."

He told me he weighed 130. "Jesus Christ," I said, "you've lost forty pounds. Listen to me. Tomorrow morning, go see a doctor. Understand? Don't worry about the cost. Man, you're the only dad I have."

"Going to a doctor scares me," he said. "I was hoping whatever it is would go away."

I took emergency leave and, when I got to Pittsburgh, my father was in Mercy Hospital. An internal specialist, about my age, met me in a hospital hallway and said, "Your father has cancer. It started in his lungs and spread to his stomach and liver."

The sight of my father made me teary eyed: a flesh-shrouded skeleton with enormous eyes, he looked like a concentration camp prisoner struggling to make it through the day. The smile he barely mustered held a faint glint of hope.

The doctor had said, "He thinks he has a bleeding ulcer that an operation will cure. I haven't told him my diagnosis. I was waiting for you. An operation would be futile. He's too weak."

"How long will he live?"

"In a case as advanced as his, I'd say three months, at most."

A day with my father progressed marvelously slowly. In the seclusion of his private room, we acted out our final roles with each other. I tried to make his last days of life as happy as he had made my childhood days. Helping him to shave and bathe took up most of a morning. Because his hands shook, I shaved him by standing pressed against him from behind, substituting my arms for his, duplicating strokes I would have made in shaving my own face. He had shriveled and I towered over him. Staring at his face below mine in the mirror was like viewing my future. I felt closer to death than I had in combat. I practically lifted him in and out of the bathtub, sponged him more gently than I had bathed my baby daughter, found fascination in the pale blue veins that showed through his alabaster skin, skin that looked thin enough to tear at a touch. I massaged his neck, arms, legs, and back more tenderly than I ever had touched a woman.

I read to him from Roger Kahn's *The Boys of Summer* while he faded out and in. We played a lot of Sixty-six, a German card game that uses nines through aces. It was the first adult card game he had taught me and we had played for money ever since I got my first job at 11, delivering newspapers. After a few hands, I recognized he was too weak to concentrate and play his normal game. So I underplayed my hands, losing more than I won and raising the bets from day to day, until he said, "I never played for stakes this high." He opened the drawer of his nightstand and pointed to his stack of winnings. "I never won this much at the club in a good week."

"So you're a hundred ahead," I said. "You've been getting lucky hands. The cards'll turn around."

"Wanna bet?" he said and his eyes brightened.

Because the hospital food looked unappetizing, I brought daily treats: corned beef on rye, pastrami on pumpernickel, an icy pony bottle of Rolling Rock, a hot fish sandwich on a poppy seed roll, potato pancakes, whatever Pittsburgh restaurants offered. Although he ate only a bite or three, my reward was complete when he said, "Thanks, Champ. I wish I could eat more. Finish it for me." He liked watching me eat.

Ralph and Vince Murovich, two of his nephews, sent a huge basket of fruit that contained black grapes the size of golf balls. He ate one of the grapes and raved about it so much that, on my way to the hospital the next day, I stopped by Market Square and bought bunches of a variety of grapes. I piled 10 pounds of them on his bed, but he missed the humor of overkill and said, "You're throwing money away."

"They won't go to waste," I said. "The nurses'll love them."

I brought him a pack of unfiltered Camels, his favorite. At that point, what did it matter? Before lighting up, he said, "I cut back since my appetite went away." He talked about his upcoming operation and how, after being cured, he would stop smoking altogether. He told friends who telephoned, "There's nothing to worry about. I have the best doctor in town. He's running tests. Pretty soon he'll operate and I'll be good as new." That routine carried over from the doctor's visits and father's asking, "How're the tests going?" and the doctor's answering, "We'll run a few more," while expectantly looking at me.

Avoiding the facts was dishonest. Had I been in my father's place, I would have wanted to hear the truth. The next time after he hung up from a phone call, I said, "You shouldn't tell people you're going to be operated on."

"Why?" His milky eyes drifted as if unable to focus. "The doctor's going to operate, isn't he?"

"No." I tried to look into his eyes, but he turned his head. "If they were, they would have done it by now. An operation won't help. There's nothing any doctor can do to make you better."

"It's cancer," he told himself.

I kissed his lips but doubted he felt my love.

"I want to be buried from Nativity," he said and disappeared behind a mask of resignation, softly addressed a power beyond the two of us: "Why? Damn it, I tried to lead a good life. There are so many things I still want to do."

And I had done everything I wanted to do. Had it been possible, right then I would have traded places with my father.

That afternoon the doctor met me in the hall and knew what I had done just by looking at me. "It's easier to hear bad news from a family member," he said.

"I'm taking him to Florida. I have a house on Navarre Beach." I pictured the two of us serenely sitting on my patio and watching the waves.

"We can help with the details," the doctor said. "He'll have to travel in a wheelchair." He started to walk away, but turned and added, "The liver biopsy we performed this morning will help to determine his extent of damage."

I walked into my father's room and before I could explain my plan, he handed me his Kaufmann's credit card. "Go buy yourself something nice," he said. "Buy something for your girlfriend, too."

And then I could pay the charge account, I thought and nearly laughed.

"What happened to that blonde I met when I visited you, the one you bought the diamond watch for?"

Oh, shit, not now, I thought and walked to the room's window, gazed out at a wedge of the city. "We got married."

He groaned and I hoped it was from pain rather than disgust.

Embarrassed by my weakness, I forced myself to add, "We're getting divorced."

He sighed. "How much will that cost?"

"I don't know." Fuck, what did it matter?

"For what?" he said, rhetorically cross-examining me.

I almost said, "For no self-control. For rolling in it shamelessly. For more fun than any ride at Disneyland." Instead I took him on eye-to-eye. "You saw her. You know."

His milky eyes shifted: anger or envy? He was beyond being read. In a voice I hardly recognized, he said, "Did you have children with her?"

"No. I would have told you that."

He made a face that left me uncertain as to whether he approved or disapproved. "Are you taking care of Karen?"

"I pay monthly child support. Straight off the top. The Air Force sends it directly to Jane."

"Promise me you'll always take care of Karen."

"Always" sounded like an overly long contract, but he was dying. If I promised and reneged, he was clean. The sin was mine. I said, "I promise."

He closed his eyes. It wasn't an appropriate time to talk about moving him to Florida.

Minutes later, he awoke and complained about a pain in his side, where he had been jabbed with a needle for the biopsy. I called a nurse who shot him with a painkiller, patted his head, and told him, "This should help you sleep through the night."

I went home and was sound asleep when the head night nurse phoned me. "Your father is hemorrhaging internally. You might want to be here with him."

When I arrived back at the hospital, she told me, "Bleeding isn't unusual after a biopsy, but it's not a good sign. We've started a transfusion."

I sat beside my father's bed, held his hand, and stroked his head. Along with the transfusion, he was being fed oxygen. The hours unwound. At some point I said, "I love you, Dad." To my surprise, without opening his eyes, he answered, "Love you, too, Champ." Then the room grew chilly and our world stopped.

I must have dozed off because the next thing I remembered was a terminally gorgeous, freckle-face, strawberry-blond nurse asking, "How's he doing?"

I shrugged.

She said, "Can I get you something? Coffee? Orange juice?"

"Juice," I said and followed her down the hall.

We ended up in a tiny alcove where she handed me a half pint carton. We stood close to each other. I told her she reminded me of all the angels in the Sistine Chapel ceiling, and then I couldn't remember if there were any angels painted there, but it didn't matter because she said, "Wow. What a line."

A moment later another nurse looked in on us and told me, "You might want to go to your father."

A wall clock read 4:17 am.

I found another nurse putting my father's belongings into his suitcase.

"Is he...?" I said.

"Yes," she said softly.

His eyes were open. Had he been searching for me in his final moment? I reached out and stroked his eyelids closed. "Why didn't somebody tell me?" I said and bit my lip. No one else was to blame: my inattention resulted in my father's dying alone.

I went into the bathroom, closed the door, and sat on the edge of the bathtub. I draped a towel over my head. I deserved to be beaten into unconsciousness. I wanted to cry but tears would not come.

I arrived home by taxi at sunrise, walked into a place where I had been living all week. I entered my father's room, where I seldom ventured, and saw that his aged Baby Ben alarm clock had stopped at 4:17, exactly. I opened the doors of his armoire, pulled out a drawer, and atop a stack of handkerchiefs, saw a prophylactic in gold foil. I pushed the drawer closed and shut the doors. I didn't want to learn his secrets.

In my room, I emptied the contents of my pockets onto my dresser, as I had done every night since arriving home, but for the first time I noticed a folded piece of copy paper on the corner of the dresser. How had I overlooked it for so many days? I unfolded it and read:

When I have trod that great uncharted road
That holds for each no promise of return
Weep not for me, lest this, my last abode
Be dank with tears a father did not earn
And when this deep mist that crowns the peak
Bows to the sun—and all the world is glad
If you should feel a cool breeze brush your cheek
Say a swift prayer and softly murmur, "Dad!"

I read the poem a dozen times, perhaps more, committed it to memory.

Aloud I said, "I love you, Dad."

The next night when I was sound asleep in my childhood bed—

Wait a minute. I hesitated a long time before writing about what came next: a hint of the supernatural intruded upon my world. Until my father's death I had believed that when a person died, that person was dead. Dead as the dinosaurs. Dead forever. There was no afterlife, no heaven, no hell, no reincarnation. Only death. A big fat period.

So...

In the middle of the next night, while I was sound asleep in my childhood bed, a chill passed over me, exactly like a cool breeze, and brought me wide awake. I sat up, trembled for a moment, and looked at my travel alarm clock. It read 4:17. Not believing what I saw, I ran to the living room and checked the time on my father's carriage clock. It read the same.

The following morning, the same thing happened. A chill awoke me at exactly 4:17 am and I sat up as if responding to a summons from my dad, a call I perhaps had failed to respond to when it was needed.

The summons came every morning until I returned to Florida.

I placed a pearl gray homburg inside my father's casket. I remained at the cemetery until the gravediggers filled the hole and covered it with sod. I already had instructed Fire Captain Pete Kalaba, my father's best friend, a short, bear-shaped man fondly called "Russian Pete," to give my father's clothes to the winos on the Lower North Side. My father had given a pat on the back and no less than a quarter, which bought at least a shot and a beer back then, to any panhandler, sometimes a guy he had known since grade school days.

I gave the remainder of my father's possessions to relatives and then emptied the bank accounts and safety deposit box he had put in both our names.

★ ★ ★

Yes, I had a mother: Louise Agnes Murovich. Wife. Mother. Homemaker. Excellent cook, with occasional adventuresome recipes my father and I endured for her sake (Dad was a steak-and-potatoes, no-meat-on-Fridays guy). Tutor. Disciplinarian (her rules emerged after the fact: "Don't do that again"). Avid reader of contemporary novels. Crossword puzzle pro. Sister to Vincent, Ann, Annetta, Betty, and Edythe.

She dressed me far better than my fellow Perry High public school students. After classes, she and I rode streetcars to entertaining events. In suit and tie at six, I met and shook hands with Admiral Richard Byrd. At 11, I saw Franklin Delano Roosevelt drive down Liberty Avenue in Pittsburgh. She and I ate an early dinner at the Rosenbaum department store restaurant on Thursdays—my dad's bowling night—and then sat through damn near every late-thirties and early-forties romantic/melodramatic motion picture shown at the Stanley and stately Penn theaters. The angst of Joan Crawford and Bette Davis overwhelmed me. I taught myself to tune out entire stories. I preferred a movie at the Stanley because it usually included a stage show such as Spike Jones. The shows were like a variety television performance but in real life.

This does not suggest my dad did not pal with me. As a newspaper reporter, he received free passes for sports events in town. He took me with him year-round. We watched boxing at Duquesne Gardens, Aragon Ballroom, and Zivic Arena; Hornet's hockey Wednesdays and Saturdays—before the Penguins got an NHL franchise; Steelers and Pitt Panthers football; and Pirates baseball at Forbes Field. No "school night" restrictions applied. Sports took top billing followed by near-midnight ham sandwiches at Zeyfang and Thomas'. Believe it or not, we saw the Harlem Globetrotters lose to their Washington patsies and laughed all the way home.

He and I damn sure hustled downtown on that balmy summer evening in August 1945 to join the VJ-Day throng.

Dad nurtured my id; Mom strained to flesh out my superego. A massive thrombosis killed my mother at age 63, two years before my father's death.

★ ★ ★

Like a messenger with a mission, a stewardess on my flight home to Florida handed me a magazine that flopped open to an article explaining how two Navy medical researchers named Holmes and Rahe had devised a social readjustment scale to measure the effects of stresses on an individual. At the time, posttraumatic stress disorder was unrecognized. The researchers rated "life events" according to how people reacted to them. Death of a spouse or parent topped their list at 100 points. They valued divorce at 73 points. A major change in the health or behavior of a family member scored 44. Lesser problems like job dissatisfaction and moving were worth 36 and 20 points respectively. Holmes and Rahe did not list a score for the stress associated with going to war. Their research also determined that positive life events could be as stressful as negative ones. Marriage was rated at 50 points, and outstanding personal achievement 28. The scores combined over a year indicated an individual's likelihood of developing a stress-related illness. A total between 150 and 299 portended a 50-50 chance of illness. A score over 300 pushed the probability to 80 percent.

Giving combat a modest 90 points, I scored close to 400.

A sidebar written by a guru accompanied the story and told about a man being chased by a tiger. The man tumbled off a cliff but was lucky enough to clutch a small shrub growing on the cliff face. There the man hung, poised precariously between life and death. Above him the tiger prowled. The man looked down and saw another tiger waiting at the base of the cliff. If he were to survive the fall, nothing much would be left of him to rescue. Then the shrub roots started pulling loose and he knew for certain he would fall within the minute. At the same instant, he saw wild strawberries growing within reach. He plucked them, popped them into his mouth, and savored their sweetness. He thought, "How lovely these gifts of nature taste."

The story's message rang clear: Live for the moment.

CHAPTER 4

Trash Hauling

I became a serious passenger "along for the ride" when I navigated C-130 Hercules "Trash Haulers" in South Vietnam in 1967–1968. I performed the tasks expected of me but often felt like a spectator. Practically every day presented an adventure that crowded my mind with reflections on life and its purpose. Comparing values I had established to that time against new activities subconsciously influenced deviations in my personality and behavior.

In Vietnam, the frequent presence of death revised my view of mortality. Deep down I was aware that life is temporary but had not seriously related the fact to me. Our crew's first encounter with men killed in action occurred when we loaded 22 body bags on stretchers one night at Phu Bai. Describing the setting as "dank" would be a compliment to the atmosphere.

We had barely offloaded our ammo delivery when three trucks pulled up behind our C-130 and the lead driver said, "Going to Da Nang?"

"If that's what you need," I said.

The drivers and their crews commenced carrying stretchers from the beds of the trucks and into our cargo compartment. Each olive-drab stretcher held a dirt-stained, zippered, black rubber bag. The men placed them four across and five deep, with two left odd. They cinched tie-down straps across each row.

What I saw didn't fully register. I could barely distinguish forms through the fabric. Then I pictured dead men with arms crossed in front of their chests. The shapes looked uncommonly small, the size of children. "Wrong ending to the war," my mind said.

A combination of thankfulness and fear washed over me. To appease Lady Luck, I walked to the bodies, stooped and rapped knuckles against the wooden handle of a stretcher—the only wood in sight. I rubbed my knuckles against the leg of my flying suit to cleanse them of any bad karma I caught in my haste to appease fate. Stepping back, I felt a newborn buoyancy from being alive and capable of performing all manner of acts. I would not die for a long time, I told myself and felt a pornographic delight tinged with guilt that my happiness depended on the dead bodies before me.

I climbed back to the flight deck and resumed my life.

★ ★ ★

One afternoon while our crew dozed on the tarmac waiting for a load, a forklift appeared out of a watery mirage along the sun-baked concrete. It carried an unpainted wooden coffin surrounded by a putrid halo from long-dead flesh. Wearing a blue bandanna tied around the lower half of his face, the forklift driver slid the coffin onto our airplane's ramp, handed a manifest to the loadmaster, and sped away.

The paperwork said the coffin held the body of a Vietnamese infantry lieutenant killed in action. The body's destination was Dalat Cam Ly. We flew with the cargo door open to create a draft, but the odor of rotten meat still permeated the cockpit. We could not outfly death.

In contrast with the grimness of the mission, Dalat's plantations, with rows of cultivated rubber trees left from French colonialism, provided eye-pleasing orderliness. The high-altitude air was cool. Dark green jungle overlapped the airstrip like a backdrop for a play from a time before pain, perhaps a scene of Eden. The landscape showed no sign of war except for our olive-drab C-130.

We taxied to a cortege of about 50 Vietnamese civilians in European dress and headed by a middle-age man and woman standing in front of a tan stucco building with a red tile roof. Not one person looked toward the airplane. My pilots remained in the cockpit with engines idling and I walked to the rear of the cargo compartment.

Six men appeared from nowhere and—neither looking at nor speaking to me—lifted the coffin and carried it to the cortege. The middle-age man and woman—displaying no reaction to the decay before them, the airplane, or me—led the cortege down a path beyond my sight but not out of my mind.

Being so blatantly ignored filled me with an oppressive guilt, as if I were to blame for the death of a warrior son, and I formed a new irrational responsibility for the war.

★ ★ ★

Our pallbearer role included hauling gray, rectangular, metal caskets, the model used for shipping bodies internationally. One afternoon we relayed four of the caskets from Hue to Da Nang. According to their lieutenant escort, the caskets contained two American and two German missionaries—three men and a woman—who had been executed by the North Vietnamese Army. Our loadmaster wanted to stack the four caskets but the escort officer stopped him. "Regulations forbid placing a male body above or below a female body," he said. "Heads point in the direction of flight," he added, "both sexes."

★ ★ ★

We hauled the wounded as well as the dead. I auditioned for God when we diverted to Phu Bai to pick up a Marine on a stretcher accompanied by a Navy corpsman. We rushed the pair to Da Nang. In the air, I went back to the cargo compartment and learned the Marine with his head wrapped in bandages had been shot in the forehead; the bullet had not exited; the kid had been unconscious from the moment he was hit; and a helicopter had evacuated him to Phu Bai Airport, according to the corpsman.

"Can you do anything for him?" I said.

The corpsman suggested a shot to stimulate the kid but wasn't positive it would help.

"Do it," I said. If I were the kid, I definitely would want it, I thought.

The corpsman performed the act so swiftly that I had to ask, "That's it?"

"That's it," the corpsman echoed and took the kid's pulse.

Moments after our airplane turned off the Da Nang runway, four stretcher-bearers transferred the kid to a waiting helicopter that flew him to the USS *Repose* anchored off shore, a hospital ship with supposedly the best surgical equipment in the world.

"The shot improved his life signs," the corpsman told me, "but I'll bet he dies. If he lives, he'll be a vegetable." He flashed me a peace sign.

"Well...fuck me," I thought. I frequently had told friends, "If I can't feed myself or wipe my own ass, I don't want to be around." For Christ's sake, what had I done to the kid?

Thereafter, when we hauled men with wounds or injuries, I kept my mouth shut.

★ ★ ★

We commonly devoted a whole sortie to one person. Because politics and war operate hand in glove, our sunrise flight from Saigon to Con Son Island appeared logical. In other words, we flew a prisoner dressed in civilian suit and tie to a blip of dirt 50 miles south of where the Mekong River Delta fans into the South China Sea. Two armed Vietnamese military policemen accompanied the silent prisoner whose face remained expressionless even though he wore shackles on his wrists and ankles.

"Poor guy probably voted the wrong way," our pilot said.

"He's not Viet Cong?" I said.

The pilot snorted. "Con Son's for political prisoners. The French built it," he said and left it at that.

Departing the island, we circled low over the prison, and I saw cells sunken below ground level, barred pits exposed to sun and weather. Shades of Devil's Island.

★ ★ ★

As if transporting the dead, wounded, and disfavored had not been trying enough, our crew became involved in an upheaval that grew equally depressing. For days we assisted in relocating families from the Highlands to the Delta. The passengers were women and children who moved like robots with nearly drained batteries.

The women wore black pajamas and carried their possessions slung inside nets that were hammocks. An observer could inventory their wealth as they climbed aboard the plane—pots, pans, clothes, cabbages, whatever. "Wealth" was the wrong word. Their baggage contained necessities for daily living. A couple of women had an empty wooden birdcage tied atop their belongings, making me wonder what tenuous connection the fragile object maintained with the past or what hope it provided for the future. The large loads the women lifted amazed us. They spoke no English.

I imagined my wife leaving home and taking only what she could carry on her back but found no parallel. Comparing these Asians' situation to American life was like matching women from different planets.

With few exceptions, the refugee women resembled grandmothers. Far too thin, with knotted arm and calf muscles, they walked stooped over and had tired, creased faces. The children looked like their grand-children. We had been told the refugees belonged to mountain tribes. We wondered if the younger women had run away. To where? Or was mountain life so physically demanding that women went from childhood directly into old age? Were the women we thought of as grandmothers actually the mothers?

Passenger controllers who put the people aboard our plane emphasized they were being moved out of a dangerous war zone and into safe homes elsewhere. Considering the haphazardly drawn lines of battle across the country, that reasoning was difficult to accept.

On the second day of the operation, somebody said, "This's like working a jig-saw puzzle backward—taking the country apart one piece at a time."

I recalled seeing ancestors of these shuffling, silently suffering women in newsreels from the Korean War and World War II and, before that, when Japan invaded China. My memory released a vivid "war card" drawing—a baseball-card-type of artwork that red-white-and-blue-blooded American children collected in the early 1940s—titled "The Rape of Nanking." It showed an Imperial Japanese Army soldier bayoneting a pregnant

Chinese woman in the belly while a couple of his buddies held aloft a baby impaled on the points of their bayonets. Mounds of dismembered yellow corpses fleshed out the scene. The tableau had been enough to make a nine-year-old swallow the bubble gum that came with the card. The same conditions continued today to my irritation.

★ ★ ★

I belonged to the 772nd Tactical Airlift Squadron comprised of 300 men and 18 C-130s located at Mactan Air Base, Philippines. The squadron operated independently even though the Tactical Airlift Wing headquartered 400 miles north at Clark Air Force Base (AFB) owned it.

The basing arrangement helped to fulfill a scheme that avoided counting C-130 airlift personnel against the in-country troop ceiling of a half million men. To balance the books, C-130 crews rotated from the Philippines, Okinawa, and Taiwan to three bases in South Vietnam for 18 days of temporary duty, with at least three days off back home between trips. Under this deal, 772nd crews worked out of Tan Son Nhut AFB and had to find their own bed and board downtown because no government lodgings or mess facilities were available for them. The politically inspired expediency made me a mercenary—fly when ordered but otherwise fend for myself.

Many men saw the Saigon shuttle as a moneymaker. A Saigon or Cholon hotel room cost between $10–15 a day, an expense usually shared by the crew's three officers—pilot, copilot, and navigator. A crew's two enlisted men—flight engineer and loadmaster—also shared a room. Food cost next to nothing and the Base Exchange sold inexpensive booze. Each man received $25 per diem to cover quarters and food. Crewmen routinely pocketed half of that tax-free allotment.

At the start of the Tet Offensive, the Viet Cong satchel-charged the lobby of the C-130 crews' favorite hotel but failed to kill anyone. We fliers moved on base into a gigantic open bay barrack adjacent to the flight line and packed with rows of World War II steel framed bunk beds to continue our normal schedule until danger cooled down. It was a madhouse with airplanes and people constantly coming and going.

We washed next door in a gym-size shower room. Squatting mamasans watched us and pointed. Red haired guys with freckles drew their biggest laughs.

At Tan Son Nhut, staggered C-130 crews worked around-the-clock, 14-hour days, separated by 14 hours for rest. In the middle of an 18-day shuttle, a crew received a whole day off. The Tet Offensive destroyed that schedule and workdays extended beyond 14 hours to whatever overtime was needed to complete a task. In one day without end, I flew 14 sorties with Captain Maury Gaston in support of Marines in I Corps. Our play-it-by-ear schedule included resupply round trips between Da Nang and Chu Lei from where the Marines seriously engaged in war along the horizon. Working in single file, Marine F-4s supported a battle in which they took off from Chu Lei, flew a low-level pattern to the edge of our vision, dropped their bombs on one pass, circled back to the base, and landed. Waiting arming crews met them and reloaded more bombs practically before the pilots shut down their engines. Minutes later a plane would be taking off again for another tour of the circuit. I called it a merry-go-round of destruction. As if that lengthy day weren't enough punishment, Gaston got into a midnight crap game that lasted until the next morning and lost $1800. *C'est la vie.*

Regardless of its aircrews' limbo-like status, the C-130 provided the brunt of in-country airlift. Toting a 30,000-pound payload, the C-130 could land anywhere that had 2900 feet of runway—concrete, pierced-steel plank, or packed dirt—which included over 150 South Vietnam airfields.

One day, with Major Ernie Dean, we landed near Xuan Loc where a half-mile straightaway in the town's dirt road served as a runway. Jungle had been hacked back from the roadside so a C-130's wings had what looked like minimal clearance. "Can we fit in there?" I said and Dean called it a "piece of cake." He smoothly touched down the Hercules, reversed the propellers, and raised a cloud of dust that reduced visibility to zero. He rode the brakes until the plane bucked and stopped. The dust settled and we found ourselves nose-to-nose with a mournful-looking water buffalo that probably had not seen us coming. Our copilot, "Roger the Lodger," said, "Ask him where we offload."

I first went in-country a few months before the 31 January 1968 start of the NVA/Viet Cong Tet Offensive. At that time, nothing important happened tour after tour. For example, we flew sorties such as delivering two pallets stacked with cardboard cartons cold to the touch and marked "Strawberries, frozen, 5 pounds each" and two pallets marked "Ice cream, frozen, 3 gallons each"—an 8000-pound load—from Da Nang to Dong Ha. Would we come back tomorrow with 8000 pounds of shortcake, I wondered. "Does Captain Queeg run Dong Ha?" I asked, but nobody knew.

One evening we deadheaded from Tan Son Nhut to Da Nang—the length of the country—to pick up an 80-pound aircraft generator for delivery to the Marines at Chu Lai, 45 miles down the coast from Da Nang.

Another day, after being detoured to Phan Rang, we waited two and a half hours before learning a mistake had been made and no cargo pickup was required. From there, we flew an empty airplane to Nha Trang and waited two more hours before being ordered to return to Tan Son Nhut—empty. At that point, a sergeant in the Airlift Control Center told us, "There's nothing to haul. Go home," terminating our workday five hours early.

Days like those were the rule rather than the exception.

An old school flight engineer told me something like, "I don't mean to sound negative, sir, but we could do about as much good if we worked half as many shifts. There's no mission. We're just logging flying time." A first-enlistment loadmaster supported him: "I volunteered to come over here thinking I'd be doing a job important for my country. Yeah, sure. I can't wait to get home."

Of course, those who enjoyed the slow pace reminded complainers "It all counts toward twenty years."

★ ★ ★

And now for the $64 Question: Did Trash Haulers get shot at? Yes, of course. A lot or a little? The degree depended on where we were, when we were there, and what we did there. Perhaps an event that took place in the first days of the 1968 Tet Offensive provides an adequate example.

One evening at Tan Son Nhut, a round from a mortar barrage smacked a C-130 dead center. Both wings of the plane drooped and their internal fuel tanks ruptured. The spectacular fire that followed spread flaming JP-4 fuel across the parking ramp and threatened C-130s parked nearby.

A moment before the C-130 took the hit, Major Gerry Prather, our master sergeant flight engineer, and I had walked out of the Operations Building (Prather became a major general. He owns a lifelong devilish sense of humor but more so an overly zealous sense of responsibility that went into overdrive that night).

The three of us watched the growing flames for a ten count until a rocket hit two buildings away and I decided I'd seen enough. But not Prather.

He grabbed my elbow and said, "That fire's going to spread to the planes on both sides. It could spread down the whole flight line."

"It sure could," I said and tried to pry Prather's fingers off my elbow. I had noticed a nearby depression in the concrete that called for my body to fill it. I knew the fundamental rules for survival in Southeast Asia: one, don't walk under the coconut trees and, two, don't stand up during a rocket attack.

Something erupted on the burning C-130 and denser fire boiled upward, roared outward, reached toward a plane parked downwind. A safe bet said the fire department wouldn't arrive until the attack ended.

Prather said, "We ought to do something."

We were, I thought, like three rubes, we were watching the son of a bitch burn.

"We need to save the ones in danger," Prather said.

A mortar round impacted on a distant taxiway.

"Gerry," I said, "they're government property—made for war—expected to be destroyed."

Prather turned from me and told the flight engineer, "Let's crank 'em and taxi 'em out of there. You take the one on the right," and he sprinted toward the more seriously threatened airplane downwind from the fire.

The flight engineer looked at me. I shook my head: starting engines and taxiing airplanes wasn't my job. I couldn't have done it if survival of the world depended on it.

The engineer ran off as ordered.

The two men started the inboard engines and—without wing walkers or guidance from the tower—moved the airplanes beyond range of the fire.

Prather then ran from his airplane, located three man-size portable fire extinguishers, and waved the flight engineer and me to him. We wheeled the 20-gallon extinguishers upwind and sprayed CB (chlorobromomethane, a hazardous liquid used to fight aircraft fires, long since banned) at the C-130 inferno. Pissing on it would have done as much good.

At some point, the bombardment ended.

The firemen arrived in time to finish saving a scorched wing tip and outboard engine.

* * *

Mortar rounds provided plenty of motivation to move, especially on tactical emergency resupply sorties—ammo deliveries for needy friends under extreme duress, which was common at the height of the Tet Offensive.

Beginning with an assault landing that demanded the pilot's descending at an uncommonly steep angle, executing a gut-wrenching low-altitude round-out, touching down at high speed on the end of the runway, and reversing propellers to aid braking, tactical emergencies got dicey. The maneuver allowed a plane to fly as high as possible while crossing a field's perimeter, thereby reducing the chance of damage by groundfire from enemies attacking the site.

Once the plane was on the ground, its possibility of being mortared demanded unconventional offloading practices that shortened vulnerable exposure time. For example, using a "rapid offload," a pilot ignored the forklifts and, on reaching the first clear area, accelerated and taxied out from under cargo packed on sleds atop rollers. Heavyweight loads careening down and sailing off the trailing aircraft ramp often broke things: it got messy but it was quick.

The pilot made a combat takeoff by standing on the brakes, revving the four engines to maximum speed while the plane trembled with the tension of being locked in place, releasing the brakes, and leaping forward to attain flying speed in minimum runway distance to escape mortar rounds or groundfire. Bounding skyward from an outpost runway of pierced steel planking or dirt and clawing for altitude ended with audible sighs of relief—at least from me until repetition converted the tactic into a Disney ride.

On an equally light note, one afternoon while between loads at Tan Son Nhut, I was napping in an aircraft revetment and a couple of mortar rounds impacted off to my left. They sounded as if they were walking toward me. Guessing I had about 10 seconds between rounds, I ran away from the sound to the adjoining revetment. Three more rounds landed and with each boom I sprinted farther away to the next revetment. I possibly set world records for the 50-yard dash. The mortar shut down before I ran out of revetments. Fright and logic simultaneously motivated my performance, but it was funny, too: I was a cartoon mouse scampering to avoid the tread of an elephant.

Another afternoon on a tactical emergency resupply sortie into Xuan Loc, a Special Forces captain sauntered out to our C-130, climbed up to the cockpit, saluted, and asked how we liked flying our air machine. We gave him a few minutes of boastful airlift bullshit. He waited for us to run down before telling us that if we liked the plane that much, we should move it because one of his spotters reported that Charlie was setting up a mortar his troops couldn't get to right now and he expected rounds would drop on us shortly. If I recall correctly, somebody called him a "blasé motherfucker." We were barely rolling when a mortar round impacted ahead of us. Moments later, a round impacted close behind us. We were airborne before Charlie finished his bracketing.

Two consecutive nights of mortar attacks on Tan Son Nhut proved to be classic displays of gunnery. On each night, a four-round salvo scored a direct hit on an RF-4, destroying it. Both airplanes had been parked in the same revetment. To station the second airplane on the identical spot where the first had burned to ashes, the maintenance chief must have reasoned that lightning did not strike twice in the same place. On the other side, the VC gunners probably did not touch their mortar tube from one night to the next. For them, it was a Secretary-of-Defense-Robert-McNamara-dream-come-true: cost- and labor-effective out the ass.

★ ★ ★

After initially checking out in-country with Major Al Hinton, I primarily navigated for Gerry Prather, Lieutenant Colonel Tex Ritter, Major Ernie Dean, and Captain Maury Gaston. I rode along on my most memorable missions of the year to Khe Sanh, under siege by the North Vietnamese Army, making deliveries by LAPES (Low Altitude Parachute Extraction System, rhymes with "crepes") and CDS (Container Delivery System), both of which dropped loads on the fly. Logisticians calculated Khe Sanh's daily supply requirements at 200 tons, a demand easily met by 15 C-130 flights—weather permitting.

The base at Khe Sanh perched on a hilltop amid naked and fractured red earth. Approaching it on a westerly heading, crews overflew ground that slanted upward in a way that made the hillside appear to move toward the plane. Ground undulations distorted depth perception. Smudges of dishwater gray clouds tended to overlay the area. Frequent mist or light rain often hid the base. On one trip, huge drops of rain pelted the windshield with an intensity that made them appear as if they were coming through the glass. Along the eastern edge of the runway a thin lip of pierced steel planking jutted upward a few inches.

Networks of enemy trenches surrounded the base. Antiaircraft fire was common.

On one of our drops, as if we weren't in the middle of it, the guy manning Ground Control Approach told us, "Charlie is hosing your ass. I can't believe you're not taking hits. You ought to see this."

Another time, GCA got blown off the air in the middle of our approach, which hardly mattered because the basic plan was every plane for itself.

At the start of the siege, which lasted from January to July in 1968, cargo aircraft landed and offloaded conventionally. Flying safely into Khe Sanh ended in February after the NVA riddled a Marine KC-130 carrying 6000 gallons of fuel in bladders in its cargo compartment. Engulfed in flames, the plane stopped on the runway and two crewmen and four passengers died. The airlift commander prohibited C-130s from further landings and ordered them to deliver supplies exclusively by airdrops. Smaller and less costly C-123 Provider transports continued to land with three-ton payloads, a quantity one general termed "creditable but inadequate."

Early in March, the NVA destroyed three C-123s. Mortar fragments damaged one at lift-off and the pilot crash landed with no loss of life; automatic weapons shot down another on landing approach, killing all 49 persons on board; and mortar fire damaged a third while it was taxiing, stopping it from taking off, and further shelling destroyed the plane. Simultaneously, depending on weather conditions, C-130s air dropped up to 200 tons of supplies daily with the LAPES system.

Khe Sanh's runway served as the LAPES drop zone. A perfect C-130 LAPES delivery began from an altitude of exactly five feet, with the airspeed squarely on 130 knots. The flight path followed a normal landing approach pattern except the aircraft trailed a 28-foot reefed parachute attached to connected pallets of cargo. When the plane crossed the runway threshold, the copilot toggled a switch that fired an explosive bolt that unreefed the parachute. The chute popped fully open, yanked the cargo sled out of the airplane, and braked the sled to a stop on the runway.

Upon release, as the mass of cargo swiftly slid aft, its weight pushed down the C-130's tail and caused the plane's nose to rise sharply. The pilot countered the pitch-up by ramming the control yoke full forward at precisely the right moment, basing his timing on a combination of skill, instinct, and a desire to survive. His action averted a low-altitude stall—a nose-high aircraft attitude that rapidly bled airspeed and frequently resulted in a crash. The instant the cargo load dropped clear of the ramp, downward pressure on the tail released; at that point in the flight path, with the control yoke full forward, the airplane was poised to nosedive into the ground. To prevent the nosedive, in the next fraction of a second, the pilot pulled the control yoke into his lap, over-correcting the balance problem by making the airplane want to climb steeply. However, the aircraft's speed was too slow for it to climb steeply. Therefore, the pilot resorted to flying by the seat of his pants and nursing the control yoke forward in order to level the aircraft and again avoid a low-altitude stall. Overall, it was the kind of maneuver that, the first time a pilot did it, he was happy the plane belonged to somebody else. And the subsequent times, too.

Watching the maneuver while standing behind Gerry Prather and seeing Tex Ritter rock back and forth like Ray Charles at the piano, my body sympathized with every groaning rivet in the airframe while he wrestled to convince the plane to fly rather than to crash.

Throughout a perfectly flown LAPES drop, the aircraft's nose maintained a level course. Seldom were LAPES drops flown exactly as diagramed. Therefore, pilots made them with landing gear extended because, although undesirable, wheels often touched earth at some point in the maneuver, causing a plane to buck and bounce.

Air Force C-130s made only 52 LAPES drops at Khe Sanh because what could go wrong did go wrong. A C-130 inadvertently scraped the ground and tore off its ramp, causing its cargo sleds to break apart; timbers and steel planking scattered like gigantic shrapnel, killing one Marine and injuring another. Shortly thereafter, another sled lost its parachute, failed to decelerate, careened off the runway, hit a bunker, and killed another Marine. Subsequently, three more extractions took place with parachute braking failure, resulting in injuries to men on the ground. Following the second death of a Marine, rumor claimed one C-130 pilot's post-flight report stated, "We took more groundfire from the Marine Corps than from the North Vietnamese Army."

The failures dictated an emphasis on CDS maneuvers that required a pilot to approach the drop zone at 300 feet above the ground and an airspeed of 150 knots. The navigator offset the aircraft's heading to compensate for wind effect and, based on arrival abeam a predetermined landmark, he signaled release. At the signal, the copilot activated switches that caused a shearing knife to cut straps arresting A-22 containers in the cargo compartment, and the pilot zoomed the airplane into a steep climb. Gravity finished the job. The containers sat on rollers and the steeper the airplane climbed the faster the containers flowed off the ramp. A lanyard attached to the airplane deployed each container's parachute and the containers drifted to earth. A perfectly executed maneuver placed the containers a few feet apart on the drop zone.

An A-22 container—nicknamed a "bundle"—held up to a ton, and a C-130 carried as many as 16 containers: one to eight in a single row, called a "stick," or two to sixteen in a double row.

The problem with CDS was that the size of the Khe Sanh drop zone was a scant 300 square yards—"Hardly bigger than the inside of a C-130 cargo compartment" one wag complained (Does "wag" stand for "wise ass grouch?"). Consequently, a minor navigator alignment error could result in a container or two of cargo drifting into the no man's land separating the Marines and NVA. Recovering those miscues involved multiple risks. Therefore, troops on the ground sited Khe Sanh's drop zone slightly beyond the western end of the runway, which was the safest location for them when gathering loads.

The CDS tactic required navigators to choose landmarks by studying Joint Operations maps of an inadequate scale. The maps lacked the fine details required to accurately determine check points for timing. Such maps are among the few relics I still have today and running my eyes across their landscape depictions takes me on trips back in time.

★ ★ ★

Ritter, Prather, and I flew to Khe Sanh for about a week as I recollect. Getting to the base presented the biggest challenge. We took fire but suffered only a couple of hits. A round hitting our fuselage sounded muffled, sort of like a slamming door in another room. Descending through shitty weather was more challenging than being shot at. The site and repetitive activity grew familiar in a hurry. Like an audition for acting, crews that did well the first time there were asked back for more performances. But I could be wrong.

I distinctly recall we were the second C-130 to land at Khe Sanh after the siege lifted. Smothered beneath a stagnant haze from exploded shells and bombs, the place reeked of an atmosphere of dissipated destructive force. We taxied to the loading area and turned the plane's ramp toward 100 Marines in full field packs. They stepped aboard like a single person.

We invited the company commander, a stocky captain, up to the flight deck for the trip to Da Nang. "That was the fastest onload in history," I said. "You troops eager to get out of here?"

He smiled. "If you gentlemen can make it to the Monkey Mountain officers' hooch tonight, drinks are on me," he said. "At times I thought we'd never escape this hell-hole. I never been shot at so much without having a chance to shoot back."

"That's the story of our life," I said.

★ ★ ★

With Ernie Dean at the throttles, we dropped CDS bundles for Operation *Delaware* in the A Shau Valley, an area owned by the NVA for the previous two years and used as a main supply route for the Tet Offensive. Critics viewed the Army's venture into the area as a public relations stunt to convince the news media that American forces were capable of large scale offensive action. A token South Vietnamese Army unit was included in the plan, giving *Delaware* the second half of its name—*Lam Son 216*.

Each aircraft in a long line of C-130s carried 12 one-ton bundles with individual parachutes in two rows of six—a double stick—24,000 pounds of food and ammunition for the friendlies.

Prior to our first scheduled drop, the NVA shot down the C-130 in front of us, which was flown by squadron mate Major Lee Stowe. They killed all eight men on board his plane. Stowe had four young children, and after his wife's early death, rumor had it that an Air Force family adopted all of the Stowe children.

The A Shau Valley was a shooting gallery. The 1st Cavalry Division suffered 10 helicopters destroyed and 23 damaged in its first day's assault. Stowe's loss forced the brass to cancel further drops for the day. We carried our load back home. B-52s rearranged the valley scenery overnight. Around sunup, tight-assed but willing, our crew dropped first in a valley free of groundfire—a non-event—but we didn't know that for certain until after we passed through.

Flying down the A Shau Valley, which paralleled the Vietnam-Laos border for 15 miles, created a spooky aura for me. Elephant grass and light forest covered the valley's floor. The valley's walls, solid clumps of trees cemented by shadows, rose steeply to 2500 feet. We were below the tops of hillsides on our right and left and watching them slide by grew mesmerizing. Who knew what evil lurked in the infinite lines of fire between them and us?

From the southernmost village of A Shau, a loose-surfaced road snaked northwest, passing Ta Bat and ending at A Luoi, our drop zone. Each village had an airfield close to the road, which presented a touch of confusion.

For our drop, I misread the landscape, signaled the pilot too early, and delivered our load about a mile short of the target. I could hear the grunts cursing me on the ground at A Luoi. My fuckup taught me a new level of self-hatred.

CHAPTER 5

A Guy Whose Sarcasm Exceeded Mine

I spent most of my first couple of thousand hours of flying in bombers—the B-47 and B-52—aircraft in which the navigator/bombardier's performance counted for at least 80 percent in determining a crew's ability. Consequently, as a navigator, I did not show the deference to pilots that they expected (myopia disqualified me for pilot training and numerous pilots classified me as short sighted in other ways). In the Air Force, the pilot ranked as aircraft commander in all situations, which at times frosted my ass after I got promoted to major and had to follow decisions of captains with less experience in the air. By the way, the Royal Air Force designated the highest ranking officer as king—I mean aircraft commander—regardless of crew position.

I hadn't intended to wander afield here, but my mind detoured down this path so I had better find a way out. The pilots I enjoyed flying with respected my ability and gave me free rein, which was what a professional wanted. The best pilots were Ray Monge (bless him above others for his depth of understanding), John Mitchell, and Ken Smith in the B-47; Dean and Gaston along with Rickert and Prather in the C-130; Dave Woolwine and Bob Killam, with Holley atop the heap, in the AC-130.

That detour path led to Phil Combies, a guy whose sarcasm exceeded mine. We taught at Squadron Officer School in the early sixties. Combies hated the job. His one true love was flying fighters. Disliking his attitude for the first year I knew him, I learned to admire his unadorned outlook on life, but other people described him better than I ever could.

Neal Combies told me the following about his father:

The image of my father came into perfect perspective on a cold January morning, while I was standing outside of the Samuel Huntington Elementary School in Norwich, Connecticut, waiting for the doors to open. Like any other morning, I'd ridden the bus to school, got off, and milled around with the other students. But today, I felt alone, outside of the crowd. I saw several of my teachers standing behind a window, smiling, looking out at me, pointing at me. Other children seemed to grant me a distance that was new. I slowly realized they were admiring the eight-year-old son of a hero.

The previous evening the United States Air Force had pulled off Operation *Bolo* that killed seven North Vietnamese MiGs. And my father—Major Phil Combies—was one of the MiG killers. He also scored a probable kill. Walter Cronkite had talked about *Bolo* on the evening's news. My mother, three sisters, and I knew what my father had done. Now I realized that the rest of the world also knew, and I was bathing in my father's glory.

The year was 1967 and the Vietnam War was still a respectable enterprise. The Tet Offensive, Nixon's bombing of Cambodia, and the anti-war movement were still to come. In my mind, however, the war involved a lot of evil thoughts. The name 'Viet Cong' sounded sinister to me, made me picture Orientals determined to hurt Americans. Hearing the name of the nation—Viet Nam, two words at that time—gave me an eerie sensation, something like walking through a graveyard in the middle of the night. I imagined all of Southeast Asia as a dangerous place. Yes, I feared for my father's safety but, at the same time, knew he was capable of taking care of himself.

When my father received orders for Vietnam, he and my mother decided to move the family back to their hometown of Norwich. They had met there in high school, and their families still lived there. My father was the only member of either family to seek a life that extended beyond the town and state. My mother wasn't happy about my father's assignment. She accused him of volunteering for it, which may have been true. He had just finished a four year tour of duty at Maxwell Air Force Base in Montgomery, Alabama, the first year as a student at Air Command and Staff College and the last three as an instructor at Squadron Officer School. He hated teaching because it wasted years he could have been in the air. At that time he flew a minimum number of hours in propeller driven aircraft to maintain proficiency. Before Maxwell, he had been strictly a jet fighter pilot.

My father's orders assigned him to fly F-4 Phantoms with the 8th Tactical Fighter Wing—the Wolfpack—at Ubon Royal Thai Air Force Base. He eagerly anticipated the mission because it offered a chance for air-to-air combat over North Vietnam. While he trained at MacDill AFB, we lived outside of Hillsborough, Florida, in a dilapidated house that brought tears to my mother's eyes when she first saw it. We had rented it sight unseen. But like a good military wife she made the best of it without complaining.

On the morning of out-processing from training, my father received amended orders assigning him to F-4s at Da Nang Air Base in South Vietnam. That wing flew air-to-ground missions in support of army operations in South Vietnam, where no MiGs roamed. The task was meaningful but not glorious, not the ultimate air-to-air test of a real fighter pilot. My father brooded over the change for most of the afternoon: he told himself that reassignments were part of being a career soldier. By nightfall, after a few drinks of Ten High, he decided he didn't deserve such shabby treatment. He had paid his dues by sitting at a desk for four years. Now he wanted the best. So he threw the amended paperwork into Tampa Bay and used his original orders to travel to Ubon. Once he arrived there, the Wolfpack commander welcomed him.

Later in the war, my father killed a second MiG.

★ ★ ★

Combies and I met up again in the mid-eighties in Austin. Working on a novel about F-4s, I enlisted his help in providing accurate color commentary. Our work routine at my home followed a checklist: first, we sat down to a feast of Mexican food—enchiladas, tacos, tamales, avocados, frijoles—cooked and served by Jan, my perfect wife (shades of my parents' hospitality toward warriors); second, Combies pushed back in a recliner and went to work on a bottle of Ten High with a bucket of ice and pitcher of water at his elbow; third, I debriefed him, asking long lists of questions about how a MiG-killer had seen the war.

Like Neal, Jan developed her personalized assessment of Combies. She said:

> He has an honest to God *joie de vivre*. You know how some people change personalities at a party, sort of loosen up? Well, Phil's like that all the time, twenty-four hours a day. He's irreverent—politically incorrect—over the top— and he has a sense of humor—all the stuff I like about air force fliers. I know his personality has to influence the way he flies—you know, "I don't give a shit. Let's just go get 'em."

That type of audacity made Operation *Bolo* a success. Wolfpack Commander Colonel Robin Olds designed the plan for *Bolo* based on an ever-increasing MiG threat against the F-105 Thunderchiefs—lovingly named "Thuds"—that served primarily as bombers over North Vietnam.

The MiGs tried to avoid F-4s while attacking F-105s in hope of shooting them down or at least forcing them to jettison their bombs short of the target in order to gain maneuverability for self-defense. After an F-105 shed its bombs, it could hold its own with a MiG in air-to-air combat, but that was not its primary mission. Olds's plan intended to lure MiGs to battle with F-4s by fooling North Vietnamese Air Force ground controllers into misidentifying flights of F-4s as Thuds. In preparation for *Bolo*, Olds sent the F-4 crews to a four-day school where they learned to masquerade as a wave of Thuds on a bombing mission. They also refined their air-to-air tactics.

On 2 January 1967, Olds sprung the trap. Three flights of four F-4s departed Ubon with Olds leading the first, Colonel Daniel "Chappie" James the second, and Captain John Stone the third, which included Combies. The F-4s joined up with KC-135 tankers for refueling and engaged in radio chatter that simulated Thuds running their standard target-bound checklists. A solid undercast with cloud tops at about 6000 feet kept the F-4 crews from seeing the ground. Therefore, the crewmen feared the ground controllers would recognize the weather was unsuited for bombing and decide not to launch MiGs. Combies looked over the situation and said to his backseater, "Wrong weather. We'll have to wait and see."

Much has been recorded about *Bolo* and most accounts center on Olds. He shot down one MiG that day, but six other Phantom crews also scored and had tales to tell. The following is Combies' account of his action on that day as he told it to me.

★ ★ ★

Trotting along at pretty good speed, the four F-4 Phantom jets in Rambler flight hunted for something to kill. Echeloned left at 4000-foot intervals from eight thou up to twenty thou, they headed southeast paralleling Thud Ridge. The Ridge was a 40-mile-long mountain range aimed like an arrow directly at Hanoi, 20 miles away. Its peaks reached to six thou. Thuds had used the Ridge as a mask against SAMs until the NVA wised up and positioned 37-mm antiaircraft guns across the area.

Riding atop a stack of four Phantoms, Major Phil Combies knew he had his ass hung out. At any moment he expected a SAM to pop through the undercast and home on him. By the time he saw the missile it would be up to speed, humming along near Mach 2. He would have about a tick and a half to dive and turn into the missile and hopefully outbend it, hopefully watch it attempt to fly up its own exhaust-hole and thereby miss his likewise-orifice. Another fun-filled day of technoviolence, Combies thought. But if the day came off as planned—if the ruse worked—he expected to be a MiG-killer by nightfall.

Over headset he heard the "scree" of ground-based search radar as its scan swept across his fighter. He wondered if the radar was Ground Control Intercept that vectored MiG attacks or if it was *Fan Song* that launched and guided SAMs. "You watching that RHAW-gear back there?" he asked Lieutenant Lee Dutton who was in the F-4's rear seat.

Dutton also heard the sweeps. Since entering North Vietnam his eyes had been locked on his warning equipment. He answered, "Yeah."

"Yeah?" Combies repeated mockingly.

"Yeah, sir?"

"I don't want any last-minute surprises from one of those big white bastards. We don't have a lot of room to play with." The NVA would shoot white today, Combies decided, tougher to see against the clouds. SAMs came in assorted colors: white, black, and the ever-popular camouflage brown and green, practically identical to the Phantom's paint job.

"Knock off the gab and keep your eyes open. Stay alert," Combies said half-jokingly. One pair of eyes wasn't enough when over enemy territory and up against an array of technological threats. Combies expected the kid in the back seat to focus on the gee-whiz electronics inside the cockpit while he scanned the outside world.

About then the four Phantoms of Rambler flight turned over the North Vietnamese air base at Phuc Yen and headed back to the northwest, up the west side of the Ridge.

MiGs operated from five principal airfields—Phuc Yen, Kep, and Gia Lam near Hanoi, plus Kien An and Cat Bi outside Haiphong—sanctuaries where they were free from attack while on the ground because, at the time, the United States government prohibited strikes against North

Vietnamese airfields (in May 1967, the government reclassified airfields as valid targets, and USAF fighters destroyed 26 MiGs on the ground by timing raids to catch them between sorties). With such immunity, the NVAF chose to scramble MiGs and have them either feint an attack or make a slashing high-speed firing pass through the formation of grossed-out target-bound F-105s, tempting them to dump their loads early and join in air-to-air combat. Once the strike force was thus neutralized, the MiGs fled to their airfield sanctuaries. From September through December 1966, 107 of 192 strike aircraft, or 56 percent, jettisoned their ordnance when engaged by MiGs.

Since 1964, when American air strikes began against North Vietnam, air defense forces had responded unpredictably. However, USAF analysts recognized a vague cyclic defense reaction geared to the experience levels of MiG pilots, seasonal weather, and the pattern of the offensive strike forces. *Bolo* had been predicated on the latter factor. The Phantoms flew exact F-105 mission profiles—using Thud refueling tracks and altitudes, target approach routes, airspeeds, radio call signs, and other procedures. Furthermore, for the first time, F-4s carried ECM pods to jam enemy radar, a recognized F-105 capability.

Now everything was in place—Olds's flight had arrived over target at 1500 hours, Ford flight at 1505, Rambler at 1510—with the three spearhead flights poised in motion, independently trolling as MiGCAPs ahead of an inbound 84 ship main force. So the next step depended on the North Vietnamese radar controllers' reaction: would they be deceived and scramble MiGs?

Fly around and wait, Combies thought. Same story, different day: hours of boredom broken by seconds of terror. On the lookout, his head and eyes constantly moved: he searched the horizon, the sky above and below. Yet he was happy to be here. His dozen years of piloting the F-86, F-100, and F-102 had built toward this day. At the same time he was lucky to be on the perch. After *Bolo* had been delayed an hour because of clouds over target, while cranking his plane's twin jet engines, his left hand generator would not stay on line. Repairing it would have required downloading his Sparrow missiles, maintenance that would have thrown him out of the takeoff sequence and probably resulted in an abort. Knowing no spare airplane was available, he had decided to "overlook" the malfunction: it was a maximum effort day. A crew chief with a leg in a cast had been feverishly hopping about the parking ramp, readying his F-4.

With nothing happening, tension building, and as nervous as a whore in church, Combies recognized whatever would happen had better happen fast. Today the F-4s had short legs, carried only outboard fuel tanks, no 600-gallon centerline tank. The streamlined configuration left them ready to dogfight instantly.

Then "Bogies... Bogies..." crackled in his headset. It sounded as if the Olds and Ford flights had rolled in to attack. Amid radio calls between the flights, Rambler lead Captain John Stone asked, "Where are you? Where are the MiGs?" The voice of Colonel Robin Olds rumbled back, loud and clear, "These are mine. Find your own."

Listening to the battle rage, Combies grew frustrated. Then he saw them, was first to spot them—six drops of quicksilver gliding over cotton—and he called, "Two o'clock low, six bandits." The delta-wing shapes were unmistakable. In a shallow climb, six sleek MiG-21 *Fishbeds* had slipped out of the clouds about eight miles away, parallel to Combies. The nerves on his hands and forearms tingled. The MiGs seemed unaware of the F-4s above them. Fucking beautiful, Combies thought.

Rambler flight made a hard right turn and Stone called, "Lead's in." He dived at the MiGs, followed immediately by Lieutenant Larry Glynn, flying Two position. Three sat still as a dead-ass. Combies gave him a two count, then hit both afterburners and rolled into a dive toward the enemy. "Yow," he yelled to Dutton. He flashed by Three who still flew straight and level and saw him again only after the fight ended. He called, "Four in. Three?"

After four days of briefings on tactics and discussions about covering each other and working as a team, plans and promises disappeared in a blink. With the meat on the table, it became every man for himself—catch as catch can, no holds barred.

By the time the MiG-21 pilots woke up, they were out of position for a head-on pass at the F-4s. Undaunted, they executed a snap turn and started shooting. Tracers from their twin-barrel 23-mm cannons looked like flaming red golf balls as they curved away from the diving Phantoms.

Combies' whole body tingled as he leaned forward against his shoulder straps, but his mind was calm. He had one objective: get behind the bastard he had picked for a target before rolling in. Nearing his prey, he kicked the rudders, horsed the control stick with his right hand, and hot-rodded the throttles with his left, in and out and back into afterburners: Boom! Boom! Rudder rolling through a high angle-off attack, he wasn't thinking about his physical movements: the plane was one with his body, an extension of his physical being. He just as easily could have been running down a street after the bandit. The rotating horizon went unnoticed: to a fighter jock the aircraft is always right side up. Combies had only eyes for his target.

He pulled the control stick right, back, tighter right, back more. He had been warned an F-4 was at a disadvantage in trying to out-turn a MiG-21, but he was doing it and pulling only four to five Gs, nowhere near the G-load he had expected necessary to beat one of those guys. About 30 seconds after spotting his target, with unimagined ease, Combies rolled out in the MiG's seven o'clock slot. Then they started turning again, pulling about six Gs.

Combies' C-model Phantom didn't have a lead-computing gunsight, so he ignored the fancy illuminated reticle and steering dot projected on his center windscreen. Instead, he flew so the MiG appeared to be sitting on the F-4's nose radome. Eyeballs were best, he believed. The two airplanes made one tight circle before Combies knew he owned him—a big silver delta-shape MiG-21 with a big red star on each wing. "Lee?" he said and caught himself grinning inside his oxygen mask.

Dutton replied, "You got a radar lock. In range." In that situation, Dutton constantly looked behind, spotting any MiG on their tail. The F-4 was a neckbreaker. Now Dutton had anticipated Combies' need and had put his head down in the cockpit, where Combies sure didn't want his. Once a fighter pilot saw the other guy, he never wanted to lose sight of him.

Combies pulled the trigger on the head of his control column. With interlocks out, the mechanical genius of the radar fire control computer was bypassed; the missiles should have launched instantly. Instead, the radar-guided AIM-7 Sparrow missile fizzled—simply fell off the airplane. Nothing? Goddamn son of a bitch, Combies thought.

Now both planes were in a hard left turn, relatively level at around 12,000 feet. The MiG pilot pulled for all he was worth but Combies pulled a little harder. He had no idea of their speed. He went in and out of afterburner, trying not to overrun the MiG, maintaining his advantage by yo-yoing, wanting more speed while trying to conserve fighting fuel. Excited—exhilarated—yet cool and calculating, about 10 or 15 seconds after the first Sparrow failed, he squeezed the trigger again and a second Sparrow flew home—a darting journey of less than a mile.

The Sparrow's 90-pound warhead hit the MiG in the tailpipe and the plane blew up. A big orange ball of fire momentarily hid the airframe. Pieces of the plane tore loose, hung suspended in the wake of the MiG's slipstream. An instant later, the fighter tumbled forward, lost momentum, and entered its final gravitational arc.

Passing the wreck, Combies was startled to see a man hanging in a parachute. How did he get out of the airplane before the explosion? Probably he saw the rocket fire from the Sparrow's tail and decided it wasn't his day, Combies thought.

Corkscrewing downward, the abandoned airframe bored its way into the cloud deck below.

"Hey, you got one," somebody shouted.

Airplanes filled the sky.

A flow of words, gasps, pants filled the radio.

"There's one, three o'clock."

"…afterburner. Goddamn…"

"See him."

"Go get…"

"He's mine."

"Two, break right."

"Fuckin'… Check six. Check my six."

"I got him." A crow of triumph. Combies recognized the voice and thought, Stone killed a MiG. Stone and backseater Lieutenant Clifton

Dunnegan made the kill with one of three AIM-7s triggered at the target. The decider hit near the wing root and set the MiG ablaze.

"Check my six, goddamnit."

"You're clean. I got him."

Off to his left, Combies saw a smear of black smoke extending down toward the cloud deck.

"I got him."

"Good show. Now get off the air," a voice commanded. Olds's voice? Even from afar, keeping tabs on everyone and everything? Time enough to celebrate back on the ground.

Following his kill, Combies took time to glance at his armament panel: every switch was positioned correctly. Good! The Sparrow had fucked up, not him, he thought and began searching for more MiGs. Out of nowhere, another went by and he fired his third Sparrow, but the rate of closure was beyond the missile's performance capabilities, and he missed.

A few hundred feet below, Combies saw another MiG cutting a circle slightly inside of his. Putting back pressure on the control stick, he decreased his bank angle, then arced the jet's nose upward. The Law of Physics went to work: in a wink, gravity sucked off the Phantom's excess speed and reduced the angle between the aircraft. The Phantom climbed for an instant before Combies rolled it onto its back, then pulled its nose toward the MiG's six o'clock position, slicing the circle in half. The maneuver, a high speed yo-yo, placed the Phantom directly in trail behind the MiG as if the guy had waited for him.

Same delta shape, same red stars. "Beautiful. Lock on? Lee?" Combies said.

"You're set."

Combies pulled the trigger and his fourth Sparrow missile died on the rails. Fuck this bullshit, he thought. He flew like crazy to stay behind these guys and his supposed technological advantage presented the biggest handicap he had ever encountered. He would have traded his left nut for a .50-caliber machinegun.

Stretching forward, Combies flipped the T-bar switch with his left hand and changed to the AIM-9 Sidewinder missiles—heat seekers with

25-pound warheads and infrared sensors attracted to exhausts. Now in a climb, he spotted two more MiG-21s, low at 10 o'clock. Bending around to get behind them, he pulled eight Gs. In the back seat, Dutton grunted under the effects of the heavy G-force.

Off to the side, Glynn came around tightly and slid in next to Combies. The two MiG-21s zoomed upward, and Combies said, "I got the one on the right." Glynn called back an affirmative just as the MiGs performed a tactical split: Combies' target went high and left while the other guy descended with Glynn after him. Glynn and Lieutenant Lawrence Cary destroyed it about a minute later with one of a pair of Sparrows. The target exploded directly in front of them, leaving Glynn no alternative but to fly through the debris, thereby damaging the underside of his Phantom—the only damaged suffered by Rambler flight. Surprisingly, the pilot escaped from the shattered MiG and parachuted safely to earth, as did the pilot of the MiG set afire by Stone. Glynn later shot another Sparrow at another but it passed 2000 feet in front of the target.

Overeager, Combies messed up the parameters for firing his Sidewinders. In a five-G turn he fired two but they went wide of the target. Designed 10 years earlier for use against slow-moving bombers, they were almost useless against swift and hard-turning fighters. Sweating now, Combies got behind the MiG, a mile back, out of sight in his six o'clock position—sweet deep six.

At that point, the MIG pilot solved the problem: flying at 12,000 feet, he leveled his fighter and started a climb while rolling and rocking his wings, obviously confused and looking for Combies. "You idiot," Combies thought and launched two Sidewinders, his last weapons. His mach meter read 1.8, nearly twice the speed of sound. Both missiles came off the rails cleanly and tracked perfectly—parallel snakes of smoke. No way they could miss, Combies thought.

The weapons had flown almost home when a voice shouted, "F-4, break hard right." In response, Combies racked the Phantom into a steep turn, dived madly, found himself flying for his life. His mind raced as if turbocharged. Had he fallen into the fighter pilot's oldest trap? Intent on destroying one bandit, had he allowed another to line him up? Twisting through space, his eyes grabbed patches of sky, expected to find a MiG on his tail. He found nothing but blue above and white below. Realizing the warning had not been directed at him, his mind asked, "Who the fuck called break?" Back at Ubon, Combies learned the warning had saved Stone from a MiG-21 firing at him.

Scanning the area where his Sidewinders had the MiG pinpointed, Combies saw a man hanging in a parachute. No MiG was in sight. From where had the 'chutist come? When Combies had fired his Sidewinders, this guy's airplane and Combies' Phantom had been the only two in that chunk of sky.

As it turned out, the "Break" call had caused everyone to panic, and nobody saw whether Combies' Sidewinders hit or missed or what became of the MiG. Under the absolute values of crediting aerial victories, the guy in a parachute provided no validity. But the scene justified claiming a probable, which was as satisfying as almost getting a piece of ass.

In a moment with nothing happening, Combies flipped his oxygen control lever to 100 percent and swallowed deep breaths of cool pure oxygen before he peripherally saw two MiG-21s hightailing it in formation. He turned after them. Dutton said, "What're you doing?"

"I got two MiGs visual," Combies said.

"And what're you going to do," Dutton quietly asked, "throw rocks at them?"

At that point, Combies would have tossed in his right nut too in exchange for a .50-cal. Dutton was right; they were out of missiles and hurting for fuel. Breaking off the chase, he searched for the rest of Rambler flight.

★ ★ ★

The results boosted the morale of USAF fighter pilots worldwide—seven confirmed kills—nearly half of the NVAF's inventory. USAF losses: zero. Olds's intense debriefing of the crewmen reinforced what they had done correctly and corrected mistakes. He succinctly summed up the operation: "Well—you see—to make a wonderfully long story short—the MiGs lost."

The victory party rocked and rolled across Ubon—staggering from Officers' Club to NCOs' Club to Airmen's Club. Combies recalled the day as "One helluva afternoon in the air. And that night on the ground was something I wouldn't want to relive. I think we finished up at daybreak in nothing but skivvies and flying boots."

CHAPTER 6

That Goddamn Fucking Steel Mill

Like me, Neal Combies' heroes were soldiers. His fondest recollection in that respect was an afternoon when Phil took him to Andrews Air Force Base to meet General Olds, who they found eating a burger and French fries in the base operations snack bar. Seeing Olds without the moustache that had been prominent in his Ubon photographs surprised Neal. It was their first meeting, but Olds greeted Neal as if they had been buddies for years and offered to share his fries. "Can you believe how I felt?" Neal said to me. "I'm ten years old and Robin Olds is passing me salt and ketchup and sharing his fries with me. What could be greater?"

When possible, Phil made his son a partner in his activities. "When Phil became Director of Operations for the 49th Tactical Fighter Wing at Holloman," Neal said, "he took me to the final briefing before they deployed to Germany. We entered the hanger and somebody shouted, 'Ten-hut,' and the room popped to, just like in the movies. It took a second before I realized they'd done it for my father."

Neal attended fighter pilots' reunions and schmoozed with several famous fliers. Displaying encyclopedic knowledge of aerial achievements—information gleaned from a dedication similar to how sports fans worshipped their favorite team and players—Neal easily fit into the group. He most enjoyed talking to Bob Pardo, renowned for the "Pardo Push," a classic aviation maneuver in which he kept a battle-damaged Phantom airborne by repeatedly nudging it from below. After speaking with Neal one night and well beyond sunrise, Pardo, who became a brigadier general, told Phil, "Your kid knows what I did better than I do."

Neal easily described the authenticity inherent in his heroes:

> Fighter jocks are a tight group. Phil would do anything for anyone. He was generous and a loyal friend. When he was nearing forty years old, with a receding hairline, a wife and four kids, he still walked with a swagger. But he wasn't Tom Cruise in *Top Gun*. He saw that movie and walked out before it ended. He said, 'That's not the way it works. That's bullshit. But spectacular flying!' And he wasn't the Great Santini. He was my dad—the pilot.

Phil himself took a realistic view of his trade. Watching a flight of four fighters sequentially pitch out for landing, like acrobats in a rhythmic performance, Neal asked Phil, "They do that so perfectly. How do they know exactly when to break like that?" Phil said, "Charley, it's simple. You just have to learn how to count to four."

Combies called his son "Charley," a nickname Neal never fully understood but one that pleased him so much that for a while he considered changing his name.

My identifying with Neal was easy: he loved and respected his father as much as I loved and respected mine. The nickname routine clinched our bond. My father had frequently called me "Jim," mostly using the term when he sought a favor, such as "Jim, how about getting us a couple more beers?" when entertaining a guest. After Dad died, I learned that in the hobo world "Jim" pretty much served the same purpose as "Dude" did among a later generation.

Although Combies often visited my home, I only met Robin Olds on the telephone. In the mid-nineties, a few years after publication of *The First Ace*, my novel about Phantom operations in Vietnam, I got an urge to write Olds's biography, referencing what better source than the man himself. I sent him a proposal letter. When, after several months, he hadn't answered, I phoned him. We talked briefly: he told me he wasn't interested and I shouldn't bother him. Because I offered much with no strings, I started to say, "So you're going to fuckin' die and nobody will ever hear your side of your story." But I didn't. My hesitation came from a vestige of ingrained R-E-S-P-E-C-T. The man was legend, but

I should have challenged him. If anyone loved the truth, it had to have been Olds.

As it turned out, Olds granted an interview to John Darrell Sherwood—the "Official Historian of the United States Naval Historical Center" for Christ's sake!—in 1997; Sherwood devoted a whole 37 pages to summarizing Olds's life in *Fast Movers: Jet Pilots and the Vietnam Experience*. A crime of omission.

General Olds died in 2007. In 2011, his daughter, Christina Olds, with the help of Ed Rasimus, published *Fighter Pilot: The Memoirs of Legendary Ace Robin Olds*. The book is a good read. Buy it. Olds had expressed his opinions in minor interviews like the one mentioned above, and shared his ideas about combat flying with the History Channel, but his memories would have been far more dynamic if he had compiled them on his own. Especially with my help.

This brings us to one of the wildest bombing missions I ever heard about. In her book, Christina Olds talks about that mission from Robin's point of view but, before then, Combies had already related his version of the mission to me. The following recollects how Phil experienced a morning drive to a popular North Vietnamese production facility.

★ ★ ★

Phil Combies' first low-level pop-up bombing mission to the Thai Nguyen iron and steel complex, located 35 miles north of Hanoi, was a masochist's wet dream. For years after, the word "suicidal" loomed up in his mind when he thought of Thai Nguyen.

He had gone to Southeast Asia with the aim of dogfighting his F-4 Phantom against MiGs in traditional fighter jock fashion. When he mentioned that fact to his wing commander, Olds, who had scored 12 kills in World War II, Olds said, "Let's face it, Phil, wars aren't what they used to be. But at least we have one."

An Air Force general explained the situation in 1967: "Any MiG kill is a bonus. The objective of the air offensive over the North is to destroy the North's ability to support operations against South Vietnam. Air superiority is necessary only to protect the strike force so that ordnance can be placed precisely on assigned targets with the least possible loss of American crews."

Unfortunately for the aircrews, the North Vietnamese knew their nation's prime targets were grouped within a hundred-mile radius of Hanoi. Therefore, the North Vietnamese Army packed the area wall-to-wall with antiaircraft defenses: SA-2 *Guideline* surface-to-air missiles (SAM) capable of boosting 300-pound warheads to an altitude of 65,000 feet; antiaircraft artillery ranging from 23-mm to 130-mm, the largest of which lobbed projectiles up to 40,000 feet; plus the whole array of early warning, height finding, and intercept radar systems; along with assorted small arms fire from anyone that had a weapon. The North Vietnamese could afford to be prodigal with firepower; the Soviet Union and Communist China paid the bills.

Before hitching up with F-105 Thunderchiefs to form 50-100 plane armadas reminiscent of World War II and Korea, Phantoms flew four-ship, low-level, pop-up missions against the North. Their *Operational Procedures Manual* described a maneuver for crews attacking "a high priority target in a SAM environment" by recommending: "The aircraft approaches the target area in low-level penetration to enhance survivability, achieve deception, and surprise the defense."

Combies read The Manual and said, "Shit, the defense would be more surprised if we didn't show up."

"Low-level penetration to enhance survivability" was also moot. The SA-2 *Guideline/Fan Song* package was a medium- to high-level missile/radar system, which meant it couldn't track fast-moving aircraft flying below 3000 feet. Therefore, by staying below 3000 feet fighter-bombers were safe from surface-to-air missiles. However, they were then inside the small arms envelope where they were exposed to being gutshot by anyone that owned a pea shooter.

The Manual spelled out a pop-up tactic: "...the aircraft is maneuvered until the target falls within a desirable angle extending from the nose of the aircraft to the target. Airspeed is increased, and at pop-up point the aircraft initiates a wing-level pull-up, climbs to an apex altitude above the target suitable for bombing."

Combies read the procedures several times and with each reading the instructions grew more amusing, grew into classic understatements. Theory took place in a vacuum. Practice happened in steel-filled air. Combies thought of such an attack as a "charge into oblivion." At the briefing for the attack on the Thai Nguyen iron and steel works, he told his backseater, Lee Dutton, "My family is in the iron and steel business—my mother irons and my father steals," which was their last laugh of the day.

Combies flew tail end in a flight of three Phantoms. Olds led with Major George Greaves directly behind him. Each airplane lugged six 750-pound bombs. In comparison, one B-52 Stratofortress carried a load equivalent to 15 Phantoms, but political restraints kept B-52s out of the North until December 1972. A scheduled fourth aircraft aborted on the ground and the spare failed to taxi for reasons Combies didn't hear. Later, Dutton said, only half-jokingly, "They knew something we didn't. They were smarter."

The day's plan of attack was simple: fly as fast as possible between the hills and into the murk. Olds, Greaves, and Combies planned to blast off from Thailand, roar in formation above Laos where they would refuel from an orbiting tanker, then flash down to the deck and burn a streak across North Vietnam—157 miles at 540 knots: 17 minutes in, 17 minutes out—at no more than 30 feet above the ground in the valleys and no higher than 100 feet over the mountains. Olds believed low level meant low level.

Combies read the frag order and thought, "You've got to be shitting me."

In accordance with The Manual, "deception and surprise" were relative. The North Vietnamese Army (NVA) knew the bombers were coming. An hour earlier a flight of four Phantoms had flown the same route against the same target. The timing exemplified the questionable thinking of Seventh Air Force planners located at Tan Son Nhut in Saigon: using identical tactics ensured the enemy was wide awake and scanning the sky.

Early on the way inbound, NVA gunners shot at the three low-flying Phantoms haphazardly. Dutton map read to check out the inertial navigation computer and make certain they were on course. Combies kept an eye on Olds and Greaves while flying as low as possible and avoiding scooping grass into his engines' intakes.

A large patch of raunchy weather presented cloud decks a hundred feet off the mountains with visibility of a half mile. Eighty miles from the target, the Phantoms climbed to 3500 feet to clear the area's highest peak. From that altitude, with clouds below, the Phantom crewmen couldn't see the ground to watch for the white smoke plume of a SAM launch. They relied on seeing the flames of the SAM sustainer engine as soon as the missile popped through the clouds, which left them with a couple of ticks to react. If the SAM engine had already burned out, no tail of flame remained visible and the lighter-weight SAM would be traveling at top speed, reducing a pilot's reaction time to nearly zero.

The final leg of the low-level route followed a narrow valley where guns lined the hilltops. Entering the valley, and having been there before, Olds said, "Okay, troops, it's time. Let's go down." The three Phantom crews punched through the cloud deck, broke out at 700 feet, and saw the Red River (the Hong River) before them. They were a quarter mile abeam of their checkpoint.

They ripped into the valley and the whole world lit up. The sky filled with streaks of glowing tracers. Looking up, Combies saw woven patterns of crisscrossing fire, a red ceiling of flak covering the valley. He heard Dutton breathing twice as loud as normal, then realized he, too, was hyperventilating. They raced along the valley floor at 540 knots and 30 feet altitude. Combies looked up again and, seeing hummocks around the guns, joyfully recognized the gunners couldn't depress their weapons far enough to hit the planes. Still the gunners kept shooting. Some blasted away down the length of the valley while others wildly sprayed fire across the valley. Small and large bore weapons—everything from AK-47s up to 57-mm—pumped endless streams of rounds. Tracers flashing from hilltop to hilltop made Combies say, "The bastards are shooting each other."

"And?" Dutton said. Thinking ahead, he knew that within a minute, they were going up into that layer of flaming steel.

Eight miles from target the Phantoms had to climb to 200 feet, the altitude necessary to permit their bombs to arm after they were dropped. At release, the bomb's high-drogue fins extended into wide X-shaped spoilers that rapidly braked the weapons' speed and converted their horizontal glide path into a vertical drop. The broad spoilers permitted the delivery aircraft to leave the bombs quickly behind and thereby escape their effects.

Approaching pop-up point, a railroad spur, Olds said, "Ready?" Greaves and Combies checked in: "Two." "Three."

Olds went up an instant before the others and an antiaircraft artillery round exploded under his right wing. The shell blew a hole completely through the wing and Combies called, "Lead, you're hit."

Olds calmly said, "I know." Fuel and smoke poured from the gaping hole in his wing.

In a climb, Combies saw flames licking off the trailing edge of Olds's wing. Then after two "cracks" and a "whump" and a "thump," the right quarter panel of his windscreen erupted inward. "Three's hit," Combies shouted and found he was upside down, 50 feet above the ground and traveling at 550 knots. Wind roared into the cockpit and he couldn't hear, could hardly see. Shards of glass were on his face, down his collar, all over the cockpit. More shards blew in at him, momentarily blinded his right eye, but the plane continued to fly.

Pulling down his clear helmet visor, he shouted, "Lee, don't go. Don't go." Instinctively he held the throttles forward: he had to maintain his speed, his primary defense. With eyes on the inverted horizon and flying by the seat of his pants, he pushed forward on the stick, kicked left rudder, and rolled the Phantom upright to a straight and level attitude.

By then Olds and Greaves were far ahead, nearing the bomb release line. Combies glanced at his engine instruments. Everything appeared normal. What the hell, what more could he ask for, he thought. He hadn't come that far for nothing. Leaning on the throttles, he tried to bend them beyond 100 percent power to catch up. Remembering he wasn't alone, he said, "Lee, you still there?"

Dutton quietly answered, "Affirmative."

Combies saw bombs drop from the other two Phantoms. Below them were three tall smoke stacks lined up north to south, and several long, three- to five-story gray buildings. If those buildings were the steel mill, he thought, the lineup looked perfect and the bombs would land exactly on target.

Pushing harder on the throttles, he thought the airspeed increased slightly. He reached the bomb release line and the buildings looked exactly like the photographs he had studied at Ubon—a lifetime ago. He pickled the six 750-pounders and mentally thanked Sweet Jesus when they separated cleanly. Then the world came apart again.

In falling behind, he had distanced himself from Olds and Greaves so that he arrived over target when their bombs detonated. His plane buffeted, bounced, and yawed in the concussions and shock waves of the bomb blasts. Then the control stick went dead in his hand and Combies' heart nearly stopped. Tracers still crisscrossed around him. If they didn't get him, his own guys would, he thought. Another lifetime passed before he regained control of his plane and, a moment later, he was through, had somehow survived the gauntlet.

Spotting Olds and Greaves turning in a right bank, he cut inside their arc and rejoined them. Olds said, "Glad to see you again." Olds's bird had holes everywhere; bands of daylight showed through his vertical stabilizer. Greaves' airplane was unmarked, had not a scratch. Combies wondered how in the hell had he done that as the trio lined up for egress.

The easiest exit would have been to bore ahead after bomb release and, flying low, follow the Red River delta out to sea, but the United States Navy owned the territory in that direction. Therefore, Air Force planners dictated the three Air Force pilots make a U-turn and retrace their inbound route. Olds led them down to 10 feet off the valley floor.

A misty veil appeared along the horizon and Combies said, "I'd call the vis 'piss poor.'"

"Or worse," Dutton said.

They tore through the valley while what seemed like the entire population of North Vietnam shot at them. They reached the end of the valley but people continued to shoot at them. Men stood in open fields and banged away with rifles.

Out of the mist, a row of hooches appeared in front of the trio. The pilots pulled up to clear the buildings and, on one of the roofs, stood an unarmed man. With the Phantoms bearing down on him, he spun about and broad jumped off the far side of the roof. Imbecile, why didn't you just stay there? Combies thought and worried that the poor guy broke his neck or arms and legs. Then he worried that they were off course.

To worsen matters, ground effect increased and made the Phantoms want to climb. Combies counteracted the aerodynamic lift by pumping the stick forward to keep his airplane low. As a result, the fighter bounced like an ocean-going speedboat leaping from wave to wave. Olds and Greaves fought the same problem. Nothing was working right.

"Lee," Combies demanded, "Where in hell are we?" The kid had inertial and computer units out the ass. What the fuck was he doing back there?

With the airplane bouncing and everything shaking, Dutton couldn't read his navigational aids. "Sir, you see that stream off to the right?" he said.

"Affirmative."

"Well, we're about a quarter mile to the left of it."

Goddamnit, thought Combies, just as he'd suspected: they were lost.

Combies flew primarily with his eyes on Olds, using peripheral vision to watch the ground streak by. Ahead, clouds merged with the mountains. Unexpectedly Olds shouted, "Pull, pull. Climb. Burners, burners."

In formation flying everybody did what the leader did. Instant response to any command was ingrained by years of training. Following orders, Greaves and Combies jerked back their control columns and fired their afterburners to give their planes maximum thrust.

The trio of jets pulled eight Gs and stood on their tailpipes. In a vertical climb, they broke out of the clouds and found themselves going up the face of a piece of karst that had been hidden in the haze—a solid rock jutting to 7000 feet. Practically close enough to reach out and touch the blackish stone wall, Combies thought that, if he lowered the landing gear, he could taxi to the top. He wondered how Olds had seen or known the chunk of rock was exactly there. If it were pure luck, all the better.

Clearing the karst, they pushed forward on their sticks and plunged back to the deck. Olds jettisoned his missiles and bomb racks to reduce drag. He alerted the tanker because he was leaking fuel. The remainder of the way out, the three Phantoms stayed in the weeds and murk.

They exited North Vietnam, climbed to altitude, and rendezvoused with a KC-135 Stratotanker that had ventured far beyond its normal station. Olds drank first. It appeared as if fuel ran out of the hole in his wing as fast as the tanker pumped it into his refueling receptacle. How had he made it that far? Combies wondered.

When it came time for Combies to gas up, the refueling boom in the tail of the tanker lowered and the probe extended out and down. In the belly of the tanker, on his stomach and facing aft, the boom operator watched through a window that put him face to face with the pilot of the plane he serviced. By controlling small wings attached to the boom, he flew the probe home to a receptacle aft of the Phantom's rear cockpit. When Combies slid into position for gas, the boom operator zoomed the probe away and said, "Sir, I can't refuel you until you put out your cigarette."

With wind roaring into his cockpit, it had taken Combies at least a dozen attempts to light the cigarette. Several seconds of dead air passed before Combies told the boomer, "Give me the fuel or I'll shoot you down."

After Greaves and Combies topped off, Olds hooked up with the boom and the KC-135 dragged him to within 30 miles of Ubon.

Olds called, "Let's go in and pitch," which meant execute a fan break over the base. Combies had been working like crazy to keep his plane flying straight and level. Olds's plane looked in worse shape than his. Combies said, "Hey, boss, I don't think that's too smart an idea for my airplane."

Olds said, "You're right. We'll make a straight-in approach." He landed first and set down hard. He turned off the runway and the plane's main wing spar collapsed, leaving the Phantom broken in half on the taxiway.

The tanks didn't have enough fuel to create a fire. Olds and his backseater walked away from the wreck.

The Wing Director of Operations greeted Combies and Dutton after they parked. He handed a fifth of Ten High to Combies who broke the seal, took a pull, then passed the bottle to Dutton. Dutton took the longest drink of straight whiskey that Combies had ever seen any man swallow.

Their airplane's fuselage looked like a colander. The airframe wouldn't be ready to fly again for a week, or more, if ever.

"Rough?" the DO asked.

Combies faked a puke.

Dutton said, "As far as I'm concerned that goddamn fucking steel mill can stay there for eternity."

★ ★ ★

A heart attack killed Colonel Phil Combies in 1990 at age 62.

Brigadier General Robin Olds died of congestive heart failure in 2007, one month shy of 84.

CHAPTER 7

Prisoner

Everyone that flew over North Vietnam wasn't as lucky as Olds and his followers on that particular day. A lot of fliers got killed and a lot spent years as prisoners of war in North Vietnam. I repeatedly have thought about life as a prisoner. I have read the concentration camp literature from World War II. I have dwelled on books by men held as prisoners by the North Vietnamese—primarily Bud Day, Rob Risner, and John Dramesi. My conclusion has been that no amount of training could come anywhere close to conditioning a person for the experience: perhaps being raised by the world's cruelest child abuser would provide a hint of what to expect.

I hate to confess the fact but, when a lieutenant in the late fifties, I spent a night in the Dallas County lockup after being arrested for public intoxication. I had decided to sleep it off in my car but the police didn't agree with the idea—because I parked in the middle of an intersection. At the jail, I surrendered the contents of my pockets along with my belt and shoelaces, and then a plainclothes policeman led me to the drunk tank. Everything was low key, relaxed to the point of friendliness. In those days, white drunks shared a spacious cell, segregated from black drunks locked in a more confining area. My escort opened the door to the white drunk tank and ordered me to enter. I took a quick look at the dazed and drooling people inside and equated the view before me with a scene from *The Snake Pit*. In a lucid stupor, I said, "I'm not going in there." My plainclothes escort said, "In," and put a hand on my back. I held my ground. Without another word, he whipped out a blackjack and slapped me behind the ear. As if stung by a cattle prod, I scurried into the cell and the door clanged behind me. The remainder of that night I sat wide awake with my back against a wall until, early in the morning, a policeman turned me loose along with the other half-sober drunks. The experience ranked as the ugliest night of my life to that date.

Loss of freedom is a bitch and a half.

A year earlier, I had attended survival school at Stead Air Force Base outside of Reno, Nevada. As a part of combat crew training, I spent three days in a mock prisoner of war camp. In the first few minutes after my capture, in the middle of being slapped in the head and poked in the kidneys by purple-uniformed "aggressors," I raised a fist toward my tormentors. Wrong move. They hauled me to a courtroom and I found myself seated at a table next to a court-appointed counselor, flanked by armed guards.

"You dared to strike a soldier of the People's Army," the counselor said. "Yours is a serious crime."

"I didn't hit anyone," I said.

A bearded man in a black suit entered the court and sat down on a bench facing me. He said, "I am State Representative Vorshinski." Reading from papers in a manila folder, he said, "Zeybel. That's a German name." He paused and studied me. "You could be Jewish. Zeybel, you're accused of being a fascist. And of using fascist tactics. You threatened a People's Army soldier. How do you plead?"

In the middle of Vorshinski's words, my counselor stood and glowered down at me. When Vorshinski finished, my counselor said to me, "You're a fascist? I don't defend fascist bastards." He told Vorshinski, "He pleads guilty, comrade."

Studying his papers, Vorshinski said, "I see that you are a member of the United States Air Force." He looked up at me. "That fact alone makes you guilty as charged. Do you offer mitigating evidence before I pass sentence."

"I didn't—"

"Forty-five years of hard labor," Vorshinski said.

Two guards strong-armed me from the courtroom and marched me to an isolated area away from the prison compound, led me to an eight-foot-deep hole in the ground. The hole was 10 feet square and cut into solid rock. One guard pointed into the hole and told me, "Dig."

The Dallas and Stead experiences gave me a keener understanding of the nakedness of an individual against the power of a state, either democratic or totalitarian. However, I had not previously reflected on the loss of freedom, a right I took for granted like most Americans. Yet that wasn't the end of the Stead story.

I climbed down a wooden ladder and, for an hour or two, chipped rock with a pick. The guards brought another prisoner to work next to me. "What did you do to end up here?" I asked him.

Before he could answer, a guard shouted, "No talking."

With two of us picking away at the rock, we built a pile of chips. I stopped digging and looked up at the guard.

"Why aren't you working?" he said.

I leaned on my pick and said, "We need a shovel to get this loose stuff out of the way."

A few minutes later, the guard brought a shovel and threw it into the hole. He pointed at me and said, "You, come up here." I climbed out of the hole. "Sit," he said, and I sat on the edge of the hole, with my feet dangling. "See if you can figure out a better way to do this work."

I watched the other prisoner dig for about an hour. The guard asked if I had any suggestions. "We need a sledgehammer," I said. "Or a jackhammer." A guard took me away to the prison's general population.

I didn't realize the result of my behavior until long after finishing Stead. Thoughtlessly, I had become a collaborator. By sitting and watching in a supervisory role while my fellow soldier labored, I had accepted a special privilege and thereby separated myself from my peers—which made me the equivalent of a concentration camp *kapo*.

The prisoner-of-war compound at Stead tried to create a real world situation. For example, between interrogation sessions, guards confined me in two types of boxes. One was a locker in which I could neither stand upright nor sit; the other was a dog house. Guards crammed me into the locker, where I alternated leaning against different walls in a semi-fetal position for about an hour, shifting positions when a cramp set in. In the dog house, I sat on the ground and baked in the heat of the day for another hour. Simultaneously realistic and unrealistic, the confinements produced discomfort that I knew had an end. At night we prisoners slept in an unheated bunker on sharp gravel, which taught us to spoon, exactly as soldiers had done under Civil War field conditions. Interrogation revolved around the details of an operation we were not to reveal, but the questioning session was primarily a mind game with merely verbal hints and feint movements toward physical torture.

Food consisted of a single daily ration of thin soup and stale bread. On an afternoon when the ladler missed my canteen and poured half my portion across my wrist and down my forearm, I tried to lick my own elbow.

Training at Stead was child's play compared to the real thing—a mere hint of pains available as we learned at war's end.

The story of one prisoner of war that received little attention was that of Colonel John Stavast. He had related the experience of his 1967 to 1973 ordeal to the Oral History Department at the Lyndon B. Johnson Library in Austin and he granted me permission to listen to his audio tape and interview him. Stavast was a major when shot down over North Vietnam. In describing his 2005 days as a prisoner, he related the following story.

★ ★ ★

We were fighting a good war. My duty was tactical recon in the RF-4C, which I first flew in 1962. We had absolutely no restrictions on us, except the restrictions of each mission. However, we could not violate the Chinese border. Marshalling yards were in China, where trains were made up. We wanted pictures of those.

I flew thirty-three missions at night, when we had no need to use afterburners or go supersonic. We flew between six hundred fifty and six hundred seventy knots at altitudes between two hundred to two hundred fifty feet. In the daytime, we went supersonic, used fuel like crazy. At night, we could see them when they were shooting at us. Most of what [the gunfire] we saw at night was behind us, and we saw it in the rearview mirror.

The most dangerous run I made in my life, day or night, was a night reconnaissance run to Kep. My backseater was First Lieutenant Jerry Venanzi. That night, they had all their guns over Kep. We came up on the Chinese border, terrain following. This particular night was light enough I could see the ground going by. Jerry said, "Time to break left." I told him, "I don't see that mountain ridge we're supposed to pop over." Being an old hand, I'd as soon rely on my eyes as on [the backseater's] radar.

As soon as we dropped into that valley, they started firing down the length of the valley. They were firing sympathetically—one gun set off the next—white hot golf balls, twenty-three millimeter especially. I could see the rounds arcing. They seemed to be firing into each others' positions. Over Kep, I made the backseater fly with the hood up, didn't want him worrying about the damn antiaircraft fire. I wanted him to look at his navigator jazz to keep us on track.

We made a fifty-five mile run in five minutes. Our recon showed eighty-two trains made up in China, headed to Vietnam. The best that we could pass on to our debriefer was that the trip was a hairy mess.

Before the RF-4, I'd been flying the RF-84 and RF-101 since 1956, daytime only. Night missions required more training, discipline, and faith. Flying out of Udorn [Thailand], I had completed ninety missions over North Vietnam, sixty over Hanoi. Once you hit ninety, the rest are [supposed to be] pretty easy, mostly counter type missions in areas of North Vietnam that were less dangerous than areas of Laos and South Vietnam.

We shouldn't have been flying on the day we got shot down. Obviously! Bad day at Black Rock. The squadron was short on combat qualified aircrews, and a Presidential-interest mission came up. President Johnson and the Joint Chiefs of Staff sent a Priority One telex message request for a post-strike look at the Thai Nguyen steel mill. It was a beautiful Sunday, a spring kind of day. I told ops I wasn't supposed to be flying and I didn't want to go flying over North Vietnam. But the mission was directed to me from a friend in Saigon who will remain nameless. He knows—and he feels bad about how it came out—he knows damn well I shouldn't have gone.

With me was a brand-new wingman on his first trip over North Vietnam. Each plane carried two ECM [Electronic Countermeasures] pods. They were most effective with two airplanes. Two pods on one airplane were too close together to do any good. But with the proper separation between two airplanes, the four pods were effective jammers.

The strike mission had been a success. Eighteen F-105s hit the mill and twenty-four F-4s bombed the railroad without losses.

We punched off our fuel tanks and went supersonic at Thai Nguyen. We had no trouble finding the steel mills. They were smoldering with dust and smoke along the railroad tracks. I don't know how in the world they expected to see anything on film. And the gunners were madder than the dickens because they had just gone through an air raid. And here comes a couple of snotty nose RF-4 airplanes busting through their airspace and giving them a sonic boom.

Now, I wasn't that concerned about SAMs because you see them coming. You don't have to be looking at them. They are so bright—like a bolt of lightning—continuous—they're moving so rapidly that you can tell instantly—somehow you can tell instantly where they're headed. That day they fired three, a salvo of three at us.

We broke left a little bit, and then broke back to the right to watch them go by—and here's the wingman out of position—and I hollered, "Get back in formation." He was upset because, just as soon as I hollered—he's breaking harder than me—here comes three SAMs from five o'clock. The first time I ever saw a SAM fired from behind.

We were going one-point-two-five mach—accelerating—when this SAM blew up right behind my airplane. It knocked the airplane— phew!—bounced it around. "Oh, my God, we've been hit," Jerry said. "What the hell was that?" He had his hood down.

"Don't worry about it. I think we just got hit by a SAM," I said.

"Oh, my God, let's get out of here."

"We're going, man."

We're accelerating through one-point-four to one-point-five mach, going down the railroad line—straight down the railroad. I climb to three thousand feet, didn't have to stay level, and tell the wingman to cross under me so we can get better coverage of the bridge. By now we're at one-point-six-five mach and we cross over Hanoi at that speed, just about as fast as she'd go with the ECM pods.

I started pulling back because the wingman had a slower airplane when all of a sudden my hydraulic system PC1 dropped instantly to zero. "We got a PC1 warning light," Jerry said.

"I know it," I said. Utility went to zero. Still had PC2. I started slowing that airplane down. I had just pulled it out of AB when it went out of control. PC2 went. We were twenty-five miles southwest of Hanoi, toward Hoa Binh on a bend of the Black River. When you lose hydraulic pressure, the elevator—the slab goes full nose down, which means the airplane goes full nose up. And we're still doing one-point-five mach. That's an awful thing to do to an airplane—awful. The G-load went way over nine.

Before I blacked out—I wasn't unconscious, but I couldn't see because of the Gs—my G-suit wasn't working properly or I would have been able to see. It happened in a flash. The airplane pitched up. Just before I lost consciousness, the right wing panel broke off—the folding part broke off and went over our heads, and that's the last thing I could see. The airplane was trembling violently and I was hollering at Jerry. The electronics in the airplane had gone dead—the interphone. I was screaming at the top of my voice for Jerry to bail out. The airplane slows down extremely fast when it presents itself flatways to the air. Finally, I was pulling my ejection handle—pulling my ejection handle—then I heard Jerry go out, then I went out.

Just after I got out of the airplane, it blew up—just went bonkers. It spun violently—rapidly—missing half its wing—crashed into the ground and blew up again. I suspect because of the strain, one of the forward fuel tanks burst, then fuel ran into the engine compartment, and that blew up first.

There we were, floating down twenty-five miles southwest of Hanoi in a very hostile environment. Thank God the parachutes worked. I was hurt when I landed—landed on my butt—compression fracture. Landed between two tall karst and my parachute was spilled by a tree—in a grove of trees. My chute spilled, then blossomed again before I hit the ground. Luckily I landed in a bamboo area—bamboo shrubs cushioned my fall, but I still hit pretty hard on my bottom. My survival kit worked fine—everything as advertised. It wasn't my equipment's fault that I got banged up. I was not aware that I was hurt.

Jerry ended up two miles west. He got out first. How did he end up west of me? Which direction was the aircraft headed when we finally got out? We were out of control at twelve thousand feet when we ejected.

Jerry announced he had been captured. They got him about two o'clock in the afternoon. I heard gunshots. I was on a path—a trail—a well-traveled trail along a little stream. I heard people coming, so I gathered my wits and tried to get rid of my parachute. I tried to pull it out of the tree, which I couldn't do 'cause it was stuck in this bamboo stuff. I could hear these chattering people. It turned out to be villagers, and they saw my parachute.

I ran up a hill with my water, my gun, and my two radios, one of which was smashed. I didn't realize that until I got to the top of the hill. I hid in some bushes when these people came up calling, "GI? GI? You OK, GI?" They walked by me—three feet—went right by and disappeared. They probably thought if they captured me, they would collect a reward. Then it got quiet for a long time. I pulled out my radio but was afraid to use it because it was so quiet. I was afraid somebody two miles away would hear me. Couldn't get a thing on the radio. Nobody was calling me on the thing. I found out later, they decided not to send any rescue missions up to that area because they had lost a helicopter there a week before—and I had met that crew.

About nine o'clock that night, it started getting dark. There was a full moon. I started thinking about moving out and heading south. All of a sudden, a bunch of these small creatures started coming out—I don't know what they were—little rats, little mice, little rabbits, chipmunks, whatever you want to call them. "What the hell's going on here?" I thought.

Then the regular army people came looking for me. They were combing the area. Next thing I knew, there was an AK-47 pointed right at me, hitting me in the chest. A guy said, "Up! Up!" I put my hands up. They treated me very well. When I ran out of my own water, they gave me water or lemonade. They let me keep my cigarettes, let me keep my boots. Had about five miles to walk out of there. Regular army treated me all right.

The first week was the most difficult. There were difficult times—most involved purges or torture of some sort or other. This first week was extremely difficult and, of course, included constant torture. For seven days and seven nights, I was tortured—in a torture cell, in a place they called the Blue Room. Some of their methods were ingenious.

The interrogator bragged that they would not leave any scars. However, they did. I have scars on my arms, back, and buttocks. Don't know who my interrogator was. I described him to guys in camp, but we didn't have a nickname for him. Most interrogators that got names—like The Rat, Rabbit, Fidel—were interrogators in the regular prison system, after we were out of the torture in what we called New Guy Village. This guy was a pretty good sized guy. He spoke beautiful English. Most of the time, he had two big helpers. These guys were big guys. Sometimes he had three helpers in there. Their job was to punish you when you failed to answer one of his questions. He did not touch me. But he directed everything. As an example, they got mad at you and put you on your knees with your hands over your head—or sometimes your hands would be tied behind you—and if you didn't answer a question or refused to do something, they'd give you a judo chop to the side of the head. Right in front of the ear. Just knock your brains out.

They didn't want information. They wanted us to confess our sins, our crimes, confess to being a war criminal. They wanted us to sign a standard piece of paper, written in our own hand. They wanted us to write a letter to GIs in South Vietnam and to Congressmen to tell them we were fighting an illegal war. I got so damn mad. They also wanted a list of names of men in my squadron. I couldn't give it. As soon as they started beating on me, I forgot all the names. Self-protection mechanism, I suppose. A psychiatrist at March [Air Force Base] told me my reaction was not unusual: I couldn't tell if I wanted to. I run into people today who were in the squadron when I was shot down and I don't know who the hell they are. I forgot my squadron commander. When I saw him later, he said, "Hello, John," and I said, "Who the hell are you?"

When I got out of torture, when I was carried to a cell, there was a guard who was to bring me back to health—a gentle, older guy, who spoke English and told me my torture lasted seven days and nights. He was supposed to keep us from getting sick. I'd had no food. Just a glass of water a day. They had moved me out to move in somebody shot down more recently. At release, I was ready to sign one of those damn fool confessions. I was at the end of my rope. I'm stubborn, but stubbornness disappears with the torture they can put you through.

One of the things almost everyone experienced was what we called The Suitcase Trick, where they take wide nylon straps—about an inch and a half wide, like parachute harness straps—and they wrap you up, starting with your ankles, and they come up around your calves, through your groin, and back around—clear around your back—and then around your front, and then around your wrists, and then they can pick you up like you're a suitcase—and you can't breathe. You cannot breathe! It's one of the most terrifying things—there you are hanging, and you can't breathe.

The other thing they did with me—they had these long spikes—looked like a giant needle that somebody would sew with. They put leg irons around you, like U-bolts. They put those on the needle that's got a hole in one end, and they pull it up by a hook and lift you up by your ankles, one side at a time. A lot of people had their ankles broken. Why the heck my ankles didn't break is beyond me. It's fantastic pain, drives you crazy. They bragged, "We won't leave any marks on you. Nobody will believe you when you say you were tortured." But they did. They broke this right arm in The Suitcase Trick, gave me a skull fracture and brain concussion from the judo chops. My right ear is totally deaf.

There was the "Bad Boy Room" where they put you on bread and water for a couple of weeks, a fan belt to the butt. The fan belt—they did that for only an hour.

The other time I got bad torture, they accused me of communicating. It was against the rules to communicate in any way, shape, or form. We talked by tapping on walls, no paper or pencils. I was in irons—wrist irons and leg irons—hanging on a wall for seven days—an extremely humiliating thing. Some guys were there longer than me. There is nothing you can do. You just hang there. You can't sleep. You defecate, urinate when you finally have to. There is no way you can do that with any self-respect—degrading, dehumanizing.

They are very puritanical about sex. In all my torture, nobody ever touched my privates. When we received shorts from home, we had to sew the fly shut.

I went from a hundred and ninety-five to a hundred and five pounds, but I could do a lot of sit-ups and push-ups. We exercised and worked problems to stay alert. You get to a healthy, hardy, super-normal mental state, develop a mental responsibility. With starvation, the brain is the first thing that goes. Once you starve your brain, you get into a dilemma. You must eat everything, get some nutrition any way you can. Otherwise, you can starve yourself to death—your brain thinks you're more and more a hero for starving yourself to death. There were a couple of guys that happened to.

[When asked if he knew anyone who did not break if the North Vietnamese wanted to break him, Stavast cited cases for me.]

Yeah. Yeah. And they killed him. He was a young guy. What the heck was his name? Lance something [Sijan]. They killed him. And another kid from Michigan [Earl Cobeil] who they beat him crazy, drove him crazy. They tried electric shock and everything to get him out of it because they didn't want to kill him. But they did. Finally when they stopped beating on him, he was so out of it—he reacted to nothing. They put him standing in the sun, and we watched him—he stood in one place, unblinking for one hour, stood stock still in the sunlight—catatonic. These torturers were ignorant—mean guys. They didn't have any knowledge of how seriously they were damaging someone. They hurt a lot of people. Ed Atterberry they killed. He tried to escape and they beat him to death for that. He was beaten to death about thirty-five feet from where I lived. I could hear it going on. He'd say, "Leave me alone. Leave me alone. I don't know what you're talking about." You could hear them beating him. They beat him with straps and sticks, like they kill their dogs before they eat them.

[Stavast described his homecoming with a touch of wonderment, a bit like a child might describe Christmas morning.]

They gave us a car—Ford gave us a car, free, for a year. My family was driving a '62 Caddy with two hundred thousand miles. Sears gave us free clothes. Everybody treated us. We went to parties—at the White House with the United States President, as guests of the Governor of California. [Although the recognition had taken place years in the past, Stavast shook his head in wonderment, nodded appreciatively.]

★ ★ ★

Colonel John Stavast died in 2004 at age 78.

★ ★ ★

Combat crewmen who flew over Vietnam, Laos, or Cambodia carried short-barrel 38-caliber revolvers. The gun held six rounds and provided damn little firepower, especially against troops with rifles. I heard old crewdogs tell new guys that the gun's primary purpose was to blow out one's brains rather than be captured. I also heard guys say they would not be taken alive. I knew one person who lived up to that declaration—Captain Larry "Dutch" Holland.

I met Holland as a fellow section commander at Squadron Officer School. He was a rawboned, superbly conditioned officer who excelled at everything he did.

In 1965, Holland's F-100D Super Sabre was hit by ground fire east of Tay Ninh, South Vietnam, while on a close air support strike against Viet Cong forces. He ejected and landed among enemy soldiers that quickly surrounded him. Rather than surrender, Holland opened fire on the enemy troops with his handgun. They returned the fire and knocked him down. He regained his feet, however, and resumed firing until they shot him and knocked him down a second time. Then they captured him. While this exchange took place, a Search and Rescue (SAR) helicopter arrived on the scene and a firefight erupted between its crew and the VC. The SAR crew last saw VC soldiers dragging Holland's limp body into the jungle. Further reports indicated Holland was later shot to death while trying to escape his captors. His body has not been recovered.

CHAPTER 8

A Sort of Leadership

After more than 50 years, Dutch Holland still lives in my mind as one of my heroes. Along with Neal and me, Phil Combies' heroes were also soldiers, nobody more so than Robin Olds who he described in these words:

> He's living proof of the old saying "The difficult we do immediately, the impossible takes a little longer." He has every attribute it takes to be a leader, not only in the air but also on the ground—the whole nine yards. Flying, fighting, and just being with the guy was one of the most tremendous experiences of my life. You couldn't ask, in our business, for a better teacher. If they ever build a memorial to fighter pilots, Olds will be part of it.

An old saying claims leaders are made, not born. A corollary taught at Air University preached that people had to learn to follow before qualifying to lead. One could argue this approach produced leaders with stagnant viewpoints. In other words, under this system, men and women who best emulated their leaders' thinking and behavior gained the greatest advancement, a fact understood from the first day on active duty, especially in the Air Force. Officers born in the year I was born (1933) and who realized the greatest success—namely those I knew and worked with and who attained the rank of general: Lieutenant Generals Carl Smith and Bob Springer, Major General Dave Forgan, and Brigadier General Tom Tobin—stuck to the rules and deserved their promotions. I did not begrudge advancement to anyone who earned it by playing the game, but I often thought the rules of the game needed fixing, specifically in regard to handling men.

My personal leadership shortcoming was an inability to follow graciously: I would rather lead a one-man band than play in a symphony orchestra—even one conducted by Toscanini. When I was a captain, one of the finest compliments I received came from a major who told a friend of mine, "That fucking Zeybel has his own way of doing everything." My problem was that I continually looked for easier and more efficient ways to accomplish any task. As I saw it, many officers felt the same way, particularly at the end of the Vietnam War. They acted accordingly when administering justice or going the extra mile for a questionable project.

Senior captains, majors, and lieutenant colonels comprised the discontented in this regard. These officers had done most of the Air Force's fighting in Vietnam and Laos and Cambodia. Disillusioned by post-war pettiness in the system, they refused to follow the old, established patterns of behavior. They thought the system was broken, starting from the top down. At least that was how I interpreted the stateside situation from 1973, when the Vietnam War ended for the United States, until 1976 when I retired.

My final assignment was as Headquarters Squadron Commander, a position that called for a captain. The Air Force was top heavy with rank and I got the job as a demotion from Chief of the Special Operations Force Command Post after I undiplomatically questioned a request from Brigadier General William Holton's secretary on his behalf. At the time, Holton commanded the Special Operations Force, a position normally filled by a colonel. The issue centered on my controllers' making early morning wake-up calls to pilots on days they flew with the general. I said to his secretary, "You're telling me these guys can't get out of bed by themselves. If left on their own and they show up late once or twice, the general might figure out who's best qualified to work for him." I might have also pointed out that the command post standard operating procedures did not include waking up sluggish lieutenants. Not long after that, I got drunk on a field trip, joked about the sexual preferences of a full colonel—to his face—that worked for Holton and soon thereafter I exited the command post. My immediate boss—Colonel Jim Montrose who ran the First Special Operations Wing and got moved aside at the same time—told me, "What you say to the general's secretary or staff is the same as saying it to the general." And he laughed at our situation.

Basically, I failed to keep my mouth shut. Psychologist Erik Erikson observed that the mark of a highly advanced technological society was childhoods lasting into the forties with a great residue of emotional immaturity. I frequently quoted Erik perhaps as a way to excuse my bad behavior. In simplified terms, his idea translated to "You're only young once, but you can be immature forever." I perfectly qualified as his poster child.

In disciplinary matters, as the squadron CO, I treated my 700 men and women the way they would be treated downtown, considering them citizens first and soldiers second. While neighboring squadron commanders levied $400–$800 fines to pot users caught with the goods, I charged my people the going rate in Fort Walton Beach and Pensacola—$25. The base commander and prosecutors in the Judge Advocate General's (JAG) office hassled me over my leniency, but regulations gave me the final word. Similarly, I chose not to punish airmen that repeatedly caused problems; instead, I told them, "Here's the way it works. If you continue to screw up, I can punish you time after time and make your life more and more miserable while building a strong case against you. Then I can take administrative action and give you a less than honorable discharge, which can create lifelong problems for you. Or you can tell me right now that you want out of the Air Force. In that case, you won't go back to work and will be discharged in three days. Of course, you're welcome to return to your job. But if you do, you have to clean up your act and not end up in my office again. Do you understand? What do you want to do?" Ninety-five per cent of the problem children straightened up. Discipline was that easy to enforce and my technique saved the JAG lawyers from reams of paperwork.

My favorite incident involved a young airman who got arrested early one evening for public intoxication in Pensacola, called his Non-Commissioned Officer in Charge (NCOIC) to bail him out, then got arrested for public intoxication in Fort Walton Beach three hours later, and called his NCOIC to bail him out again. I read the incident report and talked to the NCOIC: "It takes an hour to drive from Cola to Walton. This guy's asking for it. Right?"

"Sir," the NCOIC, a craggy technical sergeant, said, "he had an excuse for getting drunk. His girlfriend broke up with him and he wasn't expecting it."

"I see. And?"

"Well, sir, whatever happens is up to you. But he's eighteen. If you think back to when you were his age, you might remember doing something like this that wasn't exactly right."

Fuck, I thought, a few months ago I did a couple of things that weren't right and lost a cushy job over it. Around this time two full colonels had been stopped on Hurlburt for driving under the influence of alcohol and received no punishment, a well-known fact. To top it off, one of the colonels was significantly overweight but refused to step on a scale in accordance with the fat boy program, which I administered for Headquarters Squadron. Instead, he chose to phone in his current weight each week to the sergeant that monitored the program. I asked the kid's NCOIC what he wanted to do.

"Me, sir? I'd overlook what he did, sir. He's one of my best workers. No kidding. He's learned his lesson. I guarantee he won't mess up again."

He would be paying fines in both cities too, I thought. "You got him," I said. "He's your responsibility." A few weeks later the airman showed up in my office and thanked me for giving him a second chance. He didn't fuck up again.

At times my approach to leadership became debatable. Staff Sergeant Dana McCollum complained to me that his pay check had not reached his bank and he suspected an airman in finance had tampered with his records following a dispute between them.

"Have you told anybody else about this?" I asked.

"No, sir. I came straight to you because I thought it was a squadron matter," McCollum said.

I called in the airman clerk and said to him, "Why did you screw around with McCollum's pay record? Did you think we wouldn't catch you?"

He turned so pale I wondered if he was going to pass out. Then he denied the charge.

"If you didn't do it, who did?" I said.

"I don't know," he said.

"But you do know that somebody fucked with his pay, right?"

"Yes, sir. I heard that."

"From who?"

"I don't remember."

"You do have access to McCollum's pay record, right?"

"Yes, sir."

"Okay, here's what we're going to do. You go to finance right now and clean up his record, make sure he gets paid today, and make sure nothing like this happens again. If it does, I'm bringing you and McCollum in here after duty hours, and I'm letting him beat the shit out of you. I'll help him if necessary. Do you understand?"

He blinked like he couldn't believe what was happening to him. He corrected everything within the hour.

The clerk probably hated me forever, but I sure as shit won McCollum's allegiance.

★ ★ ★

After I retired, McCollum qualified for Officer Candidate School. I attended his outdoor commissioning ceremony at Lackland Air Force Base, which rain halted halfway through. He spent many years as an aide to generals before retiring as a major. He phones me on my birthday and I reciprocate.

★ ★ ★

I sat on court martial boards at Hurlburt despite the JAG prosecutors' awareness of my liberal bias. Those trials helped to firm up my belief that other middle-rank officers shared my attitude about discipline. In cases that ended in conviction, the punishment meted by the board resembled a wrist slap. None of the cases related to earth-shattering issues and board members with combat experience in Vietnam questioned the prosecutors' strict interpretation of regulations, sometimes viewing their efforts as "make work."

A day came when the JAG prosecutors had their fill of me as a board member. Upon entering the courtroom, I saw the airman on trial and instantly made up my mind that this guy would do hard time. Everything about him—from his civilian clothes, goatee, moustache, and long hair, to his slovenly posture and contemptuous glare—irritated my sensibilities. After explaining that the case involved desertion, the prosecutor challenged me peremptorily and justice triumphed. The prosecutor had unwittingly removed a biased juror who was on his side. I privately explained what he had done but the prosecutor didn't believe me. It didn't matter because the accused went to prison.

I wasn't Hurlburt's only liberal as proceedings involving homosexuality showed long before the "don't ask, don't tell" policy existed. The ultimate liberal was Technical Sergeant Leonard Matlovich who taught Sensitivity Training (originally and less sensitively called Race Relations training). I attended his classes and liked him. He understood the dimensions of discrimination; enthusiastically approached an emotional topic; and reasoned rather than preached, which was a necessity because less enlightened personnel questioned the value of the classes and resisted the teaching. His lectures included thinly veiled pleas for a better understanding of a gay lifestyle.

Matlovich became famous, appearing on the cover of *Time* in 1975, for suing the Air Force over gay rights. Well before his first homosexual experience at the age of 30, he equated discrimination against gays with discrimination against blacks, making the problem a civil rights issue in his mind. At the age of 32, he publicly admitted to being gay and the Air Force found him unfit for service, releasing him six months later. He sued the Air Force and won an offer of reinstatement, but with the proviso that he pledge not to engage in homosexuality again, which he declined to do. In 1980, court battles brought him another chance for reinstatement with retroactive back pay, but instead he accepted an upgraded honorable discharge and a $160,000 settlement without returning to active duty.

★ ★ ★

Technical Sergeant Leonard Matlovich served multiple tours in Vietnam and was awarded the Bronze Star and Purple Heart. AIDS killed him in 1988 at age 45.

★ ★ ★

A less publicized exercise in evaluating sexual behavior within military service took place when an airman assigned to me faced charges of homosexuality. The following story reviews that case and, except for mine, every name has been changed and identifying details altered to avoid embarrassing anyone who took part in the action—when the issue was truly an issue. I set the stage for our story with a view of life from Nobel Laureate Rudyard Kipling:

> And you are totally accountable for everything you do ... and there are no second chances. And a lifetime of effort and work are wiped out because of one unsavory act the results of which were understood before the act was undertaken or before the venture started and it was as if all preordained because the man knew the rules before he entered the game and was warned along the way so that his destiny was to put himself in the position where he could fail and have others say "Too Bad" and mean it and feel genuine sorrow and, at the same time, know that his disgrace was a lesson for everyone.

The accused, Airman First Class—buck sergeant—Ronald "Chip" Downey was a slight, angular man of 22 with naturally curly, dishwater-blond hair and baby-blue eyes. He radiated boyish innocence through playful and hyperactive mannerisms—a personality that, when word of his indiscretion became public, caused some people to say, "I suspected as much."

In 1975—shortly before an all-volunteer military force came into being—Pensacola, Florida, policemen arrested Downey for public lewdness. He pleaded guilty to the act and paid a $250 fine. A month after appearing in civil court, Downey was charged with violation of Air Force Manual 39-12, Chapter 2, Section B, Paragraph 2-15 (AFM 39-12), which subjected an airman to discharge for "Sexual perversion, including but not limited to (1) lewd or lascivious acts, (2) homosexual acts, (3) sodomy, (4) indecent exposure...." The regulation also said, "An airman discharged under this section should be furnished an under other than honorable conditions discharge."

Downey faced action by an administrative discharge board similar to a court-martial in structure but operated more informally. For example, rules of evidence were less stringent: hearsay was admissible if deemed fair and relevant, and board members reached decisions based upon a preponderance of evidence rather than requiring proof beyond reasonable doubt. Fundamentally, board action dealt with employer-employee relations. In many respects, it was a family gathering to decide the fate of a wayward member.

In accordance with the Uniform Code of Military Justice, Downey requested a court-appointed lawyer and got Captain Gregory DeGregorio as Respondent's Counsel. Known as "Captain Dee" to both fellow officers and enlisted men, DeGregorio was a native-New Yorker and served as the base's lone defense lawyer, a job he had earned because of brilliance as a prosecutor.

Second Lieutenant Albert Turner was assigned as Recorder, a quasi-prosecuting attorney who presented the government's viewpoint. He had been in the Air Force for eight months and Downey's case was the first he handled alone.

★ ★ ★

Chip Downey's board action took place in a courtroom that held 25 chairs for spectators. Fourteen enlisted men dressed in blue uniforms, looking like the same person multiplied several times, showed up to watch the proceedings. Five officers serving as jurors sat at two long tables. They wore the silver wings of pilots and rows of ribbons representing awards for feats performed in the Vietnam War. From among them, a lieutenant colonel was designated as President of the Board, with a major and three captains flanking him. Boards required no less than three members and the majority ruled.

In the middle of the room, side-by-side tables for DeGregorio and Turner faced a judge's bench and a witness chair. A full colonel manned the judge's bench as Legal Advisor to ensure the hearing conformed with judicial lines.

Word by word, Turner's opening argument emphasized the AFM 39-12 passage on homosexual acts, stressing that participating, proposing, or attempting such acts was wrong regardless of whether a person's role was active or passive. Similarly, habitual association with persons known to be homosexuals did not meet Air Force standards.

Intoxication was the most common excuse presented by individuals confronted with evidence of commission of homosexual acts. The excuse could be extenuating in a given case but in itself did not constitute a basis for an exception to the general discharge policy.

DeGregorio's opening remarks cited Downey's excellent performance reports as a computer programmer and suggested extenuating circumstances to justify retaining Downey on active duty.

Turner first called to the witness stand Detective Timothy Conley, the arresting officer in Downey's civil case. Conley's testimony established that he and his partner had watched two men lead Downey out of a gay bar and into the back seat of a Chrysler New Yorker. On closer investigation, the officers saw the two men fellating Downey. They rousted the two men from the back seat, but Downey remained crumpled in a corner. "We had to drag him out," Conley said. "He couldn't stand by himself. We accidentally let him go and he fell flat on his face. He wasn't faking."

Turner next called me to the stand in the role of Downey's commander. Turner confirmed my familiarity with AFM 39-12 that states, "Members of the Air Force serving in the active military service represent the military establishment 24 hours a day. There is no distinction between duty time and off-duty time as the high moral standards of the service must be maintained at all times."

"And do you subscribe to the philosophy?" Turner said.

"No," I replied. "It's overly restrictive. Once in a while everyone is entitled to let it all hang out."

Laughter rippled among the spectators.

I bowed my head toward the Legal Advisor and the President of the Board and said, "Excuse me, gentlemen. That was unintentional."

Stiffly, Turner said, "Colonel, do you believe that Air Force personnel have a responsibility to maintain an image that reflects dignity upon the service?"

"Yes," I said, "But responsibility increases with rank and—"

"Wait. Do you believe that Airman Downey's conduct in Pensacola, on the night in question, reflected dignity upon the United States Air Force?"

"He already paid the price in a civilian court and—"

"Please, Colonel, answer the question. Did his conduct reflect dignity?"

"No. Not entirely. But—"

"No further questions," Turner said.

My comment about Downey's having "paid the price in a civilian court" carried an insinuation of double jeopardy. Within the legal bounds of the Uniform Code of Military Justice, however, administrative board action that followed civil action was another consequence within the same nexus of events. In criminal matters—in court martial cases, for example—higher courts had ruled double jeopardy did not apply because more than one sovereign was involved, which meant a person could be tried for the same offense by both civil and military courts. Furthermore, a board action was not considered punishment; it was a procedure for dismissing an unsatisfactory worker.

Turner next called Downey's immediate supervisor, Captain Diane Martin, a young, perfectly tailored blonde who wore her hair in a mannish cut—looking Air Force all the way. Her husband, also a captain, piloted F-4 Phantoms. Diane Martin had a reputation for a businesslike execution of duties. She had not been present for my testimony and the two of us had not discussed the case.

Turner asked, "Captain, do you subscribe to the philosophy that states, 'A member of the Air Force is on active duty twenty-four hours a day'?"

"No," Martin said. "Not in all cases."

Turner stared at her in disbelief. He took almost a minute before saying, "Captain, do you know the reason why the respondent is facing this board today?"

"Yes. He was involved in a homosexual act."

Turner brightened. "How do you feel about that?"

"Personally?" She raised her eyebrows. "I don't care what he does on his own time. He contributes to the mission. As long as he does his job, he can work for me."

Turner exhaled loudly. He read to the board members that portion of AFM 39-12 relating to the "twenty-four hours" philosophy and rested his argument.

DeGregorio opened by calling Chip Downey's wife, Clara, to the witness stand. DeGregorio led her to admit she and Chip were separated but shared a "very good" sex life "several times a week" and "every weekend." She smiled at Downey. "We're in love. We just have trouble living together."

DeGregorio asked, "Based upon your personal observations, has your husband ever been involved in what you consider unusual sexual behavior?"

"Once," Clara said. "About a year ago, we threw a party at our place and Chip got drunk and I put him to bed. Later I went to see how he was doing and found Billy Watson this civilian friend—a man—in bed with Chip. They were hugging. I screamed and Billy jumped up, grabbed his clothes, and left. Chip was half asleep and asked why I screamed. I told him, and he said he thought he was hugging me. Like always. He'd been dreaming about hugging me. He didn't remember Billy being there."

Albert Turner approached the cross-examination like a recently stung man approaching a hornet's nest. He walked Clara through the incident, establishing that both Chip and Billy Watson had been naked.

Downey took the stand and DeGregorio made him confess to drinking at a string of bars across Pensacola before passing out. The next thing Downey knew, he was alone in a jail cell, his face and chest aching. "It's like a switch flips in my head and my memory goes blank," he said. "I don't hurt anybody, or break stuff, or do bad things." Tears filled is eyes. "I mean, bad things to somebody else."

Chip admitted to pleading guilty to the civil charges against him because he did not have enough money to hire an attorney. He had thought that taking the blame and paying a fine would end the problem.

A federal statute forbade military lawyers from representing military personnel in civil courts.

DeGregorio helped Downey to recount a childhood in which his parents divorced when he was eight; neither had wanted custody of him, their only child; and he had been shuttled off to a court-appointed guardian.

Asked by DeGregorio to describe his first sexual experience with another person, Downey lowered his eyes and said that, when he was 12 years old, his guardian performed oral sex on him. He reported his guardian to the judge who had custody of him, and the judge put the guardian in jail. Downey moved to a home for boys.

"You did the right thing at the expense of giving up the only home you ever had," DeGregorio said. It wasn't a question. "Despite everything that has happened to you," DeGregorio said, "are you capable of performing your military duties in the future?"

"Yes, sir. In the computer section, things are like they were. Nobody acts any different toward me."

"Do you desire to remain in the United States Air Force?"

Downey's "Yes, sir" was his loudest statement of the day. "It's my home. It's my whole life."

Turner did not question Downey.

In summations, DeGregorio emphasized the emotions within Downey's heart and his victimization; Turner emphasized the intentions of the law as spelled out by regulations.

Based on a finding that Downey's ability to perform military service had not been compromised in accordance with AFM 39-12, the board members denied the Air Force request for his discharge. No further findings were necessary. Downey was retained on active duty.

★ ★ ★

Afterward, DeGregorio walked into my office and dropped into an overstuffed leather armchair.

"You lawyers ever shine your shoes?" I asked.

"We'll start when the doctors start," DeGregorio said.

"Like next century? Jesus, I saw a doctor in uniform, wearing red socks."

"Could be from Boston. You nail him?"

"I said 'Nice socks, Doc.'"

"Doctors shouldn't have to wear uniforms. Their job doesn't have military implications."

A C-model AC-130 Spectre gunship firing its aft 40-mm Bofors cannon, the design used by the 16th Special Operations Squadron during the 1970–1971 dry season along the Ho Chi Minh Trail in Laos. The squadron worked exclusively at night to interdict North Vietnamese Army traffic resupplying forces in South Vietnam. (1969 USAF/Author)

An early model AC-130 Spectre gunship with an array of side-firing armament ranging from 7.62-mm to 20-mm. Note that eight weapon ports extend the length of the airframe. Deadlier weapons became necessary as Spectre raised its operating altitudes in response to larger North Vietnamese Army antiaircraft artillery on the Ho Chi Minh Trail. (1968 USAF/Author)

An experimental model of the AC-130 as envisioned by Colonel Ron Terry, the impetus behind development of USAF side-firing gunship weapon systems. The opening on the far left holds the Night Observation Device (NOD), a telescopic sensor that amplifies light and helps its operator to see in the dark. The NOD crewman stands behind it practically in the aircraft's slipstream. (1967 USAF/Author)

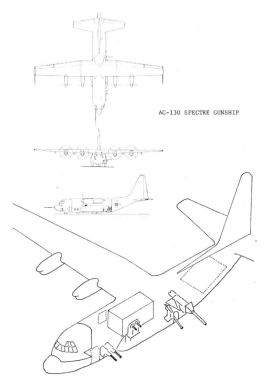

AC-130 SPECTRE GUNSHIP

The AC-130 fully loaded. Left to right: 20-mm cannons, 7.62-mm Gatling guns, 40-mm Bofors, and 105-mm howitzer. The booth in the center of the cargo compartment houses a sensor team: IR (Infrared), BC (Black Crow: a system that locates electromagnetic radiations), TV (Low Light Level Television that amplifies light thousands of times), and Fire Control Officer (FCO). The 16th SOS upgraded to this model for the 1971–1972 dry season in Laos. The aircraft also deployed to South Vietnam during the North Vietnamese Army's 1972 Easter Offensive. (1980 Author)

The AC-130 Spectre gunship with 105-mm howitzer. (1980 Author)

Major Ed Holley (far right) and his Spectre crew that escaped from three SA-2 surface-to-air missiles on 2 March 1971 over Laos. Others in the picture are: Lt Col Hank Zeybel; Majors Jim Ballsmith, Ed Coogan, and Dick Kauffman; Captains Lee Schuiten and Mike Scott; Master Sergeant Mel Bean; Staff Sergeants Billy Forrester, Jim Riffo, and Bob Savage; Sergeants Terry Snyder and Scott Wolf; and Airman First Class Chuck Heiges. All members of Holley's crew received a Silver Star medal for their actions on that night. (1971 Author)

Lieutenant General Marvin McNickle presenting a Silver Star to the author at Ubon RTAFB in September 1971. For his participation in the Vietnam War, Zeybel was also awarded eight Distinguished Flying Crosses and 19 Air Medals. (1971 USAF/Author)

The author holding the 16th Special Operations Squadron mascot "Herky the Turkey." Herky was a guest of honor at formal gatherings when officers wore their blue Spectre party suits. Each flying unit in Southeast Asia had its own distinctive party suit. (1970 Author)

(Left) Henry Anthony Zeybel, Financial Editor of *The Pittsburgh Press*. A staff member of the newspaper for 45 years, he started as a copy boy in 1921. He grew up on the lower North Side of Pittsburgh two blocks from the Allegheny River. (1963 Author)

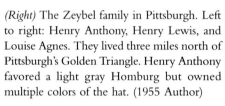

(Right) The Zeybel family in Pittsburgh. Left to right: Henry Anthony, Henry Lewis, and Louise Agnes. They lived three miles north of Pittsburgh's Golden Triangle. Henry Anthony favored a light gray Homburg but owned multiple colors of the hat. (1955 Author)

Filipino children who lived near Mactan Air Base and who the author tutored in English (enough to read the comic books he provided), soccer (they enjoyed the game), and dodge ball (they hated it) during his three days off between 18-day rotations to Vietnam. Girls who comprised part of the group (and enjoyed "Archie" comics best) were too bashful to pose for the photograph. (1967 Author)

(Left) A C-130 Low Altitude Parachute Extraction System (LAPES) delivery of a sled of supplies to Khe Sanh, Vietnam, under siege. Note the sled beneath the airplane and the trailing parachute that dragged the sled from the aircraft at an altitude of five feet. USAF squadrons resorted to this method of resupply after North Vietnamese Army artillery made it impossible to land safely at the base. (1968 USAF/Author)

(Right) Following the air-to-air destruction of seven MiG-21s over North Vietnam during Operation *Bolo* on 2 January 1967, 8th Tactical Fighter Wing Commander Colonel Robin Olds (far right) and fellow pilots nail symbolic red stars to their headquarters building at Ubon RTAFB. Major Phil Combies is on the far left. Others, left to right, are Lieutenant Dan Lafferty, Major John Pardo, Lieutenant S. Croker, and (front center) Lieutenant Steve Wayne. (1967 USAF/Author)

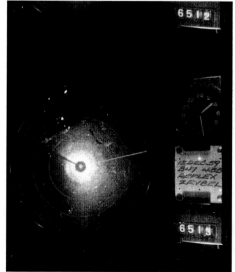

(Left) "Lake Erie to the Left." A B-47 navigator-bombardier's view of the world at-large as his aircraft progresses from Texas to the United Kingdom to serve overseas Alert duty as part of the Cold War. This crew position had no view outside of the bomber except for an optical device with a narrow field of vision ahead of the plane. Navigation was done by radar, celestial computations, or pressure pattern resolution. (1959 Author)

A Cold War nuclear-armed Strategic Air Command B-52H waits behind razor-sharp concertina wire on around-the-clock Alert at Dyess AFB, Texas. Note the KC-135 tankers in the background. Like the bombers, they, too, took off at 15-second intervals following the launch of the last bomber. The number of aircraft on Alert and prepared for instant launch fluctuated according to the degree of political tension between the United States and the Soviet Union. (1984 Author)

B-52 aircraft commander Captain Brooks Tyler wears a plzt attached to his flight helmet. With lenses made from 21 layers of lead-lanthanum zirconate-titanate ceramic, the plzt prevented flash blindness by turning opaque so quickly under intense light that light rays never reach the eyeballs of the person wearing the device. When the threat dims, the lenses fade to transparent. In the event of an Emergency War Order launch, a bomber's pilot and copilot would don the plzt for takeoff and air-to-air refueling—times when the flash curtains would be open and they might be exposed to the brightness of a nuclear explosion. (1984 Author)

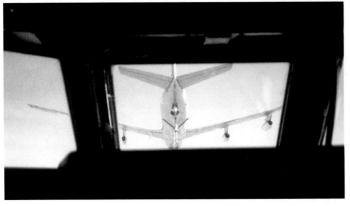

The view of a KC-135 aerial tanker as seen from the cockpit of a B-52 bomber. Enfoldment in the protective cradle formed by the tanker's swept wings, in some unexplainable way, produced the marvel of a regeneration of body and of spirit that overcame the author. (1984 Author)

Refueling, maintenance, and loading teams work over B-52 *Lady Sundown* for a practice post-strike regeneration launch so the aircraft can theoretically fly away within the hour and head for another complex of targets. The training reload includes inert Short Range Attack Missiles in a rotary launcher and gravity bombs in cluster on hydraulic lifters to be jacked into the bomb bay at Dyess AFB, Texas. (1984 Author)

A B-52 minimum interval launch. Upon command of the President of the United States, the bombers take off at 15-second intervals as the first stage of a thermonuclear war. To reduce the effects of jet wash, the first plane flies straight ahead, the second veers right, the third veers left, etc. Also rolling at 15 seconds intervals, KC-135 tankers follow 30 seconds behind the last bomber. (USAF/Author)

The M1 Abrams tank at Fort Hood, Texas. The M1 entered service in 1980 but did not engage in combat for the first time until the 1990–1991 Gulf War when 594 of them deployed to the Middle East. The tank's 105-mm main gun is supplemented by a .50-caliber machine gun fired by the tank commander. Later models of the M1 upgraded to a 120-mm main gun. (1987 Author)

Three M1 tanks from Charlie Company of the 2nd Armored Division, 3rd Battalion, 66th Regiment maneuvering for a dominant position while training at Fort Hood. Tankers' training duplicates wartime conditions as closely as possible. Central Texas provides desolate landscape similar to the Middle East. M1 crewmembers have a strong belief in the superiority of their weapon system. (1987 Author)

The author in an F-16 Fighting Falcon at Hill AFB, Utah. The rare two-seat F-16 belonged to the Reserve 466th Tactical Fighter Squadron that won the 1985 Gunsmoke bombing competition. (1986 Author)

"Did the Downey outcome surprise you?" I said.

DeGregorio grinned. "I was hoping he'd win an honorable discharge on appeal."

Administrative board actions that resulted in other than honorable conditions discharges were automatically reviewed by the General Court-Martial Convening Authority. The military was big on reviews and appeals. Every court-martial, too, was appealed automatically.

"One captain from the board," DeGregorio said, "he told me that the LC—the Board President—stood up for Downey. I know that LC. He's tough. If board procedures had permitted a peremptory challenge, I would have excused him. And then he turns around and votes for my guy." DeGregorio rolled his eyes. "I could be in this racket for a hundred years and still wouldn't understand it."

"Captain Humble," I said.

"All the guys on the board were fliers," DeGregorio said. "They all had tours in Nam. After everything that went on over there, you think they're doing a little atoning?"

"Beats me. I did time over there and I don't need to atone for a goddamn thing."

"Hey, did Al Turner talk to you before he called you to the stand?"

I shook my head.

"I'll bet he didn't talk to Diane either." DeGregorio grinned. "Young Al didn't do his homework." He stared at me, as if looking through me, beyond me. "After your display on the stand, you know, you're finished with court martial boards. Any prosecutor with half a mind will peremptorily challenge you. Same with Diane." Locked in a private world of contemplation, DeGregorio continued. "Young Al overlooked all the good twists. All the nasty angles. How about Freud? The unconscious mind? Psychopathia Sexualis. How did Chip get where it happened? Did the car know the way? And driving while intoxicated had to come into the picture somewhere. What a case. I don't believe any of it."

★ ★ ★

Base Commander Colonel Robert W. Branch, who favored an exceptionally short crew cut and virtually caricatured a cigar-chomping leader from World War II, believed all of it. He telephoned and told me, "I want Downey reassigned. Don't let him return to work."

"What if he doesn't want reassignment?" I said. According to regulations, it was Downey's call.

Branch said, "I don't want to hear that. If he stays here, things are not going to work out for him. I want him off my base. Get Personnel to expedite his request."

I called Downey to my office and explained the regulation to him. Downey said, "Thank you, sir, but I'd rather stay here. Me and Clara are trying it again. She has a good job in town. And I like the people I work with." He proudly added, "And I quit drinking."

For how long? I thought and said, "Look, it's not important what you like. A lot of people think the board's decision was wrong. They want you gone."

Downey looked distressed.

"If you stay here," I said, "nobody's going to waste time protecting your ass, especially after you turned down a chance to get away." I handed a typewritten request for transfer to Downey. "Read this and sign it."

Downey hardly looked at the letter. "I don't want to leave here," he said.

Why was this man-child that had been repeatedly fucked over still so naïve? I wondered. "Chip, sign the letter," I said. "It'll save your ass in the long run."

And Downey signed.

I told him, "Don't go back to the computer section."

"But Captain Martin told me, now this is over, I can—"

"Listen to me. Captain Martin doesn't run the base. You're leaving." I waved a hand. "Take a couple days off. Make it a week. Call it free leave. That's the best I can do." I offered my hand and Downey shook it.

Two days later, Tactical Air Command Headquarters issued orders transferring Airman First Class Ronald Downey from Hurlburt Field, Florida, to Mountain Home AFB, Idaho, 2260 miles away.

Now reread the Kipling quote and cast your vote.

★ ★ ★

Yep, that's the way the system worked back in the day: a strict structure with enough loopholes to forgive but not forget. Nailing a guy to a cross was saved for big time fuckups, but hardcore stonewallers did beat the system, a thought that demands a sequel to Kipling. Looking at those days from 50 years beyond, the problem appears to be a lack of followership rather than a lack of leadership. The full colonels and generals retained their absolute self-serving values, but younger officers—including majors and lieutenant colonels that perhaps experienced an epiphany in Nam—tended to accept cultural values of the sixties and seventies that conflicted with traditional Air Force mores. Unrestrained sex and occasional drug use became as gratifying as promotions to people that accepted a redefined value system.

Another incident illustrated the conflicting interpersonal dynamics in play on a grander scale. It involved several fair-haired lieutenants from Hurlburt that took up the sport of low-level dogfighting in helicopters, a pastime requiring them to violate numerous flying regulations. No longer facing the eventuality of going to war overseas, they created their own stylized combat in an isolated section of woods within the Eglin AFB Reservation. That led to their crashing a helicopter. The accident report reflected a powerful who-gives-a-shit attitude toward regulations and reason, outshone only by its description of the heroic efforts of a sergeant passenger who repeatedly ran back into a burning aircraft to rescue two injured men.

The lieutenants' dogfighting with helicopters had been the worst kept secret on base and, as a result, the crash led to court martial actions, which led to stonewalling by everyone involved in the dogfighting. The lieutenants erected a solid front that denied the slightest misbehavior. They called the incident an accident and said no more. The board members absolved them. I knew none of the lieutenants involved, but I read the court martial transcript. By unanimously sticking to a concocted story, the lieutenants left the board with no grounds on which to convict them. They were the only witnesses to what happened. The outcome enraged General Holton. At a weekly staff meeting, which I attended, Holton questioned the integrity of the entire officer corps, going so far as to label young officers as "corrupt." Consequently, the stigma associated with the court martial action along with low efficiency ratings ended careers: lieutenants resigned early or quit after fulfilling their obligated time in service.

If one agreed that the problem of the seventies resulted from a lack of followership more than from a lack of leadership, then one could say the psychiatrists helplessly watched the inmates run the asylum. It wasn't a totally bad time, however, because, like after any war, the participants needed a period of readjustment. At least that was how I interpreted the situation before bailing out in 1976.

★ ★ ★

Let's back up. Air Force Sensitivity Training included teaching manners for improving race relations, an endless topic in America and particularly the South—back then, long before then, and even today. In my squadron at Hurlburt Field, "Rap" Brown, a bright and outspoken black staff sergeant, interacted with me as if we were from opposing nations, which I found difficult to understand because my leniency extended to blacks as equally as to others. Maybe Brown, who was 10 years younger, saw me as an outdated old fart. Whatever, he had plenty of followers. At his request, I met privately with him and about 50 black enlisted men from our 700-man squadron for an unlimited question-and-answer period about my philosophy on racial equality. My First Sergeant—a white guy—thought such a meeting degraded my authority and opposed it. Friends told me no other commander would consider such a request. I didn't understand how but the meeting quelled Brown's suspicious attitude toward me and eased his criticism of how things were run. I had mentioned that, while growing up in Pennsylvania, during my enrollment at Perry High in Pittsburgh and Penn State University, both schools elected black students—Bill Carper and Jesse Arnelle—to the student body presidencies. Now that I think of it, Barack Obama wasn't yet born at those times.

★ ★ ★

While the school solution remained intact in advocating that people had to learn to follow before they could lead, those who did not reach the pinnacle of at least full colonel might have not learned to follow because of changing roles. Changes in the demands of duty perhaps gave them the option of not having to, or not caring to, follow. Modern warfare demanded technicians: in an air force the most prominent technicians operated the airplanes that did the fighting. Leadership among those technicians involved small groups of people working side by side: a fighter aircraft pilot and wingman at the minimum or a gunship crew of a baker's dozen at the maximum. Often in those situations, in the vortex of combat, leadership and followership fluctuated according to the demands of the moment, and all men became equal when working for a common purpose. For example, Holley's flying skill as an aircraft commander saved a lot of lives but only as a result of following orders from Ballsmith and Savage. Similarly, for Combies and the other pilots in Rambler flight, "all the plans and promises disappeared in a blink, [and] with the meat on the table, it became every man for himself." At the working level, explicit leadership became less critical.

One must remember the design of military force is to prosecute war and to defeat the enemy on a given spot; in comparison, the outcomes of conferences, staff meetings, and power point presentations are ethereal and not worth a half-hearted fuck.

The Air Force confused the issue from the start when it commissioned fliers. Why did crewmen have to be officers? Shortly after I retired, enlisted men replaced officers as Spectre sensor operators. Anyone who excelled at video games easily mastered operating the IR or TV. Although enlisted sensor operators stirred the tracking handles, an officer remained in command of validating targets. In a similar and more recent change, Air Force leaders decided "nonpilots" could fly unmanned aerial vehicles such as Predators, again emphasizing technical or mechanical skills over leadership qualities.

Ever since I became a part of the Air Force, and probably long before that time, the ranks of crewmen contained people contented to be technicians, contented to perform flying jobs for an entire career. In that case, the majority of crewmen didn't need a bachelor's or a master's degree along with additional years of education at Squadron Officer School, Air Command and Staff College, Air War College, or other institutions of up-scale military study. Like galley slaves, crewmen functioned perfectly well below deck, where they quickly learned to accommodate to demands of the moment. For example, a limited number of Air Force enlisted men flew as pilots from 1912 through 1957. One of them, Edward Wenglar, who became a brigadier general, best described his group's motivation: "We never thought about whether we wanted to be an enlisted pilot or an officer pilot. We just wanted to be pilots, and we would gladly have stayed privates forever just to have the chance to fly."

It broke my heart to see pilot friends separated from the service after failing to be selected for promotion to major, a failure usually based on efficiency ratings that subjectively reflected poor leadership potential. The primary thing these men wanted from life was to fly but the promotion system's design didn't measure that desire. The fact that the Air Force had no restrictions on the number of captains made their release from duty more unpalatable. Most of them remained on active duty as enlisted men in order to qualify for retirement benefits. Meanwhile their skill as pilots went to waste. Maury Gaston, one of my favorite pilots in Nam and at Hurlburt, got separated in this manner and ended up driving the big blue bus that carried crews to the airplanes. Every time I climbed aboard his bus, I wanted to apologize to him for the illogic of the system and the waste of his talent. A better plan would have separated the technicians from the want-to-be-leaders.

CHAPTER 9

Razzmatazz

Airplanes provided no thrills the first two times I left the ground. Reserve Officers' Training Corps (ROTC) instructors broke my flying cherry over central Pennsylvania in a C-47 Skytrain. The flight was a first for about three dozen advanced ROTC students. The old and noisy airplane lumbered around like a school bus carrying a load of discontented students. Our student fuck-this reaction was mollified by a few pleasing minutes of riding in the copilot's seat and looking outside. Otherwise, the flight wasted our time. Worst of all, for the satisfaction of the two majors leading the outing, we students had to pretend to enjoy it.

In the summer of 1954, after my junior year at Penn State, my second journey aloft came to pass one afternoon at ROTC summer camp at Greenville Air Force Base, Mississippi. I flew in the front seat of a dirty yellow T-6 Texan directly behind an engine that pulsed like an agitator washing machine ready to die. Every minute airborne in that propeller driven junker, I expected to crash. My pilot read my mood and took us home after 20 minutes. He was as disgusted with me as I was with the airplane and him.

The next day I flew in the back seat of a T-33 Shooting Star jet and it was as good as a wet dream. I blended into the plane's silver sleekness as if it had been tailor made for me. My pilot and I soared above the busy Mississippi River, and I imagined attacking the boats below. I told him, "I wish we had bombs and rockets and could sink all that shit on the river." He laughingly took me through a series of aerobatics as natural as racing around a track. G-forces gave me a beautiful and satisfying surprise. I begged him to fly under a bridge. We flew until we ran out of gas.

I remained boundlessly elated until the next morning when a physical exam revealed I was nearsighted, which I had not suspected, and unqualified to attend pilot training. At best I could become a navigator. That "Well, fuck me" summer camp roller-coaster ride took less than 48 hours.

★ ★ ★

When I was a young man courting success, I played me an impatient game—and drank a lot in the process. After two years of training, my first operational assignment took me to the Strategic Air Command (SAC) and Dyess AFB, in Abilene, Texas, as a B-47 Stratojet navigator-bombardier. I chose the job because it offered the fastest course to promotion. From 1949 to 1966, SAC had a spot promotion system that, based on performance, advanced crewmen well ahead of the normal promotion cycle. I saw officers rise from lieutenant to major in a year. The speedy jump in rank worked when a lieutenant holding a spot promotion to captain received his normal promotion to captain, and then, within a year, qualified for a spot promotion to major, which he received based on his crew's record. Navigator-bombardiers Harry Meehan and Herman Schumacher pulled off the trick as easily as putting on a new flight suit. Beyond dreams within my reach, the same gimmick worked for the leap from captain to lieutenant colonel.

A crew's standing primarily depended on how accurately the nav-bomb navigated and bombed, but mainly bombed. A wing commander submitted his preference list to SAC Headquarters at Offutt AFB—a ranking normally based on bombing reliability (meaning no unreliable bomb score) and circular error average—and SAC allocated promotions to the best of the best. A SAC publicity film told the world a crew was "no better than the navigator-bombardier's skill in those few seconds over the target" because he was "the most important crewman in terms of putting bombs on target." Only SAC gave navigators such high recognition.

In determining bombing accuracy, crews did not drop real or simulated weapons. Instead, a ground-based radar bomb scoring (RBS) system tracked a bomber's heading, speed, and altitude and predicted where a bomb dropped by that airplane would land. Scoring sites existed at major cities across the United States when high altitude bombing tactics prevailed. The development of surface-to-air missiles forced bombers to change to low-level tactics, however, and RBS sites scattered to isolated areas. Inside the bomber, on radar the nav-bomb tracked a designated target and simulated bomb release with an electronic signal. Bombing scores under a thousand feet were highly desired. The largest acceptable error was 3500 feet.

According to *The Development of Strategic Air Command 1946–1981: A Chronological History*, in December 1949, General Curtis LeMay promoted, "on the spot," 237 lieutenants to the temporary grade of captain. In 1950 and 1951, he expanded the program to include temporary promotions to major, lieutenant colonel, technical sergeant, and master sergeant.

A spot crew that failed to maintain proficiency lost its promotions. I had a friend who went from lieutenant to captain, was demoted, and then again went from lieutenant to captain in the same year. On a day when a spot major lost his promotion and reverted to captain, a wise guy at the Dyess AFB O-club tipped the piano player to tickle out a lengthy rendition of *Autumn Leaves*—"the falling leaves drift by my window"—when the demoted guy—minus his gold oak leaves—sat down at the bar.

Personnel in Air Force commands other than SAC resented spot promotions because no similar reward system existed for them. As I learned in 1962, however, as a student at Squadron Officer School where, for the first time, I met a cross-section of people from other commands, nobody in the Air Force worked as many hours and under as much pressure as SAC crewmen. General John McConnell ended the spot promotion program in December 1965, directing that crewmen who held spots would revert to their normal grades on 30 June 1966.

★ ★ ★

I joined SAC in 1957 as a bachelor first lieutenant. The 490th Bomb Squadron, the Officers' Club, and the BOQ became my limited world.

Lieutenants Dean Mucci and Nick Karras were the squadron's two other bachelors and we caught the shit details.

A large-size copilot, Mucci walked with the confidence of a big city gangster and boasted of his Italian-Chicago heritage. He hated to wear a hat because it messed up his slick coal black hair. Once when he and I met an airman without cover, Mucci hollered, "Hey, where's your fuckin' hat?" While the airman pulled his hat from a pocket, Mucci leaned into him and said, "I gotta wear a fuckin' hat, you gotta wear a fuckin' hat. Don't let me catch you without one again." His approach varied from traditional leadership techniques, but it made the point.

Karras also had coal black hair along with a ready smile. He showed pride in his Greek heritage, which included a trace of *Zorba*-like fatalism regarding the punctuality demanded of crewmen. He had the habit of arriving a moment before the starting time of any activity, whereas SAC wanted crewmen to be five minutes early and ready and waiting for whatever was to come. At the same time, Karras showed a restrained aggressiveness toward life in general. Fundamentally, he was a nice person who tried not to offend anyone.

During my first December at Dyess, Major George Jennings, our squadron operations officer, told me, "You'll be pulling Officer of the Day on New Year's Eve."

"But I already made plans to go to a party," I told him.

"Well, it's you or Karras. Mucci has OD on Christmas," he said.

"Then give it to Karras," I said and muttered something about outranking Karras.

Jennings stared me down and said, "Rank among lieutenants is like chastity among whores." To make sure I got the point, he added, "It doesn't exist." After a short pause, he asked, "So you're willing to screw your buddy so you can go to a party?"

"Yes, sir."

"Okay. But you have to tell him he has the duty."

"Okay with me."

Jennings smiled. "And tell him not to come to me with a complaint."

When I told Karras, he said, "I saw the OD list this morning. It had your name for New Year's."

"Jennings changed his mind," I said.

"Damn it," Karras said. "Why?"

"I don't know, but he said not to come crying to him. That's the way it is."

Contrary to his personality, Karras said, "Fuckin' George."

After the holidays, he learned what had happened, brought it to my attention, but didn't try to get even—as I said, he was a nice person.

At times, Jennings behaved like a character from Joseph Heller's *Catch-22*. He had pudgy cheeks, curly hair, and a mustache. On slow days, he called Mucci into his office and they talked about Mucci's love life. Jennings vicariously lived Mucci's sexual conquests. And Mucci didn't mind sharing details.

Trying to sound ultra-suave, I once told Mucci a Noxzema rubdown in the right places added zest and relief to long sexual encounters. The next day I saw him in the BX checkout line carrying four jars of the stuff. He caught me watching him and we both broke up.

At some point in our narrowly structured lives, Mucci brought his girlfriend from Chicago to live with him in downtown Abilene. Not long after, Colonel Campbell Palfrey called Mucci to his office.

Palfrey was a stiff-back West Point ring-knocking iron ass. As a lieutenant colonel he had commanded the 490th; his promotion to colonel advanced him to wing director of operations. While in the squadron, he had taken a chunk out of me. A friend of mine, who had his driver's license suspended, needed a ride to Love Field in Dallas, a 200-mile motor jaunt. He talked me into driving him there in his Plymouth Fury. Running late, I floored it most of the way, putting the hammer down on one long, smooth stretch of Interstate, most of which was still under construction in the fifties. Out of nowhere a state trooper pulled me over and said he had clocked me at 118. Because I was a lieutenant, which in his eyes somehow made us brothers in arms, he wrote the ticket for 80. I paid the fine and forgot it until a month later when Palfrey called me to his office. "You recently received a ticket for speeding," he said. "You were driving eighty miles an hour."

Right there, I learned the cold fact that state law enforcement agencies shared information with the base legal office and the base lawyers passed the data to commanders. Having no choice, I admitted my guilt.

Palfrey told me how I had violated all that was sacred within the officer corps. He ended his lecture by saying, "To make certain you've learned your lesson, I'm restricting you from driving on base for thirty days." His edict meant I couldn't keep my car on base and I would walk everywhere or hitch a ride.

Jesus Christ, I thought, if the ticket had read 118, I would have been walking until doomsday. God bless state troopers.

So, Mucci brought his girlfriend to Abilene to live happily ever after. Now, in the late fifties, living together without being married put the two of them on the outer fringe of socially acceptable behavior. In those days, marriage ruled and divorce was a giant military no-no. Old timers preached that a man who broke his vow to the woman he loved and married was equally likely to break his vow to his nation. Palfrey called Mucci to his office at wing level and said, "Lieutenant, I understand you've been leading a rather exciting lifestyle."

Conditioned by his conversations with Jennings, Mucci classified Palfrey as a fellow voyeur. He dropped into a comfortable slouch, said, "It could be better," and started to sit on the edge of Palfrey's desk.

Mucci told me, "That was the last thing I said. Man, he bombed me. I was surprised I could stand at attention that stiff for that long. I didn't fuckin' blink. I don't remember half of what he said but none of it was good. I think the Air Force won't be my career."

Being two overage imps, Mucci and I had to get even. Flying required us to work odd hours and often caused us to wander around in the middle of the night while preparing for early morning takeoffs. So when Mucci or I got up early, we gave Palfrey's home phone a single ring, enough to stir him. Of course, back then, phones didn't have caller ID, so Palfrey had no way to trace his tormentors. Our haphazard schedules formed no pattern. We considered our tactic a small victory for small people.

★ ★ ★

After duty hours, activity centered on the Officers' Club, the only place to get a drink legally in Taylor County. Except for sampling moonshine-distillers' products, the God-fearing citizens of Abilene remained bone dry. However, many of the locals cherished an invitation to the O-Club. In 1960, on the outskirts of Abilene, 29 people incorporated a small community into a town, named it Impact, declared liquor sales legal there, and opened a liquor store. Abilene's government contested the move in court but lost. Until 1978, when Abilene legalized liquor sales by a slim majority, Impact remained the only wet town in Taylor County. Gimme that ol' time religion....

Drinking and gambling set the tone of a man's world within the O-Club. After work, crewmen packed the O-Club bar in a setting that encouraged drinking by offering twofers. A single drink of the bar's best booze cost a quarter and the bartenders poured generously. After-work socializing lasted until seven or eight or nine o'clock, sometimes ten. Wives joined in the drinking only on Saturday nights.

It was easy to lose one's mind when booze was practically free. One night at dinner, Ken Lemke, whose family shared an on-base Capehart duplex with mine (yeah, I got married), ordered a martini for each of us and I told the waitress, "Make it a double." Not to be outdone, Lemke said, "Make it a double double," and we each got about a pint of martinis in a milkshake glass. To round out the drinking farce, nobody worried about driving under the influence. Police semi-looked the other way if they pulled over an officer not driving in a straight line, more often than not following him home after a warning.

The Club's back-room, Friday night, five-card stud poker game drew the biggest spenders. Games with $1000 or more in the pot provided expensive entertainment for young officers whose annual take-home averaged around five grand. The coolest action I saw took place on a last hand of the night, dealt close to dawn. The betting came down to two men. Major Scotty Couch appeared to have the pot locked when Captain Howard Bittner raised $2000, more than Couch had in cash. To call, Couch threw the keys to his Cadillac into the pot. The men showed their hands and Bittner won with a pair in the hole. The room grew absolutely still. Displaying not a trace of triumph, Bittner lifted the car keys from the pile of kitty money, slid them to Couch, and said, "You need a ride home tonight. Bring the keys and title to my house in the morning." Bittner drove the car for a week before Couch bought it back for the amount of the raise.

Because Bittner remained calm and deliberate when gambling, he won most of the time, which caused people to dislike him. Bittner looked like the actor John Forsythe and his wife reminded me of Oscar-winner Joanne Woodward. I met Bittner in the Dyess Hospital when he was sharing a room with Lieutenant Henry Lee Conn, one of my drinking buddies. I sneaked pastrami on rye sandwiches, dill pickles, potato pancakes, and a flask of bourbon into the hospital. Brain-twisting bourbon was our drink of choice, regardless of the killer hangovers. Conn took my provisions for granted but Bittner viewed my action as the start of a friendship.

Childless and older than I was (he began his military career as a seaman aerial gunner in World War II Avengers), Bittner developed a father-son relationship with me. He gave me a lot of good advice that I was too impetuous to follow. For example, when senseless new regulations pissed me off, Bittner said, "Ask yourself two questions. First, will you still care tomorrow? Second, can you do anything about it? If you can't answer 'yes' to both questions, do it and forget it." I saw his point but couldn't live it. I didn't follow the minimal advice my real father gave me. Bittner also had a keen alertness toward reading other people's reactions, which probably accounted for much of his success at poker, a skill I admired.

Bittner explained to me the reasons why he was a winning gambler: "I have a bankroll and bet only money. Other guys are betting things not on the table, like this month's rent or next month's payment on a washing machine. That puts pressure on them that leads them to make bad decisions. They fold too early or get desperate and stay in too late. Most of these young guys shouldn't be gambling, but if they're going to do it, I'm willing to take their money." Watching Bittner at play, I saw junior officers make courageous but incorrect bets against him, acting like young gunfighters trying to build a reputation by outdrawing the old hand.

I understood what he meant about betting more than money. On my first trip to Las Vegas, I'd made seven straight passes at a crap table and won $40. I dragged after every pass over concern about having enough money to reach Sacramento, my destination. Meanwhile, a guy standing next to me, who was betting $100 chips, let his money ride and won a ton. When I finally lost the dice, he flipped a $100 chip to the rake man. I said, "Why you tipping him? I'm the guy who made the passes." He said, "Right. And you're the guy who had a chance to bet." Then and there the stranger taught me I wasn't a high roller.

Bittner occasionally enticed me to gamble, but the farthest I went was to match nickels to see who bought the next bottle of champagne, a gamble in which the loser shared the winnings. However, under Bittner rules, the loser also lost the nickel.

★ ★ ★

In those days, many crewmen were senior captains on the cusp of promotion to major. They had flown in World War II, been separated from duty, and then recalled for the Korean War. Their combat experience had been in the B-17, B-24, B-25, and B-26. They seldom talked about war experiences or maybe I didn't listen enough to learn from them. I did ask Ken Smith how he earned his Distinguished Flying Cross and he said, "My B-24 sank a Jap cruiser." I said, "Did your bombardier get a DFC, too?" Smith said, "No. I didn't get the medal for sinking the ship. I got the medal for making the decision to go down and strafe the survivors." He might have been kidding, but at the time it sounded right to me.

Aircraft commander Ken Smith earned a spot promotion to major and then to lieutenant colonel. While a major, he carried a set of captain bars attached to his dog tags chain, as he said, "Just in case." Although we weren't crewed together at the time, when I received a spot to captain, he took the silver bars off his chain and pinned them on me, saying, "You have to give them back if I need them." He laughed at my irreverent comments until we began flying together. After that when we encountered a new situation ripe for mockery, he reminded me, "Don't piss in this stream just yet, we might need to drink here in the future."

★ ★ ★

Our 341st Bomb Wing shared Dyess with the 96th Bomb Wing to comprise the 819th Air Division, commanded by Brigadier General William Yancey. Previously, Yancey had bossed the 96th and his sentiments flowed in their direction, which irked our boss, Colonel Jack Hayes. The 96th had an illustrious World War II combat record from flying B-17s for the Eighth Air Force in Europe. Meanwhile, two of the 341st squadrons had spent the war patrolling the Caribbean for Nazi submarines, and the third flew B-25s in Burma.

A day came when the 96th was to present a B-17 for static display at an air park dedicated to the city of Abilene. The B-17 looked factory new. General Yancey had been scheduled to unveil the airplane along with Abilene's mayor at nine on a Saturday morning. Clandestinely, Jack Hayes led a crew of sergeants on a midnight raid on the plane, aiming to score a surprise laugh at the unveiling. However, on Saturday morning, somebody from the 96th took one last look under the sheet covering the B-17 and saw "It was rougher in the Pacific" whitewashed on the bomber's fuselage. The feces impacted the whirling blades. Yancy delayed the ceremony for an hour and personally watched Hayes and his sergeants scrub off the message.

Fucking with a general officer's pride took steel balls, even for a colonel, and Hayes's stature rose among the 341st crewmen. Of course, it wasn't their asses caught in the wringer. Not long after, Hayes retired (or was he transferred), unhappy (but not half as unhappy and pissed off as his wife) over not being promoted to star rank.

Hayes was a regular guy with the mentality of a crewman, which could have been why he didn't make general. For example, a 490th crew chief came up with the bright idea of painting white sidewalls on the tires of his B-47. He suggested it to the squadron commander, who suggested it to Hayes, who bought the idea. So one lone B-47 from SAC's gigantic fleet of 2000 wore white sidewalls on its outrigger tires. Similarly, when Lieutenant Chuck Lowe and I scored shacks—perfect bomb drops—on a *Team Scrimmage* simulated combat exercise, Hayes hugged us, and he did it long before the feel-good bullshit hugs came down the trail.

★ ★ ★

My approach to Air Force life (and most of life) barely varied from my approach to college life. I worked hard when the mission/classes demanded, but off duty I partied equally as hard. I discovered the pleasure of drinking at 16, finding it a perfect way to fill dead time between whatever. My attitude wasn't unique within the Air Force population. Many officers at Dyess, young and old, followed a similar script.

I had picked my college—Penn State (yes, it was still a college then)—based on the fact it had 69 fraternities and practically every one of them threw a beer blast on Friday and Saturday nights. The cellars of most houses had been converted into rathskeller beer halls. The sophisticated houses held occasional Sunday indoor/outdoor cocktail parties featuring Purple Jesus—a mixture of grain alcohol and grape juice—and a jazz trio to help people prepare for Monday classes.

On party nights, first floor furniture got moved into corners to make room for dancing—in the dark. Pushed out of sight, couches became make-out space devoted to hand jobs. Taking a woman to a room above the first floor—rather, being caught taking a woman above the first floor—risked probation for the house. All-nighters didn't exist. Penn State controlled its male population by controlling the schedule of its female population. Women, including those in sororities, lived in dormitories and had to follow restricted hours: they had to sign in by eleven on Friday night and by midnight on Saturdays. Sunday to Thursday, sign in time was ten.

A couple of years after I graduated—still a bachelor—and was on leave in Pittsburgh, I looked up my first college sweetheart. By then she had been married and divorced. "He was after my inheritance and there wasn't that much of it," she said. We sipped a drink or two in her swanky apartment and I made the old familiar moves. When she held back, I reminded her of how close we had been. She said, "We were children back then," and made me recall the inadequacies of our relationship.

Well—what were they—the inadequacies? They were the offspring of unintentional ignorance bred from intellect. My freshman year, in a series of guy-to-guy late-night lectures, Jim Whalen, my resident advisor who was working toward a doctorate in psychology, detailed the difference between a mere "clitoral" orgasm and a sensational "full body" orgasm for a woman—remember, this was in the early fifties and Freud ruled. I made the mistake of sharing his information—teaching my girlfriend that an orgasmic El Dorado existed somewhere beyond the shivering trickles of golden release she now experienced. The essence of new eroticism was deep and prolonged exploration, or so Whalen said, which required a quantitative performance standard that overwhelmed me. How deep? How prolonged? Penn State's environment provided no landscape for such adventure. Alas, we never got beyond the clitoral orgasm and she found a string of other explorers. Bless them all.

During my early years on campus from 1951 to 1954, the frats had little supervision: no chaperones or housemothers got in the way of boys-will-be-boys activities. In late 1954, the Inter-Fraternity Council passed a number of restrictive by-laws, the worst of which forced houses to have a chaperone attend parties, normally a puzzled old lady filling a square. But she was there. Fuck them. In my house—Delta Upsilon (DU)—I led a clan that objected to any cooperation with the Council, a suck-ass group of goodie-two-shoes that acted on behalf of school administrators seeking a more sober image for fraternities. Fuck them, too.

Until 1954, under the GI Bill, colleges enrolled a significant number of veterans—older men in their mid to late twenties—which accounted for much of the freedom allotted to the fraternities. Among the veterans that lived in the DU house, two had wives elsewhere but that didn't slow their after-hours behavior. My favorite vet was Harry Papacharalambous (his family had shortened its name from Papacharalambopolous because Immigration allowed a maximum of 16 letters), who normally weighed 150 but boxed at 125 pounds. Yep, the NCAA sanctioned the manly sport from 1932 to 1960. "Pappy" didn't encourage my misbehavior, but he didn't discourage it either. The vets set examples I found easy to follow. When the veterans disappeared, the administration clamped down on the remaining younger students. Pennsylvania's legal drinking age was 21 but, with the veterans present, the law had not been enforced inside fraternities. That changed.

Papacharalambous's family lived in Jersey City and, when he temporarily lost his driver's license for speeding, he enlisted me to chauffeur him home once a month. He owned an Olds 98 that blew by everything, except a red-headed Cuban woman-child named Rosita Pagan. We were on the Pennsylvania Turnpike, cruising at 95, when we both saw her standing well clear of the roadside. "Is that cutie hitchhiking?" Harry said and, in the time it took him to ask the question, I stopped the car. Rosita grinned when she jumped in and told me, "You the champeen stopper." She snuggled between Harry and me like we three had been friends for life. Manufacturers built cars correctly back then, with a wide bench front seat, space enough for friends to be friendly. We took her home to DU for the night. I remember her perfectly because she was one of my first half dozen. And we didn't discuss Freud.

The vets gave us a broader view of the world. For example, I still recall the first time I heard an obscentity used between syllables when former-sergeant-and-soon-to-be-lieutenant Archie Kinder said, "I always carried a re-fucking-volver." I remained in the ranks of DU pledges until the end of my junior year. I carried a B-plus GPA, but my attitude held me back from being initiated. For example, at a "bitch session"—a rite in which pledges lined up before the brothers for reprimands—the brother I roomed with told me, "'Fuck it' is not a proper response to 'Good morning.'" I said, "Fuck it! That's how I feel in the morning," even though we were not supposed to reply. "See," the brother shouted. "You're fucking hopeless." Because I argued rather than obeyed, brothers frequently assigned me with extra work chores, which I frequently ignored and they often forgot. One semester, I received an $80 fine—a monstrous sum in those days—for a drunken stunt now beyond recall. And it didn't help that my favorite topic of conversation was going down on women, which disconcerted some people.

By the way, Penn State had a ball-busting grading system. An A counted as three points, B was two, C was one, and D was zero. But F had two levels: a minus one or a minus two, quaintly called a "bar-one" and a "bar-two." The bar-two gave a professor the power to bury a student. As a result, a handful of freshmen finished their one-and-only year at State with a negative GPA. At the start of my senior year, on a rainy night, I totaled a friend's Jeep and then banished myself to a third-floor back room at DU from where I made the Dean's List. I remained sober for over a year. The disastrous memory of the crash dissolved after I left school and home and entered the Air Force.

Milton Eisenhower served as Penn State's Prexy and he arranged for his brother, President Dwight Eisenhower, to address the Class of 1955, which happened to be the University's centennial year. The school had made the leap up from college rank in 1953. Before and after the graduation ceremony, Dwight and Mamie walked around campus near Old Main like any other couple, schmoozing with the hoi polloi. Secret Service men kept practically invisible, an appropriate move because everybody liked Ike.

Regardless of the pictures I have painted, I don't blame anyone else for my drinking. By reading the white spaces surrounding the words, one should easily see I selected environments that allowed me to act as I did. In retrospect, the amazing thing was that so many people tolerated my misbehavior, particularly those in the military, but then, the Air Force needed technicians and I excelled inside an airplane. So my accomplishments at Dyess from 1957 to 1961 included marrying Wilma Jane Brewer from North Little Rock, Arkansas, who I met while on leave; fathering a red-head daughter named Karen Louise; receiving a spot promotion to captain and a regular commission; joining Ken Smith's standardization-evaluation crew; and transferring my drinking habits from the O-Club to a Capehart housing living room.

★ ★ ★

Dyess had two heroic flying performances while I was stationed there. One happened in daylight on the runway and the other took place high in the sky above North Texas at night.

Late in 1958, under a simulated Emergency War Order (EWO) launch, SAC tested the Dyess Alert bomber fleet to prove it could get off the ground in less than 15 minutes—the lag time between liftoff and arrival of ICBMs from the Soviet Union. As part of this scheme, bombers launched 15 seconds apart in a minimum interval takeoff (MITO). For the exercise, loaded with nuclear weapons, the fleet scrambled as it would if attack were imminent. Because the Alert B-47s weighed a maximum of 220,000 pounds, each airplane had a horse-collar of 33 jet-assisted takeoff (JATO) bottles attached aft of its fuselage's midpoint. Each bottle held a solid propellant that generated a thousand pounds of thrust for approximately 20 seconds, which meant the horse-collar configuration added 33,000 pounds of thrust to aid liftoff. To fully appreciate the boost, every crew made a JATO takeoff at least once but at a greatly reduced weight. Therefore, the JATO Alert launch was new only in regard to the gross weight of the airplane.

Ideally, the mathematical dynamics of a MITO took place with aerodynamic precision. A B-47 takeoff roll lasted approximately 60 seconds. With only 15 seconds of separation between aircraft, it became possible for four bombers to be on the runway at the same time: the leader scant seconds from liftoff; the next two airplanes around mid-field, one soon after and the other shortly before JATO firing; and the fourth commencing acceleration at the hammerhead. The lockstep stream allowed no time for a deviation in an emergency. Once the JATO fired, the crew was committed to fly. With no cutoff switch, the JATO bottles burned until exhausted.

On the day of the EWO exercise, when the scramble klaxon sounded at Dyess, base personnel raced to the flight line to watch the takeoffs. Faster than expected possible, the lead B-47 roared down the runway and broke ground perfectly. Number two wasn't as lucky.

Captain Don Youngmark, a broad-chested six-two at age 37, piloted the second bomber. He was the kind of guy who had little patience with people that didn't perform to the best of their ability. When he triggered the JATO bottles, one bottle ruptured in a flash, kicked loose eight bottles surrounding it, and sent them flying like unguided missiles. Two of the bottles rocketed upward, tore through the skin of the plane's fuselage, ripped into the main fuel tank, and ignited the fuel that poured from the ruptured cell.

Spotting the blazing bomber, the senior controller in the tower, a master sergeant and former World War II pilot, calmly said, "Aircraft on the roll at the five-thousand-foot marker, your fuselage is on fire."

About the same time, copilot Captain John Gerding heard and felt the explosion, looked over his shoulder, and reported, "AC, we got a helluva fire." The plane appeared to be burning from the wing root aft. "We gotta bail out."

Flames blossomed into a gigantic yellow flower engulfing most of the aircraft's empennage. Petals of fire fell along the runway. The bomber could have exploded at any moment.

Youngmark didn't hear the tower controller's call, but he responded to Gerding. "Stay calm," he said. "I want enough altitude so everybody can get out. Crew, prepare for bailout."

In the aircraft nose, navigator Captain John Dowling tightened his lap belt, checked the connectors between his seat and parachute, lowered his helmet visor, gripped a D-ring between his legs, and waited. Simultaneously, in the narrow aisle below the pilot and copilot seats, Staff Sergeant Robert Schneider gripped the emergency release handle of the entry door, his escape route. For a real EWO launch, Schneider wouldn't have been on board the airplane, but he had received special permission to fly the exercise. Both Dowling and Schneider needed 500 feet of altitude for bail out, enough height for their parachutes to fully deploy.

Youngmark and Gerding rode ejection seats that shot them high into the air, giving them the capacity to eject from ground level and still gain enough altitude for their parachutes to work properly.

Barely at flying speed, Youngmark lifted the burning bomber from the runway, climbed it to 500 feet above the terrain, and ordered the crew to bail out. With the aircraft in a nose-high attitude and seeing he had the minimum altitude for a downward ejection, Dowling pulled his D-ring. The first two inches of travel of the D-ring lanyard released a panel below his seat, a metal square like a trapdoor leading from one life to another. The next three inches of pull fired the seat: like a double exposure, Dowling was inside and outside of the airplane in the same instant. He separated from the seat, which automatically pulled his parachute lanyard, and his parachute popped open. He oscillated through half an arc and landed gently in a seated position.

Gerding went out next, but before he did, he twice shoved Schneider with his left foot, shouted, "Go. Go. Bail out." Before he ejected, Gerding saw Schneider pull the emergency release handle for the entry door. Then he too blasted his way out of the airplane and floated safely to earth.

At the point where the airplane leveled off and started downward, Youngmark also ejected successfully.

The bomber crashed five miles beyond the south end of the runway. Schneider failed to escape.

An ambulance picked up Gerding and Dowling and carried them to the base hospital.

Youngmark walked back to the end of the runway. By then launches had been halted. Youngmark spotted the 96th Bomb Wing commander in a car and hitched a ride to the flight line. Greeted by wide-eyed squadron mates, Youngmark struck a John Wayne pose and said to a friend, "Was that spectacular enough for you?"

Then he went to the hospital. The three survivors had sustained no injuries and were released within an hour.

When Dowling met Youngmark at the hospital, he said, "Ace, you saved my life."

A neighbor of mine saw Dowling riding his Lambretta scooter home to Capehart housing that evening and reported, "He was staring off into space with a big satisfied grin. I doubt if he knew where he was."

Months later, in a parade ceremony, Youngmark received the Distinguished Flying Cross for his coolness and professionalism as a pilot.

★ ★ ★

Lieutenant Colonel Don Ernest Youngmark left earth on 22 September 2015, two weeks before his 94th birthday.

★ ★ ★

Dyess' hero of heroes, however, was Lieutenant James Obenauf. At 24, Obenauf had the clear-eyed, clean-cut visage of a Viking warrior. The story of his extraordinary 1958 flight was told in a book titled *Twenty Seconds to Live* and on a *Goodyear Theater* television show, a classic tale of fellowship and self-sacrifice.

★ ★ ★

In the middle of the night, the B-47 shuddered and rocked from an explosion in number six engine. Then a fire warning light came on and the engine began shooting flames and sparks for 30 to 40 feet. Aircraft commander Major Jim Graves didn't hesitate to make the proper call, "Bail out. Bail out." Flying at 30,000 feet above Dalhart, Texas, the burning airplane could have erupted into a fireball in moments.

In the aircraft's nose, Lieutenant John Cobb reacted instantly, pulled the D-ring between his legs, and ejected downward, leaving a three-by-four-foot hole in the floor. Simultaneous with Cobb's ejection, a blast of incoming air generated by a plane traveling at 470 knots threw Major Joe Maxwell backward along the narrow aisle on the left side of the plane's interior. Maxwell had been evaluating Cobb's proficiency, which meant he had been seated on a sextant box while looking over Cobb's shoulder. Meanwhile, Graves and his copilot, Lieutenant James Obenauf, went through their ejection sequence: they stowed their control columns; squeezed the hand triggers on their left armrests, which bottomed their seats and blew off the canopy; and squeezed the right armrest triggers to fire the seats. Both seats failed to fire. Obenauf decided he had not worked his handle hard enough, so using greater strength, he repeated the sequence and squeezed the trigger again. Nothing happened. Meanwhile, Graves stepped down to the crawlway, strode forward, and rolled out of the hole left after the navigator ejected.

Obenauf glanced at the fire and thought it was spreading: the wing appeared to be burning. He stretched himself up from his seat, reached down, and pulled the lever to open the entry door, a designated alternate bail-out exit. Helmet bags and boxes from in-flight lunches jammed the door from fully opening. He stepped forward in the crawlway with the intention of bailing out through the navigator's hatch, but found Maxwell passed out on the floor and blocking his way. Maxwell had lost his helmet.

Obenauf's first thought was to roll Maxwell out the navigator's hatch, but he couldn't see how to activate Maxwell's parachute once he had cleared the plane. The three-by-four hole was too small to allow the men to exit together. Furthermore, the likelihood of Maxwell's coming awake and opening the parachute on his own in freefall was questionable. Therefore, Obenauf climbed back into the copilot's seat, unlocked the control column on the second attempt, and decided to return to Dyess, the closest field where he knew the landing pattern. To that point, the airplane had remained on autopilot.

In an open cockpit at freezing temperature, Obenauf wasn't thinking clearly and switched his oxygen setting to emergency, changing the flow to 100 percent. Then he descended to get Maxwell to an altitude where he could breathe normally and perhaps bail out on his own. He cut off the fuel flow to the number six engine, which stopped the fire but left the engine glowing brightly. By the time he reached 11,000 feet, wind and dust had blasted into his eyes and he found it difficult to see. He leveled off at 10,000 feet but his instruments looked milky, forcing him to fly largely by instinct.

Joe Maxwell started shaking his head. Obenauf slapped him awake and tried to convince him to bail out, but Maxwell couldn't find his parachute. After minutes of arguing, Obenauf saw that number six engine had lost its red glow. He recognized his mayday calls had gone unanswered because his interphone plug had disconnected. Altus AFB DF (directional finding steering) picked up his next call, and at the same time the pilot of another B-47 in the area overheard the emergency message and convinced people on the ground that Obenauf could land the bomber from the back seat. Of course, the other pilot didn't realize Obenauf was practically blind by then, couldn't see his directional indicators, and had no idea of his heading.

Under normal conditions, landing a B-47 from the back seat was a difficult task because a bulkhead in front of the copilot blocked his forward view; to see the runway on approach, the copilot had to lean far to the side, which Obenauf could not do because of wind blast.

Fat Chance GCI (Ground-controlled Interception) contacted Obenauf but came in garbled and its instructions did not help him. A few minutes later, Dyess DF and Reese DF located Obenauf and lined him up toward home. About the same time, Maxwell grew more normal, but he still needed eight attempts to find the switch at the pilot's console for turning on the landing lights.

While Obenauf flew the Dyess GCA (Ground-controlled Approach) pattern with a gyro-out steer, the ground controllers ran him into moderate to severe turbulence: he found himself in 40 to 50-degree banks and barely able to control the plane. With partial blindness keeping him from reading his airspeed indicator, he flew an 88 percent power setting and when the plane slightly buffeted or gave a hint of a stall, he pushed the power up to 94 percent. GCA lined him up on final approach but far left of centerline. Choosing not to make a go-around, Obenauf rounded out, stepped the plane down until wheels touched ground, and deployed the brake chute. Feeling almost normal, he chopped power to engines one, two, and five; turned off electrical power; and when the aircraft came to a complete stop, cut engines three and four. The normal again became abnormal when he remembered he was sitting on an armed ejection seat, and he leaped from the airplane. Seconds after his feet touched the runway, he went completely blind.

Obenauf and Maxwell spent the following day in the hospital for treatment of shock, frostbite, and wind-burned eyes.

Two mornings later, members of the 341st Bomb Wing filled the base theater to watch the SAC Commander decorate Obenauf. Everyone arrived 15 minutes early, including Nick Karras. The people on stage wore Air Force silver tans, arguably the Air Force's most dashing uniform ever. Obenauf stood center stage. To his side was Wing Commander Colonel Anthony Perna. Behind them stood Obenauf's wife, Graves, Cobb, Maxwell, and Maxwell's wife along with their five children, one a babe in arms.

On the hour, the auditorium was called to attention. SAC Commander General Thomas Powers marched the length of the theater and climbed the few steps to the stage. Everyone remained standing. An aide said, "Attention to orders," and read the citation accompanying the award of the Distinguished Flying Cross to Obenauf.

Wearing a gauze bandage over one eye along with a pair of dark glasses, Obenauf moved with the uncertainty of a blind man. Perna gently touched Obenauf's elbow in reassurance. Powers pinned the medal to Obenauf's uniform, spoke a few words to him while shaking his hand, and then marched from the auditorium.

Joe Maxwell smiled through the entire ceremony and well beyond.

In further recognition of his heroism, Obenauf received the 1959 Aviator Valor Award.

★ ★ ★

Obenauf and Youngmark became bona fide heroes from my days at Dyess, but one could argue their heroics were momentary and make the point that, on a day-after-day scale, every B-47 crewman and maintenance man displayed heroism by fulfilling the demanding peacetime duties created by SAC.

CHAPTER 10

Waiting with "The Bomb"

My first target as a Strategic Air Command (SAC) B-47 Stratojet navigator-bombardier was Foochow, a provincial capital along the southeast coast of Red China. My designated weapon for the city was a 19-megaton thermonuclear device, equal in yield to a thousand of the design of the bomb dropped on Hiroshima. Overkill was a way of life. A single sentence from the *Weapon Delivery Handbook* remains forever in my mind: "At detonation this weapon is ten thousand times brighter than the noonday sun." Blinding light: darkness at noon.

Back then, in 1958, our three-man crew was temporarily stationed at Andersen Air Force Base, Guam, as part of a 90-day bomber-fleet dispersal plan. Before being certified as "combat ready," the aircraft commander, copilot, and I briefed the 341st Bomb Wing commander and his staff on our role in the Emergency War Order (EWO). When my turn came, responsible for the target data, I stretched to my full six feet. As lean as Cassius, with a blond crew cut, blue scarf, pressed flying suit, and spit-shined black boots, I squared my shoulders, recited the designated ground zero latitude and longitude, down to the seconds, and said, "Our target significance is a population of six hundred twenty-three thousand people." Approval from the staff colonels sanctified my gung-ho role in SAC's mission. Following two and a half years of training, I was a 24-year-old first lieutenant performing the assignment I desired. I was a true believer.

Two years later, based primarily on my proficiency in radar-scored bomb runs on American cities and a rare drop of a simulated weapon on Matagorda Island, our crew advanced to "Select" status—the highest rank attainable—and I received a spot promotion to captain, putting me a couple of years ahead of the normal promotion cycle. Concurrent with our upgrade in status, we received the Kremlin as our Alert target and my ego roared off like a space shot. The system assigned the best crews to the most critical targets. Our bomb was the ninth weapon scheduled against the Moscow complex. The Single Integrated Operations Plan (SIOP), which coordinated the employment of all nuclear weapons, had programmed eight intercontinental ballistic missiles (ICBM) to arrive prior to a manned bomber. Using those numbers, I estimated a single ICBM had a 12 percent chance of success. Do the math.

At our home station, Dyess Air Force Base, at a recertification briefing, the wing commander asked me, "What will you do if you find nothing but a big hole where the Kremlin should be?" I frowned as if the supposition were new to me; in truth, a fellow navigator had warned me about a similar question. I told the wing commander, "I'll make the hole bigger." It was the correct answer because, at the time, United States military strategy followed Secretary of State John Foster Dulles' concept of massive retaliation: a head for an eye. SAC's job was to punish without restraint: an "If you start it, we'll finish it" mentality. Years after I left SAC, a friend told me that making holes bigger was no longer the correct answer. SAC had granted crews the prerogative of choosing a target of opportunity if they found their primary target obliterated.

The United States attack plan against the Soviet Union revolved around a "burn-back" theory. Before ICBMs entered the inventory and only manned bombers delivered weapons, strategy dictated the first wave of planes would hit defensive installations—fighter bases and command and control sites—on the perimeter of the Soviet Union. Follow-on waves would strike deeper and deeper into Soviet territory. With 1400 B-47s and 400 B-52s available to attack, as of 1958, SAC aimed to annihilate the Soviet Union. When ICBMs entered the inventory, planners programmed them against deep targets aircraft would not reach until later stages of the EWO execution, but traditional thinkers led by General

Curtis LeMay continued to preach that manned bombers were the only reliable weapon system.

Under the burn-back plan, the Kremlin was as far downtown as one could go. As we had repeatedly proved our proficiency, our crew's assignments had progressed from targets near Kirovsk and Severodvinsk to Vologda and Rybinsk, deeper and deeper into Soviet territory. Against targets located on the fringe of the Soviet Union, bomber routes reversed themselves for egress, and the missions terminated at post-strike bases in Norway or England. However, an attack on the Kremlin called for an all-out, low-level dash across the width of the Soviet Union, ending at a post-strike base in Turkey or Iran. The mission required the maximum in brains, balls, and belief.

For the Kremlin, I planned my actions down to the second. Every day on Alert (bomber crews spent one of every two or three weeks living in a bunkered facility beside their loaded aircraft, ready for launch in less than 15 minutes), I studied charts stamped "Secret" along with radarscope photographs of the Soviet Union gathered by U-2s, soaring aircraft with wings thinner than those of an angel. As part of the secrets within secrets and unknown to most of the world, the U-2s operated from Laughlin Air Force Base, outside of Del Rio, Texas, and without them, we would have had to rely on data of World War II vintage. Aided by U-2 radar photography, technicians reproduced sections of the USSR on ridged and pimpled metal plates; when submerged in a tank of shallow water and scanned with an electronic beam, the plates produced radar returns like those seen from the air. Technicians then connected that equipment to a booth that duplicated the navigator-bombardier's station inside a B-47. In one such booth, hidden and earthbound, hundreds of times annually I simulated flying low-level across Russia and bombing the Kremlin. Life was an infinite rehearsal.

I frequently thought about my counterpart in the Soviet Air Force, particularly about the *Bear*—Tupolev Tu-20—bombardier who drooled over Washington and the Pentagon. How good was he? How accurate was his equipment? Was he young and eager or old and cynical? Our wing had several of the latter type, Korean War retreads who viewed SAC's mission as a job rather than as the crusade I saw. I disliked them.

I pictured my enemy poring over beautifully detailed 200-Series charts of Washington, D.C., that showed every building down to individual homes, each structure numbered and labeled. I had similar charts of Moscow that I avidly studied, ran my fingers across as if reading the buildings in Braille, trying to grasp the mysteries of the foreign capital, willing my fingers to absorb knowledge my mind did not fathom. Was my counterpart's confidence of success as high as mine? At times I imagined flying his mission and destroying a major American city. His potential for destruction appeared so much greater than mine; to my way of thinking, after Moscow and Leningrad, Soviet cities offered no significant civilized value. Yet, at heart, he and I were as interchangeable as cogs on a wheel.

The EWO mission would be hellish but its challenge constantly entertained my mind. ICBMs would have impacted before we arrived, but their accuracy was suspect. Other bombers would have been dropping weapons elsewhere. Planners assigned each sortie with an entry and exit corridor, along with a designated drop time. I intended to fly my track and time perfectly, anticipating that other navigators in at least one of a thousand possible ways would fuck up their deliveries and heighten the danger for our crew. However, their failures enhanced my value because I knew my crew would reach and destroy its target and survive. I envisioned our refueling and rearming at a post-strike recovery base in Turkey or Iran and flying a second mission—a restrike sortie—to clean up a target that had somehow escaped the initial attack. I believed my crew's destiny was to slay the chosen few that had lived through the impossible, to destroy miracles. Few crewmen thought that far ahead. Facts justified my infinite conceit. In the fifties and early sixties, SAC ruled the world, controlling 95 percent of the Free World's striking power. Its nuclear strength was the one thing that Nikita Khrushchev and his Presidium feared. SAC's power was my power.

★ ★ ★

My mind still retains the impetus for my hunger for destruction—the December 7th when in my Pittsburgh bed, I cringed with the fear of an eight year-old child who expected the Japanese to bomb him exactly as they had bombed sleeping Pearl Harbor that morning. My knowledge of geography and my computations of time and distance collapsed under the weight of my fear. My mind replayed newsreel scenes of London burning in darkness beneath the blitz of Nazi bombs. That night, a lifetime ago, I suffered my first exposure to a recurring childhood dream in which, like the buildings of London, my home was set ablaze by bombs, made to flare like a bonfire, before it crashed inward upon me. That night I died the first of many deaths.

Four years later I was reborn from the ashes of Hiroshima and Nagasaki. By cremating those cities, American aircrews repaid the Japanese for the fear with which they had infected my sleep. I fell in love with "The Bomb." What was real became magical. Hiroshima and Nagasaki showed me a god on earth. How could a heavenly god be more powerful? What was human became divine. The sacrament of confirmation that followed a summer later was meaningless to me. The circle of my religious belief had been closed with the birth of atomic power.

While in SAC, I felt no tug from the gravitational trajectory that linked me to a Soviet—or Chinese—child with dreams of death more valid than mine.

★ ★ ★

Upon entering SAC, I was surprised to find that crewmen exhibited a somewhat blasé attitude toward thermonuclear weapons. Nobody openly admitted to being awed by them. People showed a degree of respect and that appeared adequate. Perhaps one reason for their lack of awe was that the weapons weren't much to see. Even the casing that contained the 19-megaton device, the largest yield in the inventory, was painted a dull olive drab, like the others. I had anticipated seeing a streamlined, silver or chrome shape and wouldn't have been disappointed if it had glowed in the dark. Instead, the brutish object with its blunt nose and square fins filled the B-47 bomb bay like an amorphous lump.

Perhaps men became blasé about thermonuclear weapons because they had been desensitized to their effects. Much of the final week of my six-month advanced high speed navigation and bombardment course at Mather AFB, California, had been devoted to motion pictures of atomic- and thermonuclear-weapon effects. Day after day, the class of 20 lieutenant navigators watched footage from every US detonation to date. At first, viewing grainy color close-ups of pigs and goats tethered and exposed to the heat and blast of a test device instilled a feeling of criminality in us. When the flesh of a few of the animals peeled away, the "Holy Shit!" light flashed on: we were to become the bearers of uncontained violence. Later, sheeted in scars, half naked victims of Hiroshima and Nagasaki passed before the camera like an endless freak parade, too grotesque to be believable, too agonized to be human. Injuries that initially were breathtaking slowly became common sight. At some point, somebody called out a number to rate a woman's degree of disfigurement. After nervous laughter, a few of us joined in the judging. Then a stunned boredom set in among us and, by the final day of viewing, nothing that we saw impressed us.

One person fell out of step from the group. On the final day, Bill Reardon, a devout Catholic, said, "I don't know. I don't think I can drop one of those bombs. Even if I got to my target, I'm not sure I could drop." I determined he wasn't being trained or paid to think in that direction and told him, "You better make up your fucking mind before then."

A couple of decades sped by before I awoke to the fact that the motion picture program could have been designed to give new guys a respectful appreciation of the power delegated to them. Shouldn't we have reacted with unmitigated fear rather than mockery and boredom? Had we been too stupid to recognize the truth? We individually would receive more power than anyone in history in order to protect the Free World by destroying a significant part of the world at large. The concept was as reasonable as destroying a Vietnamese village to save it. Of course, too many important people have not experienced anything like my belated epiphany. It's not easy to become sane.

★ ★ ★

In the late fifties, crewmen were expected to know everything there was to know about thermonuclear bombs. Once each quarter, in a semi-electrical engineering class lecture, crewmen watched weapon instructors practically dismantle, then reassemble, one of each type of bomb in a wing's inventory. For days, the instructors ploddingly reviewed the bombs' fusing and firing circuits. At the end of a week, each crewman had to pass a written test that covered every weapon; failure meant additional training classes. On the first day of an Alert tour, each crew was tested as a team. Using a simulator that contained the monitoring equipment inside a B-47, the crewmen proved to an instructor that they collectively could cope with malfunctions related to the weapon they were assigned for that week.

Many crewmen grew bored by the weapons classes. When the houselights dimmed for a slide show, eyelids went down at the same time. Instructors accepted the challenge and emphasized new information by stomping their feet and raising their voices. In the 1950s, SAC taught its crewmen how to build thermonuclear bombs and it seemed to be the proper and natural thing to do. What could have been the greatest irony of the era was that many crewmen resented their having to master the detailed information because to them the mission was simple: kick the tires, light the fires, and kill Russians.

Weapons were unimpressive not only for their drab external appearance but also because of their primitive internal construction. Our wing's inventory contained an early-model weapon that required the navigator to finish its assembly by crawling back to the bomb bay and inserting the nuclear component—a mass of heavy metal, the "m" like in $E=mc^2$—into the heart of the bomb. Not quite as large as a bowling ball, the mass had the weight of 10 balls. Planners scheduled this "insertion" to be accomplished "in-flight" while target-bound, following descent for air-to-air refueling over Canada. Inside the shadowy, yellow-green bomb bay, the navigator would stand on a foot-wide fold-down ledge to accomplish the task. First, he unscrewed the weapon's nose plate to reveal a yellow sphere of explosives. The sphere's outer design resembled the hexagon pattern of a soccer ball, except that each section of the design was much larger. The navigator disconnected wires attached to detonators implanted in the sections nearest to him, then lifted out these wedge-shaped, high-explosive sections, known as "lens mold" charges, designed to focus trigger force inward. In that way he cleared an avenue to the hollow core of the bomb. Next, he unclasped the lid from the "bird cage," a three-foot-tall canister that contained the dull gray nuclear component. He lifted the component from the bird cage by screwing a crowbar-sized rod into it, creating a contraption as unwieldy as 100-pound barbell with the weights on one end. Transferring the component into the hollow heart of the weapon was a critical maneuver because if the navigator struck the heavy component against the detonator of a still-in-place charge, he would reduce the scale of the weapon. Instructors hinted he might cause the detonator to fire and every crewman knew "One in-flight explosion can ruin your whole day." After the navigator seated the component, he unscrewed the rod and set it aside. He then repacked the wedge-shaped, high-explosive charges as tightly as the pieces of a jigsaw puzzle and reattached electrical leads to their detonators. He finished the in-flight insertion by screwing on the bomb's nose plate. At that point, the weapon was complete, but it remained unarmed until the navigator crawled back to his station and operated black boxes to close firing circuits inside the bomb. On a mock-up weapon, every navigator practiced in-flight insertion at least once per quarter, but with both feet planted firmly on the ground and under the supervision of a weapons instructor. Few navigators in our wing became smoothly proficient or overly confident with the procedure.

In March 1958, to prove in-flight insertion could be accomplished in flight, SAC assigned a B-47 crew from Hunter AFB to perform the procedure at 10,000 feet. The navigator completed the task but, before returning to the cockpit, he paused to catch his breath in the rarified air. For no reason except that decreed by fate, he thoughtlessly grasped overhead for support and grabbed the long cable connecting the shield-guarded, red-painted emergency bomb release handle at the navigator's station to the U-hook clutching the sling holding the bomb. The navigator unwittingly suspended his weight from the cable. His first 20 pounds of pull unlocked both the U-hook and the bomb bay doors. The bomb fell onto the doors, its weight spread them, and it continued its fall to earth, landing in the yard of a farmhouse in Mars Bluff, South Carolina. Only the bomb's high explosives detonated, blasting a crater 75 feet wide and 35 feet deep. The explosion injured six civilians.

Around this time, higher-ups in the chain of command decided that crewmen's human frailties constituted the major weakness in the control of weapons. Practically overnight, crewmen no longer had a "need to know" and the system of handling weapons changed. A single black T-249 control box with an "Arm-Safe" wafer switch and one red press-to-test light replaced several pieces of monitoring equipment, thereby ending the necessity of thinking on a crew's part. Concurrently, weapons were improved internally. Now, the navigator twisted the T-249 wafer switch and the bomb armed or didn't arm; in either case, the crew dropped it. Design dictated any malfunction was elsewhere than inside the weapon. In fact, for crewmen, weapons ceased to have insides. New policies forbade weapons instructors from answering questions that went beyond rotating the wafer switch or pressing to test the red light. Their stock answer to questions became "Improved designs in thermonuclear circuitry have made malfunctions virtually impossible." What we knew yesterday was to be forgotten today.

★ ★ ★

Further changes took place as upper-echelon thinkers also recognized a need for an absolutely foolproof system of control of weapons, particularly when two nuclear superpowers faced each other on equal terms—and the possibility of nuclear proliferation existed among lesser nation-states. Starting a war by mistake became SAC's primary fear.

SAC Alert—the concept of constantly maintaining armed strategic bombers ready for launch in less than 15 minutes—had become standard practice in late 1957 because of the threat from Soviet ICBMs. Three footnotes help here. First, SAC's 15-minute launch parameter was predicated on the flight time of ICBM's fired from the Soviet Union. Second, SAC's motivation for assuming Alert status grew from national concerns about bomber and missile "gaps," intelligence estimates that incorrectly gave the Soviet Union parity with the United States in both areas. Third, originally "Alert" was briefly called "Red Alpha" and then "Quickstrike." In 1986, while writing a novel about SAC, I spoke with the Command Historian and he told me those earlier names were new to him (had my memory deceived me or were official records incomplete?). A decision-making network encompassing the Distant Early Warning Line above the Arctic Circle, SAC Headquarters in Omaha, and the Pentagon in Washington provided American leaders with timely upper echelon command and control of the Alert bombers, and in the offing was completion of the North American Aerospace Defense Command Cheyenne Mountain facility in Colorado Springs—hardened, heavily guarded, overmanned, spacious, and lavishly furnished. Multiple primary and backup communications networks linked these command centers every second of every day.

Meanwhile at base level, where Alert crews and their loaded bombers waited, conditions significantly differed. At nights and on weekends, one high-ranking sergeant along with one lieutenant—designated as the Wing Duty Officer (DO)—locked themselves into a back room of the wing headquarters building and from there ran the show with two standard landline telephones and a special red telephone hot-wired directly from the SAC Headquarters Command Post.

Acting as Wing DO, a lieutenant who was a combat crewman filled the role played by a major or lieutenant colonel from 0700 to 1700 on weekdays. Because the duty came around only every month or three, the lieutenants acquired little proficiency in fulfilling the assignment. Furthermore, the duty occasionally served as punishment for lieutenants who habitually fucked up in minor ways. Nobody questioned the arrangement despite SAC planners' belief that the Soviets would attack at night on a weekend or holiday—especially Christmas, which held no significance for godless Commie bastards.

When the red telephone rang at our base-level command post, the lieutenant on duty permitted the sergeant to answer it. A call from SAC Headquarters demanded more skill than anyone who showed up less than once a month could handle in the allotted time. Formatted messages had to be copied accurately on the first reading, decoding had to be accomplished, and authentications had to be validated without the slightest hesitation. A message normally required scrambling Alert crews to their airplanes and relaying instructions to them. These tasks were duties the sergeants had been specially trained for. Therefore, the attitude expressed by most lieutenants was "If there's anything I can do to help, sergeant, let me know." Otherwise, they kept out of the way and hoped the sergeant didn't screw up because the DO shouldered the blame when things went sour. Furthermore, because the next message could be the real thing, we lieutenants failed to view the exercises as learning experiences. Media estimates, confirmed for us by secret briefings, kept us in a constant state of agitation over the Eurasian horde's activities, exactly as George Orwell's *1984* imagined.

SAC exercised its Alert crews close to daily. Under an Alpha scramble, we crewmen raced to our bombers and, upon arrival, copilots checked in with the command post controller who logged our response time; under Bravo, we started engines before logging in; and under Coco, we taxied to the hammerhead of the runway where our arrival time was recorded. No exercise included an actual launch; that came later. One night by 2330, we still had not been exercised for that day and, on a hunch, the crews ambled out to the bombers and climbed aboard. When the Alpha came at five minutes to midnight, the entire force clocked a zero response time. We paid for being presumptuous: SAC scrambled us again, three hours later.

At the beginning of the Alert program, commanders unquestioningly trusted the men in the command and control network. No concern existed about possible aberrant behavior in communicating messages between levels of command. However, the network was most vulnerable at the base level where, for example, either man in the makeshift command post could have easily overpowered the other and then prevented or delayed an EWO launch. Similarly, the same type of person could have unilaterally launched his wing's Alert aircraft to fly as far as a Positive Control Point, geographical coordinates north of Canada where the crews turned around if, en route, they did not receive a Go Code message—two letters that, if they matched two letters sealed inside a packet chained around each aircraft commander's neck, authorized the expenditure of nuclear weapons. An unauthorized launch threatened severe consequences: it could have degraded SAC's EWO posture and, more importantly, it could have triggered a response from the Soviets if they viewed the scrambled bombers as a pre-emptive strike. Either case would have increased the probability of a nuclear incident because with loaded bombers airborne any number of mishaps became possible.

Command and control was equally vulnerable at the aircrew level because copilots bore sole responsibility for handling messages from the command post. Aircraft commanders and navigators trusted them unquestioningly. One afternoon, when we were scrambled to our B-47, standing on the entry ladder, I watched copilot Captain Milo "Yankee" Myers furiously copy a transmission while the AC started engines. Tossing his checklist aside, Myers yelled at me, "Fire! Close it up. Let's go." I dropped to the ground and because the crew chief still had not arrived, pulled the chocks and moved the auxiliary power cart while thinking, "Fire?" The term had no meaning in regard to launch. Around me, with jet engines screaming, other bombers started taxiing. At that point, for me, "Fire" translated to "Attack." By the time I pulled up the ladder behind me and closed the outer and inner doors, we were rolling. I tried to hustle forward to strap in but Myers grabbed me and said, "There was a fuel spill a couple of rows over. The fire trucks're washing it down. The command post wanted us away from the area in case there's a fire." With my heart pounding, I barely understood him. I had expected confirmation of my thought that had equated to war. The event demonstrated that a crew did whatever its copilot told it to do. As strange as it sounds, I felt slightly unbalanced by recognizing we were not headed to war.

I observed similar reactions after the 1962 Cuban Missile Crisis when every bomber in the fleet stood poised for launch. Many of the B-52 crewmen at Bergstrom AFB, Texas, from among whom I watched a telecast of President John Kennedy announcing war had been averted, emitted no sighs of relief at his words. If anything, I sensed disappointment among a few of the men who, earlier, had expressed a desire to "sink that fucking island." Based on the trend of years of secret briefings, they believed the Soviet Union would surpass the United States in nuclear capability by the following year and our chance for an overwhelming victory was slipping away, maybe forever. While we filed out of the Alert lounge following Kennedy's speech, I muttered Captain Bernie Mohan's softly spoken but often-repeated message: "Better to waste your time pulling Alert than to end the world in twelve hours." But I didn't believe his advice.

To tighten command and control, and to cope more effectively with the limitless contingencies involving men and weapons, SAC adopted a series of Red Dot, Blue Dot, and Green Dot messages, which covered exercises as well as EWO situations. A myriad of options under each color instructed the crews to do everything from waiting in the bombers with engines shutdown to launching for strike without possibility of recall. The complex system frequently left SAC rookies still flipping through a thick binder of checklists, searching for the correct format, when a message ended. Now, instead of only the copilot copying messages, every crewman was taught to handle incoming orders and was required to prove proficiency by individually taking a test every day he was on Alert. The only passing grade was a perfect paper. SAC's philosophy to ensure expertise among crewmen was "training overkill." Practicing a task 100 times was better than 10 times. The goal was flawless execution. Shortly after I joined a B-52 crew (three more crewmen, two more engines, several more bombs), my aircraft commander, a lieutenant colonel who had been in SAC for much of his career, transcribed a single wrong letter on his test answer sheet. He had decoded the correct response on his worksheet but had copied the answer incorrectly. As a result, despite his vehement protest, he had to complete a four-hour block of instruction designed for new guys. Our copilot, Lieutenant Bill Bushman, said, "There's a reward for getting ten thousand correct answers—a new number two pencil and a clean sheet of paper to start the next ten thousand."

★ ★ ★

Bomber crews did not only sit and wait on Alert at their home bases. Depending on the degree of international tension, B-47s dispersed to smaller stateside or overseas bases. The tactic, called "Reflex," allowed more aircraft to get into the air in less time by shortening lines of bombers. It also placed SAC bombers closer to their targets in the Soviet Union and Communist China, which complicated Soviet targeting of our forces. Reflex took crews away from their families for two-week to three-month periods, which made the action unpopular with the great majority of wives who didn't mess around.

While I was stationed at Dyess, to start 1958, our entire wing deployed to Andersen AFB on Guam for 90 days. With access to government run fishing boats, nearby beaches, and inexpensive taxi hops into Agana, we enjoyed bonus pleasures of a south sea vacation.

For the latter part of the year, our crews reflexed for two weeks at a time to Elmendorf AFB, Alaska, where we spent all but a day or two on Alert. The following year, we reflexed to RAF Greenham Common for three-week periods, and vacation-like bonuses returned because we had the middle week free to travel anywhere in Europe. Better yet, the Air Force sometimes provided transportation to a popular destination. In a half dozen reflexes, I made it beyond London's magnetic pubs one time. A week in Copenhagen provided me with a stage for playing the role of immature, drunken tourist to perfection. I loudly savored every bite of food, gushed over scenery, and drank enough beer to float the *Queen Mary*. But what the fuck, I had the next week to sleep it off.

London taught me to admire the anti-war soapbox orators in Hyde Park and the brilliant efficiency of British policemen—the Bobbies. In the fifties, they did not even carry a nightstick. I watched a Bobbie stop a street fight by walking close to the combatants, who were rolling around on the ground and punching each other, and telling them in a slightly raised voice, "Gentlemen, behave yourselves." And they did, instantly.

I also learned how to navigate through a foreign city blanketed by fog from concentrated pollution that, in some neighborhoods, limited the field of vision to the point where people could no longer see their feet. Sightlines of less than half a block were normal.

★ ★ ★

I can't recall exactly when but, around the time crewmen became the usual suspects, the game of "What If...?" originated among staff members. As every commander lived in fear of a nuclear incident—an unauthorized weapon expenditure or accident for which he was responsible to the whole world—identifying fallibilities in the command and control system became a career for staff officers. They developed "What If...?" to identify and clarify dangerous exceptions to the rules among crewmembers. But, of course, there were no exceptions, which was what the game intended to prove. The favorite suppositions of staff officers followed preposterous lines. For example, "You're launched without authority to expend your weapon. You meet your tanker and offload your scheduled fuel. You reach the Positive Control Point but still have received no authority to expend your weapons. What do you do?" The proper answer: "We orbit until we receive a message or until fuel dictates we divert to our assigned alternate base." After a crewman responded, the staff officers piled on eventualities that demanded new decisions: "En route to your tanker, you'd seen mushroom-shaped clouds over major cities in the United States and Canada." "You learn that SAC Headquarters has been destroyed." "You learn that Washington has been wiped off the face of the earth." "You see other bombers continue beyond the PCP and fly out of sight toward the Soviet Union." "Your radio receivers are inoperative." "You regain use of your radios in time to hear and recognize the President's voice, and he orders an attack without using a message format or authentication." Et cetera, et cetera, et cetera.... Yada, yada, yada.... The staff officers aimed to drive a crewman to a point of indecision. As soon as a crewman hinted that, in a unique situation, he might consider expending a weapon without receiving a properly formatted and authenticated message, the staff shifted the game to Eric Berne's "Now We've Got You, You Son of a Bitch." In the guise of Parent-to-Child, staff officers could have given lessons to Berne as they declared the rules had no exceptions. I detested their methodology. Frequently the questioning caused animosity to erupt between staff members and crewmen. For example, I watched Lieutenant Colonel "Pappy" Roe, an aircraft commander, grow tearful over the thought that, after seeing Washington disappear in a fireball, he still could not retaliate without a proper message, and Roe shouted down the staff inquisitors, telling them, "Your system stinks. If that's the best you can do, you ought to start over." It wasn't stretching the point to say a crewman or two viewed nuclear war as a vendetta.

Detecting a weakness in command and control procedures usually generated a new contingency plan, which redefined and further emphasized the limits of an aircrew's actions. Crewmembers, who had been the most trusted men on base, slowly evolved into the most suspected persons. A new SAC Two-Man Policy forbade a lone crewman from so much as walking around a loaded bomber; while on Alert, crewmen had to accomplish duties in pairs. Even in pairs, however, crewmen were not permitted access to a bomber until they exchanged numerical passwords with an armed guard by adding or subtracting from a base number that changed daily. For a short period, crewmen received a daily duress number for use by a person being forced to board an airplane; guards were instructed to kill anyone directly behind the man who spoke the duress number. First the commanders and their staffs didn't trust crewmen and then they tried to teach crewmen to distrust each other.

Crewmen bitched about the restrictions placed on them and rightfully so, but their complaints had no effect on policies that demanded for them to answer to everyone for everything and be perfect every time. Nobody answered to them. When a crewman questioned anything in the EWO or SIOP, he was treated like a new Martin Luther tacking his theses to the church door; by challenging the system he identified himself as a troublemaker. Intelligence officers and staff planners made it clear they did the thinking and crewmen were expected only to react. I overheard one staff officer tell another, "We're too intelligent to be crewmen." Secretly, crewmen told each other, "We'll win the war despite the plan. When the time comes, we'll do it our way." The fact was that crewmen uncompromisingly gave themselves to their duties.

In everyday peacetime operations crewmen demonstrated dedication reflecting heroism. In 1958, two B-47s crashed on 14 March, one on 31 March, one on 14 April, and two on 15 April when their wings came off for no apparent reason. Three of the first four aircraft exploded shortly after takeoff, killing everyone on board. When our crew flew over that span of days, I felt tingles of concern for my safety but, like me, no crewman refused to fly, no crewman challenged the wisdom of continuing daily training missions. Meanwhile, engineers magnafluxed the B-47 fleet and found planes with fractured wing roots, a problem that could cause the wings to tear loose under stress, especially with a heavyweight takeoff. Engineers beefed up the fractured areas with a "boiler plate" modification of metal braces. Throughout the ordeal, crewmen stoically understood flying was a day-in-day-out struggle against reality and everything that reality entailed, which led them to accept the fact that standing down the fleet was impossible because it would completely degrade the EWO. Similarly, crewmen, without complaint, spent the majority of their duty hours in windowless cinderblock buildings, isolated from wives and children. Hidden from the eyes of the world, these men had the world hidden from them. The degree of commitment inherent in planning and executing both peacetime as well as EWO operations proved the crewmen's loyalty and heroism.

★ ★ ★

Within EWO planning, nuclear parity scrambled America's Judeo-Christian beliefs regarding the value of the individual. As Americans lost ground to the Soviets, each weapon gained greater importance. Therefore, kamikaze tactics evolved as part of the EWO plan. What had been a list of acceptable reasons to abort a strike mission rapidly reduced itself to none. Even with inoperable navigation and bombing equipment, a crew was expected to raise its flash curtains, dead reckon a quarter of the distance around the globe, and release its weapon at the estimated time of arrival over target. Crewmen mocked the plan with scenarios such as "We've been blindly flying this heading for twelve hours and fourteen minutes. Our estimated time of arrival is—now! Bombs away!" Such haphazard tactics pissed off a lot of navigators who expected to find safe corridors for entry and exit. Planners also drastically reduced separation time between weapon deliveries. On one target, the first bomber was supposed to lay down three small thermonuclear weapons, and 10 minutes later a second bomber was supposed to streak through the three mushroom stems and plant a larger weapon among them. If the first bomber was late, the second was supposed to orbit 75 miles from the target and wait. Our crew had that mission for a while and for the first time I questioned our likelihood for success and survival.

Other significant planning changes involved fuel. Before Sputnik, a crew that missed its aerial refueling and didn't have enough gas to reach its post-strike base was permitted to land at an en route base where it was topped off and rescheduled as part of a follow-on wave. As more and better Soviet missiles entered the game, post-strike bases became less and less likely to survive and the rules changed. Soon, a bomber crew was required to have only enough fuel to clear Soviet territory after delivering its weapon. Then, a crew needed only enough fuel to escape beyond the range of its own weapon's effects. Finally, the hero factor reached infinity when the EWO criterion became "dry tanks at bombs away over target." Stanley Kubrick's *Doctor Strangelove* nailed the situation when Slim Pickens rode a bomb down to a target. At annual recertification, a wing commander was certain to ask, "What do you do if your tanker fails to show?" A crewman metamorphosed into some sort of existentialistic Patrick Henry when he answered, "No sweat, sir. From takeoff we have exactly enough fuel to make it to flameout at bombs away." That magnitude of dedication warmed my red, white, and blue blood. Crewmen cynically agreed it hardly mattered if they ended up inside the fireball because there wouldn't be anything left to come home to in the United States.

Planners knew that, after Soviet ICBMs followed gravity's rainbow, bombers still on the ground were doomed. Therefore, by 1960, SAC attained its goal of having one-third of its bombers and tankers constantly on Alert, ready for launch in less than 15 minutes—within an ICBM's flight time. In 1961, Kennedy placed 50 percent of the bomber fleet on Alert. As a result, crews went from being on Alert one week out of three to every other week, in sickness and in health, 'til death do us part. Alert duty was the only duty for which there was no reason to be excused. Lord Alfred Tennyson clearly described the SAC mentality: "Theirs not to reason why, theirs but to do and die." Yet deep in our hearts, we crewmen cherished the task.

Also in 1961, after two years of test operations, SAC began flying nuclear-armed B-52 Airborne Alert missions, called *Chrome Dome*, thereby freeing those few aircraft from being trapped on the ground. This tactic countered the threat of submarine launched ballistic missiles and their shorter flight times compared to ICBMs. I flew *Chrome Dome* missions out of Bergstrom AFB that lasted twenty-four and a half hours, transiting the eastern United States, paralleling the west coast of Greenland to latitude eight-four degrees north, crossing the Arctic Ocean, loitering over Alaska, and then returning home, avoiding over-flying Canada. We had help from KC-135 tankers over the North Atlantic and Alaska. An alternate *Chrome Dome* route crossed the Atlantic Ocean and circled the Mediterranean Sea before returning to the United States.

★ ★ ★

Because SAC's rules were hard and fast, anyone with half an intellect recognized an obligation to challenge them. Major Ray Gamble and I spent hours on B-52 Alert devising ways we could bomb an American city. A *Chrome Dome* mission provided the perfect opportunity. We settled on New York City as our target. If two men on a crew collaborated, the task would be too simple. Using multiple weapons, they could have cratered significant chunks of the east coast. Therefore, our objective was for one man, acting alone, to strike New York City with a thermonuclear weapon, survive, and be found innocent of the crime.

Our *Chrome Dome* aircraft carried a pair of two-megaton devices in the bomb bay and two Hound Dog missiles, each with a two-megaton warhead, under the wings. Our routing took us over New York State three hours after takeoff, a schedule that provided ample time for one man to defeat the four other officers up front on a C-model B-52. A gunner sat isolated in the aircraft's tail. Although putting drugs or poison in coffee or food was the easiest methods to disable the other officers, it was not the most reliable; therefore, my plan opted for physical force. On a B-52, two navigators worked side-by-side on the lower deck, aft and out of sight of the pilot, copilot, and electronic warfare officer, and that starting position automatically put one of the navs in control of the situation. Ray and I agreed the most obvious flaw in the system was the ease with which a crewman could take weapons such as guns, hatchets, and knives aboard an airplane. Navigators carried two or three large bags of equipment and nobody examined their contents. For that matter, any crewman could have carried a small arsenal aboard a bomber without risk of detection.

My violent plans were one-way tickets to a court-martial and death sentence, but Ray's schemes were convoluted enough to give him room to maneuver at an inquiry. His best scenario fabricated *Mission Impossible*-type ruses that used a latex mask to create a mistaken identity, sleeping potions, injections, and amnesia-inducing drugs that tilted guilt toward the other navigator who remorsefully committed suicide following his foul deed. Awakening after the fact, the pilots returned home with Ray and the electronic warfare officer unconscious. Regardless of whether or not a person got away with the act, Ray and I agreed one man could hijack a bomber and do an appreciable amount of damage.

We understood that merely inventing our game was potentially self-destructive. Had the wrong person overheard one of our conversations, we could have been removed from crew duty and had our Human Reliability clearances revoked. Men in our position had no need for thinking as we did. For that reason, we did not report the weaknesses we uncovered in the system.

★ ★ ★

The best warrior was schizophrenic: bulletproof but simultaneously wishing to die a heroic death if necessary. The Air Force Hymn told him, "We live in fame or go down in flames." Naturally, before dying he expected to take a toll from the enemy that far exceeded the value of his single life. I bought that way of thinking until the Vietnam War. In the 1970–1971 Laotian dry season, my AC-130 Spectre gunship crew destroyed or damaged 1084 trucks along the Ho Chi Minh Trail. We egotistically took credit for the technoviolence generated by machines, attributed to ourselves personalities that matched their power. But machines lacked imagination, and we provided a spirit of victory. Too many nights were glorious, but they grew sad as I came to understand that we crewmen had more in common with the men we fought than with the men who led us.

Along the way I learned to respect Khrushchev, Fidel Castro, and Ho Chi Minh—men who argued and fought for the little their nations possessed, exactly as Americans passionately protected how very much they owned in comparison. Why did we hate them when they demonstrated the characteristics Americans cherished: determination, perseverance, fortitude…?

In the 1980s, I argued for unilateral nuclear disarmament. My convoluted reasoning would have dazzled Gandhi. "Scrap the thermonuclear stockpile," I wrote, trying to convince friends the United States should righteously stand unprotected. "It doesn't matter if the Soviets fry us tomorrow. For at least one day I want to bask in the purity of having done the right thing. For one day, I want to stand before the world totally free." Yes, I believed that national martyrdom could convince the rest of the world to live in peace. I've yet to meet a person who will wear that suit without alterations. Only by giving away everything can people learn the value of what they have, I preached. I had proved the belief to myself by giving away everything I owned, except for uniforms and summer clothes, before my second tour in Southeast Asia, and I had felt absolutely saintly. My friends considered my goal of unilateral nuclear disarmament to be naïve, joking, or pure bullshit. Their philosophy mimicked a Chris Hedges (the Pulitzer Prize-winning journalist) declaration: "War is a force that gives us meaning." Recognizing I was so far out of step that I was marching alone, I gave up my screed: once I had been the problem, but I would never be the solution.

★ ★ ★

My turn to emcee the game of "What If…?"

What if Ray or I had attempted one of our plots and made it work? Imagine the outcome of a nuclear detonation—even a partial yield—on New York City in 1963. At the time, while thinking the unthinkable, Herman Kahn had suggested that in a nuclear exchange with the Soviet Union, twenty million American casualties would be acceptable and the

United States could claim victory. Would the reality of the destruction of New York City have shown the fallacy of his thinking? How would Americans have reacted to three or four million deaths? Consider such a disaster in the perspective of the reaction to 3000 slain at the World Trade Center. Could our action have triggered a thermonuclear exchange with the Soviets? Or would the destruction have generated a national or international movement for nuclear disarmament? Could the destruction have turned Americans inward, thereby avoiding foreign war in Vietnam and subsequent overseas actions? Did Ray and I miss an opportunity to give SAC's nuclear power an ultimate significance?

What if we had...? Well, Ray has been dead for years and years, which meant he had less to lose. And for me? I wouldn't now be living lean, dumb, and happy, fucking around from day to day until it became my turn to die meaninglessly.

CHAPTER II

The Pornography of War

Cowboys and writers share and appreciate an old saying: "Once you find a horse you can ride, ride him till he dies." For writers the saying means that once a person finds a subject he truly knows (or can sell), he should write about it until he can't find any more to say. The adage isn't always obeyed. Unlike cowboys, some writers continue to ride dead horses. This phenomenon occurs primarily in the field of fiction where writers beat to death the common problems of limited successes and major failures found within the uneventful lives of their protagonists—the sort of characters that manufacture their own tragedies—or they repeat the coming of age theme as if their characters are the first ever to get laid, get pregnant, get stoned, or not get what they want at the earliest possible age.

I grew up loving John Steinbeck and Ernest Hemingway, authors who found honest-to-god heroes in everyday life. Tom Joad's journey to California in search of a new life involved a real problem, a true character building odyssey—not some self-indulgent *On the Road* wandering. A great story transcended the description of a 400-page trip to the mall experienced by characters in Raymond Carver or Richard Ford's novels. In that regard, I was so happy when Rabbit Angstrom died that I almost sent John Updike a case of champagne. Of course, these authors did show what sorry-ass, conventional lives Americans led during the second half of the 20th century, but who gave a shit? People could receive that message by looking around their own homes if they ever tore their eyes away from the tube.

Because war and its permutations constituted the soul of me, it became my theme as a writer. Surprisingly, my narrow air force point of view did not disqualify me from expanding my perspective into non-air force matters. As a writer, to get stories, I occasionally played army games.

Visiting a military installation as a reporter frequently embarrassed me. Military personnel treated me with a kindness disproportionate to my expectations. In particular, commanding officers seemed unnecessarily cautious toward me, viewed me as an enemy although I came in peace. I carried credentials as a reporter, but in my heart I was still one of them, still a soldier, a fact they could not see. Furthermore, I represented editors who loved the armed forces.

Perhaps the commanders I encountered as a reporter did not recognize that playing with an M1 Abrams tank or flying in an F-16 Fighting Falcon jet (yes, a few F-16s were configured with back seats, although I had to travel to Hill Air Force Base in Utah to find one) topped a vacation at Astroworld. The activity itself was pay enough. Getting to write about my experience and then receiving a check for doing it were bonuses beyond belief. For perhaps the first time in my life, I had enough sense not to bite the hand that fed me so generously. For example, at Dyess AFB for a week, I lived in a general's suite in the VIP quarters, an area off limits to me years earlier when I was stationed there. Naturally, the brass doling out the special treatment aimed to flatter me. Instead they showed me a horribly inverted system: my plush quarters should have been in daily use by people theoretically in the line of fire, and short-time spectators like me should have roughed it in a single room of lesser quality. Among the crewdogs, I joked about "my promotion," but I didn't mention my feelings to the top bosses, believing they might categorize me as a troublemaker—a label familiar to me from active duty days. Looking through privileged eyes, commanders developed their own perspective of the world, which was the reason I could not believe that truth was the last word spoken by the highest-ranking person in a room. As it turned out, the vision of those leaders might have been better than mine. Did they see reactions in me I didn't recognize? Had I been unconsciously using my credentials as a means of bidding a final goodbye to all of it—kind of tiptoeing my way toward a second retirement from the military.

Shortly after retiring from the Air Force in 1976, while I continued to live in a house on Navarre Beach, Florida, a headhunter phoned from Los Angeles and introduced himself with an ego-boosting spiel: "I recently talked to a couple of men who know you, and they said you're an extremely intelligent and hard-working person. I can find a position for you if you'll move here."

"Who told you about me?" I asked. The headhunter wasn't at liberty to say but stated "they" had told him nothing but the best. We chatted and he hinted at a starting salary around $50,000, almost twice what the Air Force had paid me. He smoothly segued into a checklist of personal questions: Married? Do you drink? Do drugs? Homosexual? I answered truthfully and asked, "What kind of work would I do?"

He said the job involved the defense industry, primarily hosting and coordinating with high-ranking officers in the military services. Without hesitating, I said, "Right before I quit, I received promotion orders to permanent lieutenant colonel. I could have remained on active duty for eight more years if I wanted to deal with those assholes."

Need I say that the headhunter didn't phone back?

As a writer, I found myself again dealing with high rankers.

★ ★ ★

As a reporter, to make interviews of senior officers friendlier, I did not use a recorder or take notes. I simply listened intently to what each man said. After a long interview with a wing commander, I told my host officer to delay our next activity and, for about 20 minutes, sat in a corner and wrote out everything I remembered from the exchange. At the end of the day, the host officer told me, "I explained to the CO about how you wrote down everything after you left his office. He said, 'I'm glad to hear that. I started worrying when the SOB didn't take any notes.'" As a payoff for her honesty, I treated my host officer and her husband to dinner.

Another example of unnecessary catering to me also took place at Dyess. The wing director of operations arranged a lunch in my honor, attended by his best crewmen and their wives. The meal turned into a lovefest as each person—men and women—related the joys of being part of SAC. From the gathering, however, I did learn that the Officers' Club no longer served as the hub of off-duty activity and the Officers' Wives' Club now played an almost non-existent role in the social scene.

Today, on many bases, political correctness dictated the proper term as "Officers' Spouses' Club."

★ ★ ★

It took a while for me to recognize I had become a public relations man, pushing toys for grown boys. With that mentality, I wrote so many glowing reviews and sidebars about the new and controversial M1 tank and its components—for *National Defense* and *Army* and *Tanks* magazines—that Chrysler Corporation translated one of my pieces into Mandarin Chinese as promotion for its foreign military sales program.

It turned out the Chinese didn't buy the M1. Egypt purchased 777; Saudi Arabia 315; and Kuwait 218. The United States Army and Marine Corps bought the remainder of the 8800 manufactured by Chrysler. I wondered if my reviews helped sales. If so, I deserved a percentage.

I hooked myself on this type of writing after Kevin McCommon, a young financial expert/philosopher/writer/and behind-the-scenes politician, taught me the art of selling magazine articles. Before meeting McCommon, I had considered myself a novelist, a long-distance runner. I had written two novels, was in the middle of a third, but hadn't sold anything. My sales approach was something like "What do you mean this isn't the greatest thing you ever read? Fuck you." McCommon taught me how to shift gears.

"Magazine editors want you to tell them what they want—what they need," McCommon said. "They sit in an office day after day. They can't keep up with everything that's going on in the world. They depend on writers to supply ideas for them. Just explain how your piece fits into their magazine." Until then, I had been trying to sell short pieces about flying to magazines where they didn't fit, tailoring stories into totally inappropriate formats. In other words, I wrote like a fucking dunce—assumed a voice that wasn't mine.

McCommon aimed me toward two magazines—*Eagle* and *National Defense*—and he was dead on target: without hesitation, editors Jim Morris and D. Ballou accepted my proposals and articles for their magazines. For Morris, I rewrote stories fictionalized in my unsold novels, telling them as fact and using real names—and my own irreverent voice. Ballou gave me the credentials necessary to travel on fact-finding trips to military installations.

Banging out a 3000-word story and seeing it in print a few months later was more encouraging than a beautiful woman's smile. Morris, an ex-Green Beret, provided extra motivation by frequently phoning to chat and by printing every word I mailed to him. Although expanded for this book, the tales about the heroics of Holley and Combies first appeared in *Eagle*.

Jim Morris could write, too. His *War Story* ranked as one of the lesser-publicized Vietnam War books worth reading again. He left *Eagle* to become an editor with Berkley and then Dell. Later he moved to the west coast and wrote *Dumbo Drop*, which Walt Disney Pictures made into a movie starring Danny Glover, Ray Liotta, and Denis Leary. It's a facetious winner.

Morris made it possible for me to sell my novels. New York agent Adele Leone read my stories in *Eagle* and phoned to ask if I had tried writing a book. I mentioned two manuscripts sitting on the floor under my desk. She read them and within a month sold both for a grand total of $15,000—taking a 15 percent commission.

At the time, I was working on a third novel, which I sent piecemeal to Leone—in two packages a few months apart, each 320 pages in length, making the final manuscript 640 pages. She sold it, too. Then the fun began.

The edited manuscript returned to me contained only the first 320 pages. I phoned my editor and asked him where the rest of my work had gone. He said, "That's all I received." I explained that it told only half of the story, and he said, "Now I see why it had such an existential ending." Then he added, "I probably wouldn't have bought it if I knew it was that long." I laughed and said, "You bought half of a novel," which did not endear me to him. Shortly thereafter, he ordered me to cut a hundred pages from the manuscript, which was like saying, "Chop off an inch of your dick," but I did it—for another $7500 minus commission. I write about a finished page a day, so cutting a hundred pages was like throwing away three or four months of my working life.

The shit hit the fan after publication of my *First Ace*, a story about F-4 Phantom crews flying over North Vietnam. A book reviewer for the *Austin American-Statesman* interviewed me and told the world: "Hank wants folks to know that you can't judge a book by its cover. He is distressed that the New York artist who designed the cover for the book used a tank driver's helmet as a model." She forgot to include "...and a tank driver's jacket." What she said, however, was enough. My editor read the interview and chewed out Adele's right hand man; in turn, Adele counseled me about the disadvantages gained by making an editor look like an idiot. I applied her lesson when *Wings of Fire*, which focused on B-47 operations, hit the shelves. I kept to myself the fact that B-47 crewdogs didn't wear leather jackets like the ones on the cool dudes on the book's cover and the aircraft in the background were B-52s. What the fuck, I was dealing with civilians and how were they to know? Of course, they didn't show me a cover prior to publication.

In comparison, when Pan published my books in England, artist Chris Moore designed classic portraits of the planes—F-4, AC-130, and B-47—featured in each novel. Pan mailed me courtesy copies of the covers before publication. The Brits have manners.

In evaluating my second book *Spectre: Gunship of Death*, the editor who reviewed it wrote:

> Zeybel does for Spectre what Robert Mason did for the Huey in *Chickenhawk*: this is a grunt's-eye-view memoir of the nuts and bolts of battle as it was fought from a single type of airplane. The reader comes away feeling he knows the AC-130, its layout, armament, capabilities, and vulnerabilities, as well as the men who flew them. Mixing in stories of friends and other crews along with his own happy hunting sorties, Zeybel pulls together a definitive portrait of one narrow theater of the war and is content to leave anything else to those who actually witnessed it. Contempt for journalists and armchair historians of the war simmers

beneath his preemptory prose, as if to say: I was there; this is what we did; take your jeremiads back to your air-conditioned Saigon hotel rooms.

This manuscript could capture an audience identical to Mason's. It is superbly well written—frighteningly so considering the racist, jingoist, near-lunatic dedication to male animal aggression extolled on its pages. Zeybel is somehow a cross between Lieutenant Calley and Yeats' "An Irish Airman Foresees His Death," and his singular tale of *Animal House*-like buffoonery mingled with blood lust rings authentic nearly throughout. There is a calculating, icy edge to the writing, which prevents it from degenerating into B-movie melodrama. I believe Zeybel's story. How his kind of fuck-all cowboy can write so tightly is a mystery.

Someone will publish this manuscript; it is much too good to ignore. It is valuable as Air Force history and will find a solid readership there. The question is whether a sensitive editor will go for a higher audience by expunging the more infantile posturings and deleting the occasional rambles into reactionary politics, while maintaining the killer edge. Zeybel had his eyes open in Vietnam and his little reminiscence tells more about that war—and about young imperialists in general—than a roomful of Pentagon documents.

Definitely *Advertisements for Myself*. Norman Mailer long ago sanctimoniously validated authorial chest pounding. I saw the purchasing editor's review only after Simon & Schuster published the novel. Until then, had someone cared about whether my sensibilities could endure honesty?

Along with the English, the Japanese also published the novel, in hardback, yet. The Japanese treated my fictionalized account as straight history and produced a layout with photographs of every weapon system mentioned in the text. I still wonder why the Japanese found the story attractive. It glorified killing their cousins.

★ ★ ★

The Spectre Association provided Jan and me with a delightful weekend in Fort Walton Beach, Florida, in return for a guest of honor speech at its 1988 Reunion. The Association—founded in 1974 as an excuse for war buddies to gather, get drunk, and go nuts—is a socially conscious group of past and present AC-130 gunship crewmen who, at least once a year, gather, drink, and go nuts. Spectre's enlisted men are the backbone of the Association. Their unity is rooted in membership in the "Gunner

Hooch," a notorious Ubon Royal Thai Air Force Base hangout where the unwritten motto was "Nothing in moderation."

The gunners' civic awareness first emerged at Ubon during a fund drive for a Thai charity. The local armed forces radio affiliate was collecting nickels and dimes from individuals who paid to hear song requests. After half a day of requests, the Spectre gunners pooled several hundred dollars, enough money to buy the remainder of the radio day. They then pooled a larger amount of money and bought the following radio day, meanwhile pledging the same sum for every day thereafter. The gunners' only request was for "Ghost Riders in the Sky"—the squadron anthem—to be played over and over and over. After 24 hours of the same, the base commander ended the charitable drive, declaring it a success. By then, the gunners had contributed more money than anticipated for the entire drive.

Over its many years, the Spectre Association has sponsored little-league teams in several sports, special Olympic activities, and awards for outstanding military personnel in the Fort Walton Beach area. The Association also presents two college scholarships annually. Furthermore, since 1991, the Association has provided a fund for children of Spectre crewmen killed in the Middle East.

Being the guest of honor and after-dinner speaker challenged my creativity and originality. Drinkers wouldn't sit still for anything that smacked of a lecture and the men in the audience knew as much about Vietnam and gunships as I did. So I cooked up a humorous mix with a ladle of surrealism. My peers had selected me as the outstanding speaker at Squadron Officer School in 1962 and at Air Command and Staff College in 1967. Both times I had won because I hadn't viewed life as seriously as the competition.

I said to the Spectre gang....

★ ★ ★

Rumor has it that you invited me as your rent-a-mouth because of a novel I wrote about Spectre. Earlier tonight, somebody asked me, "Why did you write the book?" I told him, "Because I—me alone—want the world to know what we did."

Pilots in the audience with reading problems—that's all of you—you'll be happy to hear that a California publishing house—Fantagraphics—is working on a comic book version of the story.

But enough of this ad-libbing.

To coin a phrase, I want to make one thing perfectly clear: I told the Spectre story the way I remembered and evaluated what I heard and saw and did while in Southeast Asia. The story was told through my eyes only. I hear you asking, "If that's the case, how come Spectre had to be painted by a guy who wears glasses?"

In my defense, you should know that I took a long, hard look into my memory—and notes. I spent five years finishing the book. I wrote four versions. And no agent or publisher would touch any of them. So I wrote another war novel that took a year and nobody liked it either. That was around 1981. Hold that thought while I digress by telling a story about a man who's obsessed.

We'll call the man Rex. Rex's life is one long sexual adventure—with a cast of thousands. More than Wilt Chamberlain. One day Rex is stabbed to death by a jilted lover—or shot dead by an irate husband?—and he wakes up to find himself in a motion picture theater. No—no pearly gates for Rex. For those who don't recognize symbolism, let me spell it out: the motion picture theater is Rex's version of hell. You see, Rex hated movies because he believed real life was more exciting and interesting than anything he'd ever watched on a screen. Now the audience in Rex's personal hell is made up of everyone Rex respected and everyone who had even a hint of respect for Rex. Mom and Dad. Grandmothers and Grandfathers. Former wives. Girlfriends ages fifteen to fifty. His kids. The favorite high school teachers. The football coach who was Rex's second father. Get the picture?

The houselights dim and the movie begins. It's a video of Rex's life with one glitch. It shows only Rex's sexual activities—the last thing he wants to share with people in the audience. We're talking hard core—pure, unadulterated, two-hundred-proof porno. Including physical violence—between consenting adults, of course. Perhaps a bit of sexual depravity? Did I mention self-abuse? You name it, it's there in living color—flesh colors.

The audience is stunned—disgusted—appalled. The movie grinds on in slow motion for ten, fifteen, twenty years. Remember, this is hell. There's no time keeper.

Gradually, a strange thing happens: the attitude of the people in the audience begins to change. The change is generated by—dare I say it?—by admiration based on Rex's relentless intensity. The audience now recognizes dedication where before it saw only depravity. Miraculously, the purpose of Rex's actions ceases to matter. Rights and wrongs are forgotten. What counts is how much Rex is doing and *how* he is doing it—because, by God, he is spectacular.

The audience ends up loving Rex more than ever.

What's the moral of the story?

To figure that out, we have to think backward. Remember America's reaction to the pornography of violence called the Vietnam War? In the sixties, over martinis and TV dinners, American citizens watched hour after hour of specially edited footage of spilled blood and guts on television, and they said, "Tut-tut-tut, that's horrid." Walter Cronkite and Dan Rather pointed fingers and declared, "Bad, bad, bad. Wrong. Immoral. Ugly." And today—twenty years later—those same experts endorse and narrate videos that glorify the tremendous individual efforts that were put into that same war, glorify those same combat action scenes, the exact footage they censured and abhorred.

Let's now go back to my two manuscripts—the novels nobody liked—that glorified killing. You know one major reason why nobody liked those stories? Because, when I wrote them, the Vietnam War was not an honorable topic. Those two manuscripts sat on my closet floor, side by side, for three years.

Here comes the funny part.

About ninety percent of both novels are truth converted to fiction. Because I couldn't sell the fiction manuscripts, from them I dug out the best stories and rewrote them as non-fiction articles, which I sold to magazines such as *Eagle* and *Gung-Ho*. The war magazine editors hung graphic titles on the articles:

The Pilot Who Outflew Death
Red Ceiling of Death
Whispering Death
Eat Death, Comrades

Are you getting an impression that death is a major selling point?

A New York literary agent read the articles and phoned me. I sent her two manuscripts. She sold them in a month. While they had sat on the floor, the news media had blessed violence, destruction, and death, and Hollywood had made Saint Rambo the idol of war-crazy movie fans across America. The *Deer Hunter* and *Apocalypse Now* grabbed everyone's attention. And those bloodthirsty stories were thought up by people who had not fought in Vietnam, who had not been in the war. In that way history is written. Or better yet say, In that way history is created. The only thing I can add is "God bless Sylvester Stallone"—he sanctified the Vietnam War and its pornography.

The entire episode hinged on point of view and point of view is a killer. It chokes a lot of writers. Point of view also strangles readers who open a book and expect the story to be told from their perspectives.

For example, Steve Ryf wrote me a letter wanting to know why I picked on copilots in the Spectre novel. He reminded me that a copilot's job was tough. Copilots had to hold altitude within three inches and airspeed within micro-knots while the aircraft commander thrashed around trying to line up the fire control display—or groping for his pacifier. Steve missed the point—of view. I didn't pick on copilots. I simply described the angle from which I saw them.

To further prove that we evaluate experiences from our single point of view, let me tell you a story that I have not written.

In the Easter Offensive of 1972, the North Vietnamese Army moved a bunch of 130-millimeter guns into the game. Some brain in the chain of command got the idea that, with infrared sensors, Spectre crews could find the guns. The brain in the chain believed that hot barrels emitted easily recognizable heat signatures. Major Ed Thompson and I volunteered to go to Ubon and honcho a search for the 130-millimeter guns. A few days before we arrived at Ubon, the NVA shot down two AC-130s. Therefore, the last thing on the minds of the crew members was hunting for artillery hidden in the jungle. The crewmen were too busy looking over their shoulders. And rightfully so. They had sense. The guns were finding them.

Like a rookie, I didn't recognize the mood among the Spectre crewmen. We shared no common core of fear. My point of view was locked in the mind-set of the previous season when Spectre crews ruled the world. Or at least ruled Laos. When I'd been there full time, we didn't lose sleep over triple-A because we didn't lose an airplane. We took hits, but we didn't get hurt.

With that grossly distorted invincible point of view, I walked on stage to present our gun-hunting briefing to two hundred crewmen and performed the neat trick of stuffing two size-ten flying boots into my mouth: I said, "Remember when you were training at Hurlburt and I lectured you that flying with Spectre was like playing in the Super Bowl every night? Well, I didn't promise that you'd always win."

The room got as quiet as the Pentagon on Lieutenant Calley's birthday. But what did they expect from a born-again agnostic? I honestly thought my comment about not winning every game was funny. If you can't laugh about death, what can you laugh about? Remember the old knock-knock joke?

Knock-knock.

Who's there?

Death.

Death whogggggh...

Who dares to find fault with the insensitive innocence of my mind that glorified the pornography of war by writing:

The gunship was a perfect toy.

My first walk through the AC-130 was like a walk through the imagination of an executioner.

A first truck kill is a lot like a first piece: it ends almost before it begins, it produces thrills that live beyond the spastic moment, and it inspires dreams of doing it again and again and again.

I willingly confess that my days with Spectre were the most exciting days of my life. Every mission was a life in itself. Nothing from yesterday had value. There was no tomorrow. Everything was now. In overpowering ecstasy, we lived for what the moment provided.

Now, it's twenty years later. Sins are abolished. We're going to be pals—communists and capitalists—Russians and Americans and Vietnamese—real buddy-buddies. I'll buy that. But I leave you with two thoughts.

Once upon a time, we had fun trying to kill them.

And you know they felt the same way.

★ ★ ★

I didn't bother to tell the audience that after my disastrous briefing of the Spectre crews, I voluntarily flew on missions to An Loc, which was a hell hole of utter confusion under continuous bombardment. The North Vietnamese Army antiaircraft weapon of choice was the shoulder-launched SA-7 Strela. While I was there, one Spectre needlessly took a hit when the TV sensor operator stupidly left the 2KW searchlight operating in the infrared (IR) mode in daylight and the missile homed on its IR beam. It didn't happen to my airplane, but the hit changed my point of view about the battle.

Ed Thompson and I accomplished nothing. The gun finding plan turned out to be totally worthless.

★ ★ ★

Good deals continued to enhance my life. As I mentioned earlier, researching the F-16 Fighting Falcon and M1 Abrams gave me a few fits of rapture. Soaring—in every sense of the word—in an F-16 was the best flight of my life. Unfortunately, I wasn't a member in the Mile High Club. Describing the F-16 for a magazine article, I wrote:

> The F-16 cockpit is the most pilot-oriented environment I have experienced: the ejection seat is as comfortable as a high-priced living-room recliner; the instruments are small and bunched together, but perfectly readable; auxiliary equipment is located out of the way so the pilot has ample room to turn around and search the sky; the bubble canopy permits a splendid three-hundred-sixty-degree field of view, including the deep six position.
>
> The thirty-degree seat-back angle of the ejection seat makes a world of difference when pulling six or seven Gs. An hour of air-to-air dueling invigorated

me. By comparison, the previous week I visited Dixie Bombing Range [near Austin, Texas] in the back seat of an F-4D, and an hour of sitting upright and pulling Gs in that cramped cockpit made me feel as if I had been wrestling Hulk Hogan the entire time.

The real thrill of the F-16 is its ease of handling. The plane seems to respond to the driver's thoughts. With forearm resting on supports that cantilever from the right cockpit wall, the pilot guides the plane with a side stick control much like the grip of a video-arcade game. Twitches of the fingers or flicks of the wrist are enough to fly the fighter through the most difficult maneuvers. Full throw of the stick is about a quarter inch of movement.

Designers call the cockpit a "nine-G environment." They have arranged everything so the pilot can smoothly function under that stress load.

Basically, the plane is a robot that encases a man. The levers, wires, and pulleys that once tied stick and rudder to flight surfaces are long gone. F-16 control is digital, with four electronic paths for each signal that drives actuators and poppets. Wings have leading and trailing edge flaps that automatically change contour to suit angle of attack flight and speed of the aircraft. The airplane almost flies itself.

Did that description sound like a commercial to make you want to rush out and buy your own Falcon? Well, it was supposed to.

While at Hill AFB in 1986, I interviewed a group of pilots that appreciated their jobs to the fullest. They manned the 466th Tactical Fighter Squadron, the only Reserve unit equipped with the F-16 at that time. Fliers like Majors Tom "Waldo" King, Danny Hamilton, and Wayne Conroy exemplified everything ever said about professionalism. Under the leadership of Colonel Bane Lyle, they won Gunsmoke '85—an Air Force-wide bombing and gunnery competition. Each man had over 3000 hours of fighter time and had flown multiple combat tours in the Vietnam War. All scored among the top ten Gunsmoke competitors. Lyle, who finished second overall, had a bombing circular error of ten inches, which meant every one of his bombs impacted on a target tank, with all but two hitting the tank's turret.

Lyle modestly told me his performance more than likely wouldn't be duplicated in combat. "I flew the same airplane for a month before the competition, and our ground crews fine-tuned it beyond belief. Bombing turned into a matter of rote," he said. "And, of course, we weren't being shot at."

I spent one morning at Eagle Bombing Range on the Great Salt Lake Desert and watched a couple flights of 466th pilots weave their low-angle attack magic. Their "average" bomb deliveries were an F-4 pilot's lifelong dream: three meters, shack, four meters, shack, three meters, two meters… The releases grew predictably dull until the plotter called, "Twelve meters at four o'clock." Spotters in the tower looked at each other as if asking, "What did he do wrong?"

I believed a few 466th pilots were disappointed that high-performance maneuvers in the F-16 didn't make me sick. By the time of my visit to Hill, I had been retired from the Air Force for almost 10 years, and my hair had grown inordinately long by military standards. At a bull session, one of the jocks asked me point blank, "Why don't you get a fucking haircut?" I said, "My wife suggested that. So I made a bet with her that I just won. I bet her that one of you guys would say exactly what you just said." A few from the group smiled, but the jock who asked the question continued to sneer. I believed he didn't want me in his fraternity. I think it further irritated him when I doted on the shit we did in the airplane. In fact, I craved more but one flight was my limit.

A year earlier, before visiting Fort Hood, I had my hair clipped short, wanting the soldiers to appreciate that a retired Air Force officer still possessed a touch of military bearing. I first visited Hood in 1984, four years after the Abrams tank entered the inventory but while many people still questioned its capabilities and battle worthiness. Later the 6th Cavalry gave me a tour of its AH-64 Apache helicopter operations. A day with the tank crews convinced me to commend the M1, a conclusion the editor of National Defense longed to hear because the industrial side of the military-industrial complex paid his rent (and part of mine, too).

The following accounts are consolidations of articles I wrote for National Defense, Army, and Tanks magazines based on field visits and additional research.

Here was how I came to view the peacetime United States Army, a few years before it returned to combat in the Middle East.

★ ★ ★

On a scrub country gunnery range in the heart of Texas, I watched Charlie Company from Fort Hood's 2nd Armored Division, 3rd Battalion, 66th Regiment rip through individual M1 Abrams tank qualifications. The crewmen demonstrated the "Woodmansee tactic" in which tanks attacked in pairs, like a lead fighter plane and its wingman. Lead did the firing; the wingman helped to spot targets while protecting the flanks. The maneuver was developed by and named after a former 2AD Commander.

The crewmen displayed their skills, but the M1 tank was the star of the show.

At the start of the first run, hunkered in a depression in the conventional hull-down defensive posture, the lead M1 reminded me of any other tank. It popped forward, fired its 105-mm main gun, then slithered backward into its lair. The tank appeared above ground for one to five seconds each time it fired. Every round hit the target.

When the range officer introduced enemy armor into the scenario and presented moving targets, the M1 took on a different personality. It became an offensive monster, springing from its hole like Walter Payton bursting through a gang of tacklers. In the role of a blocking back, a second M1 advanced parallel. Gathering momentum, the lead tank fired continuously, blasting targets while on the move, randomly sidestepping to avoid counterfire. The tank worked its way downfield, moved in from a range of 1500 meters to under a thousand, then, slamming to a stop, it simultaneously salvoed smoke grenades overhead, activated a ground-level smoke generator, and slipped into reverse. Essing backward, it became invisible to anything in front of it.

Seeing was believing, I thought, then reminded myself I had watched merely one crew in action. Within moments, minus the smoke razzle-dazzle, another crew performed with identical firing accuracy. And then another. And another. About the time I wished the M1's critics could be there, the fifth crew screwed up, hit short with most of its rounds while charging forward.

At the time, I was hitching a jeep ride with the Charlie Company Commander and his Executive Officer, Captain Dave Rich and Lieutenant Mike McGonagle, who followed every tank downrange, evaluated maneuvers, and scored rounds.

"What're they doing wrong?" Rich asked.

McGonagle gave him an explanation in terms I didn't understand—something about the computer.

By the end of our first trip downrange, a layer of caliche dust, like a coating of powdered sugar, covered the three of us. The layer thickened with each trip. Rich and McGonagle ate the dust without comment, were at home in it. I imagined them complaining when they didn't find it sprinkled over their morning cereal. Leather-faced from the eternal Texas sun, the two leaders were lean muscled, looked fit and combat ready, like everyone in Charlie Company.

After McGonagle's explanation about the computer, Dave Rich said, "Don't go too hard at debriefing. But make sure the crew learns not to repeat that mistake. That's what counts."

Later, between trips downrange, sitting in the baking shade of an M113 armored personnel carrier (APC), Rich told me, "In the M1, once you sight something, from there the gunnery is simple. The computer will hit it. The important thing is having the computer set correctly at the start. Human errors cause most of our misses. If you miss, you probably did something wrong earlier." He sprang to his feet and said, "Come on, I'll show you."

A minute later, I'm tucked into the gunner's seat of "Combat Cruiser," an M1 commanded by Technical Sergeant Lou Bush who gives me a three-minute course on switchology, aiming reticle placement, and firing the 105-mm gun. Lou Bush has 13 years in M60s and M1s; he exudes expertise and confidence.

The crew's regular gunner, Sergeant Ralph Sartin, is demoted to loader while I fill his seat. Sartin bites his lip when I wrinkle my forehead and search for switches that are in front of my nose. Everything at the gunner's position is up-tight, a finger flick away.

Reticle placement is controlled by movement of a steering yoke, much like an airplane's control. Tilt the yoke back and the reticle moves upward, climbs; push forward, it dives; twist the yoke right, the reticle moves to the right; bank left, it glides left. The big gun's barrel follows with clicks and clanks.

After my crash course, Bush lets me take my time and, using optical sighting, I punch a hole in a bull's-eye at 1100 meters with my first round. Fish in a barrel.

Practically stroking my left shoulder, the 105 recoils 12 inches. The gun produces a whoosh of concussion more than a noise of blast. The tank interior fills with a biting odor that reminds me of ammonia fumes rather than the heavy cordite aroma I had expected. Rich later explains the M1 rounds use a beaded, fast-burning powder to produce muzzle velocities much higher than the old howitzer rounds with which I'm familiar.

Seated behind and above me, Bush says, "That was too easy. Want to try it at combat speed?" I nod. He scans with the optics; I look where he looks, but I have 10-power magnification. He calls, "Enemy tank. You see it? Hit it."

A moving tank silhouette appears on the right edge of my sight picture. "Got it," I shout and fly the aiming reticle onto the target's center, depress the laser-ranger button with my left thumb—read a digital "1470" in the sight picture—squeeze off the round with my left trigger finger. Whoom! Bam! On the money.

It's that easy—when the computer's correctly set in advance.

Sartin is ready to shove another round into the breech. I raise a hand. "Hold it. I'm convinced." I see no need to perform the same magic trick over and over.

Bush tells Sartin, "Save it."

Sartin re-inserts the round among rows of 105 rounds in a magazine separated from the crew compartment by a steel door that opens and closes as swiftly and softly as an eyelid. "Blastproof," Bush says and pats the door. "If we take a hit in the ammo magazine, the explosion and fire will be vented away from the crew compartment. We won't be harmed." Bush also explains that the M1 has a Halon gas fire extinguisher system so sensitive that it puts out a flash fire before crewmen can recognize a danger exists.

"If you don't want to shoot," Bush says, "let's go for a ride." He directs me to a standing position in the loader's open hatch and we back out

178 • ALONG FOR THE RIDE

of our hole. There is little sensation from a 1500 horsepower turbine engine at labor, no great noise. The engine revs with a swoosh of air that sounds like a helicopter engine. It dawns upon me that, all day, the tanks have moved relatively quietly, most noise clinking from their treads.

Bush verbally guides his driver, Sergeant Kelly Roller, across rough open terrain. We move slowly, almost daintily. I am surprised by the numerous sharp but fluid turns, tiny zigs and zags. I get the impression Lou Bush could tiptoe the M1 through a mine field. We reach a dirt road and Bush says, "Open her up." The tank takes off like a Formula-1 racer.

My gee-whiz publicity handout claims "zero to twenty miles per hour in six seconds." But we accelerate from a walking pace to 45 miles per hour in that time. I wonder if we have sprouted wings. Standing in the slipstream with 60 tons of flowing armor beneath me, I am flying low, buzzing the ground.

We slow, turn off the road, and head cross-country at a good clip. The treads level the rough, rolling terrain. Momentarily, I recall somebody telling me, "The M1 is a more stable platform the faster it goes." But then, approaching a jagged looking depression, I take a white-knuckled grip on the edge of the hatch and clench my jaws; we traverse the jagged dip with no more jolt than jumping off a step. And I'm a believer.

Seated back in the dusty shade of the APC with Dave Rich, I mention how quiet and responsive the M1 is. He tells me that infantrymen nicknamed the tank "Whispering Death." "When the wind's right, you don't hear the treads," he says.

I imagine an M1 creeping up from behind, crushing me flat before I know it's there. Involuntarily, I glance over my shoulder.

The only complaint about the tank concerns its tracks. "There's lots of tension on the tracks. They last only five to six hundred miles, depending on where you drive. You get eight hundred and fifty miles in the desert. But that's not far at ten thousand dollars a set," Mike McGonagle says. The Army is developing a new track with removable pads, which is like resoling old shoes rather than buying an entirely new pair. Despite the horsepower and speed of the M1, thrown tracks are not a major problem because armor skirts cover the top halves of the treads and help to keep them on their guide wheels.

"The M1's smooth speed is impressive," Rich says. "At *Phantom Sidewinder*, operating in broken desert scrub, we ran light reconnaissance dune buggies to ground, rounded them up like cattle."

"You think the light recce guys would agree with that claim?" I ask.

"I don't know," Rich says, "but it was supposed to be a four-day operation and they went home after two days."

Earlier, a tanker had told me, "The first time I rode in an M1, the driver took it up to a hundred kilometers, right at sixty miles an hour. When he started making turns at that speed, he scared me. I asked him to slow down."

Gunners claim they shoot more accurately on the move. "Of course, we used to shoot on the move in the M60, too," one crewman said, "but we couldn't hit anything." Gunners unanimously agree that hitting while on the move is what counts and no tank does it as well as the M1.

"I used to think tanks were defensive weapons," Rich confesses. "The M1 made tanks into an offensive team. Night operations are a dream," he says straight-faced.

For night and all-weather sighting, the M1 gunner uses thermal imaging, a passive system that picks up heat generated by man-made objects or men and makes them stand out from nature like neon pop art figures. Crewmen are trained to identify thermal images, friend or foe. Both the tank commander (TC) and gunner have thermal sighting, complemented by light-intensification sighting for the TC and driver. As a last resort, the TC also has night goggles. Everyone I talked with agreed that, using thermal sighting, "the tank shoots better at night." Rich says, "That equipment makes tanking simple."

Tankers firmly believe the M1 is worth its $1.75 million price tag. The Army paid thirteen billion dollars for 7500 M1s—3300 of the basic model and 4200 with improved armor and a 120-mm main gun. When questioned about the 120-mm smooth-bore weapon, staff officers said, "Same ballistic computer, same accuracy. Heavier firepower. A definite improvement. What else is there to say?"

The tank crewmen provided me with a crash course in ammunition. Tank-versus-tank combat uses three basic rounds: sabot, HESH, and HEAT.

The sabot, a hyper-velocity projectile, carries no explosive charge, but it is the deadliest. A sabot is the plastic bushing that surrounds a projectile in order to make it fit tightly in the bore of a gun. The champagne-cork fit builds tremendous pressure and produces muzzle velocities beyond 5000 feet per second. As soon as the round clears the muzzle, the sabot outer casing splits into three pieces and falls away. What remains is a solid two-inch thick, foot-long piece of dense tungsten-carbide—a 15-pound chunk of heavy metal that is rear-fin stabilized and humming along at a mile a second—fast enough to hit a road runner. The sabot projectile relies on kinetic energy for its destructive force. It splinters layers of hardened steel as easily as if they were wood. By the time the projectile shreds its way into a tank crew compartment, it has created splinters of metal that fill the tank's interior with high-velocity ricocheting shrapnel.

The HESH (high-explosive squash head) round flattens against armor much like a Monty Python bomb: Ker-splat! Then its explosive charge sets up shock waves through the armor that cause spallation, fragmenting of the tank's interior walls. Again, the closed space literally erupts into high-speed shrapnel that ricochets around and around, only this time it is the tank walls themselves that have been converted into deadly projectiles.

The HEAT (high-explosive antitank) projectile, called a "shaped charge" or "hollow charge," has a hollow conical windshield that causes the charge to detonate at a given distance from armor surface. The explosion liquefies a second metal cone, turns it into a high-pressure, high-velocity jet of molten metal that focuses into a kind of drill. The pressure of the liquid-metal jet is so great that steel is pushed aside much as a high-pressure jet of water pushes into a bank of earth. When the jet pierces the armor, the crew inside gets a red-hot lava shower.

M1 crews are mainly concerned with hammering such deadly rounds into enemy armor, but the crews also recognize they can be on the receiving end. They're betting their lives on the latest technology. Along with other defensive bells and whistles, the M1 has laminated armor that, the crewmen are convinced, is capable of defeating most known threats—kinetic energy or armor piercing.

At lunch break from gunnery range activities, I dropped the big question on Captain Dave Rich: "How do you think you will do in actual combat?"

"I think about that quite a bit," he said. Rich was an enlisted man for three years before winning a competitive appointment to West Point. "I believe we'll win, in armored warfare, mainly because our equipment is superior, even though on paper we're outnumbered."

Outnumbered six-to-one on paper doesn't mean you'll face six enemies at once in the field, I thought. Rich knew that.

He said, "I've talked with defectors—armor officers—and they admit the M1 is superior to anything the Soviets have. What we've learned from the Israelis and from some of our other friends confirms that."

I mentioned combat experience and Rich told me, "The battalion has a dozen or so E-6s and E-7s on crews, men who earned their CIB [Combat Infantryman Badge] in Vietnam. They're blooded, but few have armor experience in battle. Vietnam wasn't an armor war."

Thinking out loud, I said, "Yeah, but how much battle experience do Russian tankers have?"

"Right now they're getting more armor experience in Afghanistan than we got in Vietnam," Rich said.

"But Russian tankers aren't facing enemy armor in Afghanistan, aren't fighting tank-to-tank."

"The Russians are rotating troops through Afghanistan just like we rotated people through Vietnam," Rich said, "trying to get them experience. I don't know how valuable that experience is. I hear that many of their troops are becoming disillusioned by that war, the same as some of our people did in Vietnam."

"What if the Russians are just plain better soldiers than your guys?" I said.

I expected the note of irritation, bordering on hostility, in Rich's voice when he replied, "Sure, that's possible. Combat ultimately comes down to man-to-man. That's possible." He paused for several seconds, relaxed. "Have you looked at my men?" he asked rhetorically. "They're professionals. Including the ones who aren't career. Look at them. They're ready. Clear eyes. No fat. No drunks, no drug users. Russian soldiers can't be better. I know the Russians aren't better trained. If both men are equal, the man with the better equipment should win. And we have the better equipment." Then he added softly, "The better soldiers too."

Multiple analysis programs and built-in safety sensors greatly improve the M1's reliability and save money. Analysis programs predict failure and identify replacement parts based on current conditions rather than length of time in use. For example, oil analysis can predict hydrostatic steering failure, telling maintenance men to pull a transmission and rebuild it; this costs $4000 compared to a new transmission cost of $175,000. Similarly, safety sensors tell a driver of impending engine failure and stop him from destroying an engine in peacetime operations; however, under combat conditions, he can override the sensor.

Sergeant Lou Bush had the last word on the subject when he refuted the M1's early reputation as a moving maintenance problem: "I have nearly five thousand miles in M1s without one breaking down on me. The secret is good preventive maintenance, which isn't any big secret."

★ ★ ★

The Fort Hood training ranges provided a bonanza of reportable experiences for me. Their desolation adds a surreal touch to activities. In central Texas the sun bakes the scrub landscape with eon-old ferocity. From where I stand, atop a low rise on one of the ranges, I watch a lone silhouetted buzzard glide undisturbed in slow orbit. The planet appears as if it has drifted back to prehistoric time.

I hear a whisper of wind behind me and turn to see an AH-64 Apache helicopter slowly unmask from behind an adjacent rise, lift its bulbous sensor-laden snout as if to sniff the air, then sink from sight like a techno-grandchild of Grendel. Minutes later, from behind a different rise, the monster reappears; simultaneously, one of its mates lifts up from a third position. Both nod and drop from view. Steel dragons of death, I think, recognizing the ambivalent lethality and fragility of the beast. Is the Apache predator or prey?

The Apaches' stealthy maneuvers are part of a quest for new tactics—tactics that ideally will mesh with M1 tank battle plans. "Presently there is no doctrine for the AH-64," a 6th Cavalry Brigade lieutenant colonel told me. "We're in the process of inventing ways to use the AH-64's capabilities most effectively."

The McDonnell Douglas Helicopter Company (now Boeing) AH-64 Apache matches the fondest dreams of combat helicopter pilots, and at the same time perhaps creates new nightmares for them. The Apache's mission is anti-armor—tank busting—a task planned for execution on an electronic battlefield, a new environment for helicopters. Technological advances make the Apache far more fit than its predecessors for that battlefield, and those advances provide planners with tactical options not previously feasible. At Fort Hood, aviation tacticians view the attack helicopter as a maneuver unit, a role that ground commanders often find difficult to accept. Traditionalists among ground commanders see the Apache as little more than fancy artillery limited to a fire support role or, at most, a close air support anti-armor weapon.

Aviators abhor the close air support role, contending the Apache is too vulnerable for the mission because it lacks the necessary speed. However, equipped with the laser-guided Rockwell International Hellfire missile and a Martin Marietta sensor package that includes forward-looking infrared, low-light television, and direct-view optics, the Apache has an extended standoff range and day/night/adverse-weather capabilities that make current anti-armor tactics obsolete.

Because it possesses more than double the effective firing range of the M1 Abrams, for example, aviation tacticians believe the Apache would be wasted if deployed alongside a tank. In one scenario, they see the Apache engaging targets well forward, employing direct fire before passing off targets to tanks. In another scenario, tacticians envision the Apache lurking well behind friendly lines, engaging targets with indirect fire, remaining mobile but isolated from threats the AH-1 Cobra and UH-1 Huey must face to do the job.

Although the Apache's ability to fight either independently at night or in adverse weather are firsts for the helicopter, its tactical potential coincides perfectly with the night fighting capabilities of the M1 Abrams and M2 Bradley. "The Apache and friendly armor must operate as a combined arms team," a staff-level aviator explained to me. "The M2 is supposed to add to the M1's capability, and the Apache should augment both of them. If you ask me, the Army gets new equipment and then continues to use outdated tactics. The M1 isn't being used to its full capacity. Commanders fail to take advantage of the M1's speed and ability to fight at night. They fail to recognize the M1 will do what the M60 wouldn't. What the Army now is looking at is a wholly modernized brigade that needs wholly modernized tactics and doctrine." A 6th Cav lieutenant colonel agreed: "Only a combined doctrine will do the job. There's nothing new in that. Combined doctrine has always been the answer. Even fliers like me who have Vietnam experience need to rethink the problem."

"Right now our basic tactic is to run a lot and hide," an Apache pilot said. "We're learning defensive maneuvers, how to protect ourselves, how to escape and evade if caught in the open."

Defensive maneuvers were what the Apaches were practicing when I watched them flying nap-of-the-earth. "Nobody flies as low as we fly," a pilot said. When I told him that I'd experienced extremely low level in a B-52, size and speed being relative, he shook his head and said, "B-52s follow terrain contours. Apaches live inside the contours of the terrain. We fly within the obstacles."

At a briefing before the start of daily maneuvers, part of a week-long troop exercise, a squadron commander told a tentful of Apache pilots, "Forget about making plans for Friday night. When we return to base we're going to review everything we did this week and then brainstorm what we have to do to improve."

I raised the question of helicopter air-to-air combat and was told dogfighting is a last resort. According to Apache pilots, the AH-64 possesses no weapon adequate for air-to-air. Its 30-mm cannon has no shoot down capability for chance encounters. A pilot said, "The Hind [Soviet Mi-24 helicopter gunship] is a big and powerful machine, and it's used for close air support. To battle Hinds we need to use flanking attacks, something where we're waiting in ambush, have them outmaneuvered before the fight begins. For air-to-air, our best bet is to outguess the Soviet deployment pattern." Another pilot said, "The Air Force should examine the A-10 as an air-to-air weapon for that role."

While visiting the 6th Cavalry Brigade, I imagined a Congressman questioning procurement of the Apache: "Why has the Army ordered so many of something it doesn't know how to use?" I recalled my experience with the AC-130 Spectre gunships along the Ho Chi Minh Trail. For Spectre to survive, every year improved equipment was provided for crews who, more or less on an individual basis, learned to use that equipment through trial and error while in combat. A lot of mistakes were repeated annually. At the end of the fourth year of Spectre operations, Major Dick Kauffman and I wrote the squadron's first tactics manual. We were a little late. A year after that, the North Vietnamese introduced surface-to-air missiles to the contest and chased Spectre out of Laos. At least the Apache drivers won't have to learn tactics and develop doctrine while on the job under fire, I decided. My recollection revived an old question: Does technology lead tactics or do tactics lead technology?

On an earlier visit to Fort Hood, I'd watched a combined force of 1st Cavalry Division Cobras and Bradleys and Air Force A-10 Thunderbolts attack an enemy armor brigade. Families turned out for the demonstration. Mothers and children sat in bleachers or sprawled on hillsides, watching daddies practice war with live ammunition. Over a public address system, an announcer spelled out the phases of the attack. I got the impression the women knew the drill as well as the announcer: I was sitting among the players' wives whiling away another day at the ballpark. The attack force's live fire was deadly accurate and conclusive. The Cobras were particularly impressive, unerringly hitting targets at maximum range with rockets. Furthermore, even from my elevated vantage point, the black Cobras were difficult to see as they maneuvered through sparse vegetation. They crept forward, sidestepped, and backed out of firing positions with a style that, as paradoxical as it sounds, I only can describe as motionless. And that was in daylight.

The Cobras' stealth flashed my mind back 20 years to an evening at Pleiku, in Nam, where I watched two Hueys race to perimeter defense, like cavalry to the rescue, and create a firepower display of bold and pyrophoric beauty. Over the base perimeter, the first Huey dropped virtually unseen from the darkening sky, abruptly announced its presence with a stream of golden orange fire that, as the gunship rapidly descended, linked aircraft to ground, grew into a pedestal of flaming steel. The gunship continued firing until it reached treetop level. By then its tracers had no time to burn out before hitting the ground and ricocheting in a shower of sparks that reminded me of molten steel being poured into ingots—awesome memory of my Pittsburgh youth. The moment the first Huey bottomed out from its descent and flitted into the night, climbing rapidly, the second Huey swooped downward, spraying fire across the identical area. And then the first Huey was on top again. The stream of tracers remained uninterrupted as the two shadowy gunships gyrated through a lethal dance.

Today the flaming sparks of that promiscuous display are as cold as the sparks of my Pittsburgh mill. Few Apache aviators harbor the notion they will dash to battle with unbridled care, charge like cavalry to the rescue as if the helicopter were an invulnerable Pegasus. They know on tomorrow's electronic battlefield the bold Vietnam maneuvers will be anachronisms. Doctrine that sanctions such permissiveness will be equally outdated. Future helicopter doctrine must match the sophistication of new machines capable of subtle methods of delivering destruction, and of changing the course of battles.

★ ★ ★

Regardless of how much I enjoyed the hospitality of M1 and Apache units, I would be remiss if I did not present follow-on studies of M1 and Apache performances in combat that revealed weaknesses in training for the employment of both.

The Department of Defense summarized the battlefield proficiency of the M1 in a comprehensive 2000 report that said 594 M1 Abrams tanks engaged in combat action for the first time in the 1990–1991 Gulf War. Overall, 10,000 armored vehicles engaged in intense combat operations around the clock. The technological advantage of US combat vehicles over "Iraq's older, mostly Russian-designed armored vehicles" included "superior sighting and sensor equipment [that] almost invariably allowed US crewmen to see and engage Iraqi forces first." Iraq's best tank—the T-72—had a "125-millimeter cannon with a maximum effective range of eighteen hundred meters"; however, the US M1A1s "routinely scored kills at twice that distance." Furthermore, "Iraqi tanks, anti-tank guided missiles, and infantry anti-tank weapons failed to penetrate the DU [depleted uranium] armor of any…M-1A1s…." Iraq lost more than 4000 armored vehicles to US air and ground fire. Meanwhile, "fewer than ten US combat vehicles were destroyed by hostile fire (a smaller number were damaged or destroyed by mines)."

In the Gulf War, armored units fought much of the war at night and under poor weather conditions. Heavy rains, low clouds, sandstorms, and blowing smoke hampered visibility. At dusk and pre-dawn hours, crewmen appeared to experience the greatest difficulty in using thermal sighting.

Seven battles involved damage resulting from friendly fire by M1 crews when US vehicles became disoriented and moved counter to the general flow of US forces. The Battle of Norfolk, which involved the 2nd AD, was "the largest friendly fire incident of the war," resulting in the destruction or damage of five M1s and five Bradley M2s. Overall, incidents of friendly fire involved six M1s and fifteen M2s. Of 146 U.S. service members killed in action during the war, 35 were killed and another 72 wounded by fratricide.

The M1s fired depleted uranium rounds that, in almost every case, penetrated and passed completely through the Bradleys hit by mistake. In one case, two DU "rounds passed through both sides of the [Bradley] and struck another Bradley parked twenty feet away," which "caught fire and, in the words of its driver, 'melted to the ground.'"

In the Gulf War, the Apache helicopters used ground-attack tactics that primarily targeted tanks and fighting vehicles, according to a 1992 *U.S. News & World Report*, but their actions deviated from the designed plan. Trained to fly low, use hills for cover, and pop up to fire, Apache pilots were forced to modify their tactics because the desert provided few hills high enough to hide behind. Therefore, Bravo Company devised "high-energy" and "low-energy" tactics. Basically, six helicopters lined up shoulder to shoulder, in three teams of two spread across a 3000 meter front. Low-energy tactics involved flying at an altitude of 30 feet and creeping forward just fast enough to leave the dust from rotor wash behind with the hope of springing surprise attacks. High-energy tactics involved advancing at speeds of 40 miles per hour. The plan was to get close, shoot, and get away fast.

The Apaches' most notable success was destroying Iraqi air defense radar sites with Hellfire missiles to start the war. As a result, follow-on Allied aircraft attacked without opposition. The Apaches also proved successful in attacking tanks and armored personnel carriers. In the final action of the war in the Euphrates Valley, patrolling Apaches intercepted and destroyed 32 tanks and 100 or so vehicles of retreating Iraqi Republican Guard forces within an hour.

Apache pilots were involved in a case of fratricide in February 1991. Missiles fired by Apaches killed two American servicemen and wounded six in one incident, according to a 1993 Office of Special Investigation report. Another report speculated that an Apache set fire to an M1 with "a large shaped-charge round—probably a Hellfire anti-armor missile."

★ ★ ★

Fast forward a dozen or so years to Afghanistan where there ain't no tanks to bust. Jesus, after all the staff thinking and planning, does the Army now leave the Apaches stateside? How do commanders best employ its sophisticated Hellfire missiles and rockets and 30-mm cannon? Sadly for our planners, targets dictate tactics and in Afghanistan the enemy targets are primarily people. Consequently, the Apache has been forced to revert to the "outdated tactics" of close-air-support—raining fire on foot-soldier attackers—a use that American troops, especially those in southeastern Afghanistan, roundly applaud. Is it proper to say, "We proceed unhampered by progress?"

★ ★ ★

The Gulf War clearly confirmed that technology can compensate for deficiencies in other aspects of combat performance. Numerous Gulf War photographs of decapitated Iraqi tanks with their turrets lying nearby in the desert attested to the M1's striking power emanating from the DU round that entered the inventory just prior to the war. A sabot-kinetic energy round, it featured a long rod penetrator made of depleted uranium with a density two and a half times greater than steel. It provided higher penetration characteristics than the old tungsten-carbide slab as well as a pyrophoric effect. Continued redesign of the DU round resulted in longer and heavier penetrator rods. Newer rounds also have improved sabots and propellants, which combine to increase accuracy, muzzle velocity, and penetrator performance.

And you thought that stuff taught in high school physics classes was just book learning.

★ ★ ★

For a writer, a little success can be dangerous. Shortly after Pocket Books published my novels, other writers sought my advice. They acted as if I possessed knowledge of shortcuts to getting published. As much as I hated to admit it, I once held similar beliefs such as knowing the right person would compensate for my misdirection, deficiencies, or idiosyncrasies that I didn't understand how to cope with in writing. A couple of years before selling my novels, I had gone to the University of Texas for help. Actually, curiosity overpowered me and I enrolled at "The University" to learn what experts had to say about writing. I studied under the brilliant Guyana-born Wilson Harris—and David Ohle, a counter-culture legend who moved on to teach at Kansas, and I monitored lectures by Angela Carter, who emphasized a need to "find the rapture of life." As teachers, the three encouraged their students to write in styles that departed from accepted standards, to find perspectives of imagination beyond the norm.

Unfortunately, my fellow students disappointed and irritated me. With but a few exceptions, they were lazy and lacked a sense of deadlines. Of course, an appreciable age difference existed between us. By my standards, their ability to produce quality work was nonexistent. Too late, I recognized my carrying over of military values and expectations went beyond their training and desires. I am positive they viewed me as a curmudgeon.

After classes, Wilson Harris permitted me to walk him to his condo-minium, a 20-minute trip that invariably left me humbled. The depth of

Harris' intellect defied description. He knew the world and the people who inhabit it as if he had lived for 5000 years. He spoke of real and imaginary figures—referencing mythological gods and goddesses—as if he knew them personally. He analyzed character in historic terms, putting the lives of common men on a par with the views of presidents. He offered what amounted to proclamations as softly spoken suggestions. In explaining the depth of imaginative fiction, he showed me how much I didn't know.

Harris believed fiction described the lives of people who did not appear in the history books. As he saw it, fiction contained truths equal in importance to what historians presented as facts. I had understood that idea while writing about Vietnam. I had fictionalized my characters by creating composite characters and describing real-life actions they performed. Now, Harris helped me to look at my combat experiences in greater depth. He said, "I cannot do what you have done. But I can learn from what you learned. You must show me."

At the risk of sounding overly dramatic, I confess Harris made me recognize the possibility of an existence of a soul in what, for me, had been a relatively soulless existence. He brought out a touch of conscience in me, an attribute I had pretty much ignored for half a century.

Based on my limited success as a writer, Brigadier General Richard Baughn contacted me for advice. He had enjoyed an illustrious career reaching from World War II to F-105 combat over North Vietnam and diplomacy in South Vietnam. However, his heart remained forever in the cockpit of a P-51, which he flew in combat against the Germans and which served as the core of his novel in progress. Along with telling Baughn how I wrote, I pointed out techniques that other writers followed as "best practices." In 2006, Baughn's manuscript saw publication as *The Hellish Vortex: Between Breakfast and Dinner.*

Along the way, I received drafts of stories from others who sought writing advice. Their manuscripts ran between twenty and a hundred pages resembling tentacles groping out to survey the surroundings. Did they submit their best or their worst material? I wondered if they were testing me.

★ ★ ★

In conducting research for magazine articles, my meetings with people that operated weapon systems was the best feature about visiting military installations. Watching them from a neutral position gave me a keener appreciation for what I had experienced on active duty. As a crewdog, I had an inner sense of entitlement, recognizing that I ranked among those on the bottom of the totem pole but knowing the pole couldn't stand without our holding it up. Therefore, I had bitched about the bad things and seldom found time to appreciate the good. Often I wish it were possible to do it all again, only this time while wearing a smile. But then, would I still be me?

CHAPTER 12

World-Class Warriors

After more than 20 years the dreams continued. Strapped in the darkened belly of a Strategic Air Command (SAC) B-52C Stratofortress, I perform celestial computations on a navigation leg to an unknown destination. Or I make a bomb run on a target difficult to identify. Confusingly, I have mislaid information needed to complete the mission; unexplainably, I am alone in the airplane. The heat of raw frustration soaks me with sweat. My body twitches in tempo with the drumming of my heart. To complicate matters, the dream is lucid: I know I have no right to be there. I retired from the United States Air Force nearly a decade ago. The C-model B-52s now rest in the aircraft bone yard in Arizona or have been chopped into scrap. I hesitantly perform duties I once executed reflexively, maddeningly ponder why I am there. Is this the real thing—thermonuclear war? Without knowing the facts, I cannot escape from the dream. If it is war, responsibility that spans two decades dictates that I must not fail.

★ ★ ★

In 1984, concurrent with my persistent dreams of navigating bombers, I stepped through what resembled a time warp and emerged as a pseudo member of SAC's 96th Bomb Wing at Dyess Air Force Base, Texas. From 1957 to 1961, I had logged over 1000 hours as a B-47 radar-bombardier flying from Dyess. On arriving at the base, I quickly recognized that Thomas Wolfe was wrong: You can go home again. The base had evolved through numerous minor changes, but its basic features had remained the same. Beyond the physical, however, the major change was an intensified intellectual complication of the mission.

I had flown the antiquated B-52C model from 1961 to 1963. Now I would be an observer on Captain Brooks Tyler's B-52H crew. The upgrade in aircraft models was as pronounced as switching from counting on your fingers to owning a high-powered computer. Actually, under the auspices of the editors of *National Defense, Eagle, and Airpower* magazines, I was a guest tasked with evaluating a generation of changes in strategic bombing tactics.

One thing that hadn't changed with B-52 operations was crawling out of bed in the chilled middle of the night to prepare for a 0815 takeoff. SAC had proved several thousand times that, under Emergency War Order scramble conditions, an Alert bomber could be airborne within minutes after the warning klaxon sounded. However, for a training flight SAC still required a crew to show up three hours before takeoff time.

"Does all of this feel familiar?" one of Tyler's crewdogs asks as we grope through the night toward base operations. All I can think about is the stack of huge, fluffy pancakes that used to be served in the Flight Line Snack Bar that now is dark, hasn't yet opened for the day. At least the cooks have common sense, I tell myself.

Until we get to the airplane, the routine is pretty much as it used to be: weather briefing, mill right, file a flight plan, mill left, latrine call, stand and wait, pick up flight lunches, shuffle aboard the blue bus.

Today we will be flying aircraft 0010—called "Balls Ten"—crewed by Staff Sergeant Randell Baker, who affectionately named the bomber *Lady Sundown*. His name and the title are stenciled on the left side of the fuselage, above the entrance.

Like shaking hands with an old friend, I run a palm along the slick white paint that covers the underside of the bomber. We called it "thermal paint" because it reflected heat and reduced the chances of flash burns from a nuclear-weapon detonation. As if…

The B-52 is the heaviest and most powerful bomber America ever built. It grosses out at over 500,000 pounds, more than double the gross weight of a B-47 and 100,000 pounds more than the B-1. The B-52's drooping wings span 185 feet and provide 4000 square feet of lifting surface. Walking beneath a wing, I am under an aluminum overcast.

From long-ago habit, I stroll back and check the bomb bay. For practice bomb runs on training flights, the bomb bay doors are cycled. Therefore, nothing that could accidentally be dropped should be loose inside the bomb bay, which is 30 feet long, as wide and as high as the airplane. The top of the aircraft's fuselage stands nearly two stories tall; the tail towers over four stories. Despite its size, however, the bomber is still smaller than a Boeing 747 Jumbo Jet.

I walk forward and kick one of the four tires on the front main landing gear, part of a double-truck/two-outrigger configuration. The tire is as tall as I am.

An old rhyme comes to mind: Kick the tires and light the fires. Time to saddle up.

A body enters a B-52 through a hatch in the belly: crouch, duck under the fuselage, then stand up with head and shoulders wrapped in blackness. I'm home again. The first deck, approximately four feet off the ground, is a compartment where radar-bombardier and navigator sit side by side, the place where I used to ride. The two-man nav team now is called The Offense.

Behind their stations, a vertical six-foot ladder that has a fireman's pole attached for quick egress leads to the flight deck. Up there, aft of the ladder and facing aft sits The Defense: electronic warfare officer and enlisted gunner.

The last of this venerable line of bombers, the H-model is much more confining than the C-model aluminum cloud in which I floated around. Areas I remembered as wide-open spaces are now stuffed with equipment. For example, in the C-model the navigators had control panels scattered in front of them, with a few to the left of the radar position. Today's H-model navs are enveloped in electronic gear: an unbroken wall of black boxes faces them, curves around on both sides of them, descends from overhead. A claustrophobic wouldn't last ten seconds in there.

The rest of the aircraft interior reminds me of a wholesale electronic warehouse with black boxes piled upon black boxes. Over the years, the H-model has been systematically packed with newer and newer equipment to keep it survivable in a constantly changing combat arena.

After banging my head a couple times on unfamiliar projections, I reach the flight deck. I move forward and twist my way into the instructor pilot seat, located between and slightly aft of the pilot and copilot seats. Along with front, side, center, and overhead instrument panels, the three of us fill the first ten feet of the airplane's nose. Inside this 157-foot-long airframe capable of carrying enough fuel to give it a range of 12,000 miles—halfway around the globe—along with enough firepower to obliterate Texas, each crewman is bound into an ejection seat that occupies a space roughly three feet by three feet by three feet. My makeshift seat is a metal folding chair. If ordered to bail out, my procedure is to hustle downstairs and roll out one of the openings created by the navigators who eject downward. The other four men fire upward. In the design of warplanes, comfort is not a critical criterion. Ironically, man is both the most and least important cargo. Wedged into my seat, my thousands of hours of flying experience involuntarily come back in a rush. My fingers take over and, with nimbleness that surprises and pleases me, they connect the hoses, wires, and straps for oxygen, interphone, and parachute. Do my fingers activate the equipment or does the equipment activate my fingers?

At first sight, my acceptance of Captain Brooks Tyler's six-man crew was hesitant. Every one of these guys is young enough to be my son, I thought. At 29 and the crew's oldest member, Tyler has the clean-cut, all-American good looks of Christopher Reeves, a la Clark Kent, right down to the horn-rimmed glasses. As if to complete the comparison, his skill and confidence in flight approach the dynamics of Superman. More about that later.

Each of the other four officers is 26, and the gunner is 23. Inside the bomber the men become ageless.

Tyler's copilot, Lieutenant Rod Gillis, is a smooth-faced, seemingly worriless, young man who soon will be promoted to captain and who stands fourth in the 96th Bomb Wing line to upgrade to aircraft commander. Tyler continually preps Gillis, primes him for what is to come next. Although Tyler has not been shot at in anger, he instinctively understands that in combat, or in an emergency, a crew's best insurance policy is a highly qualified copilot.

The two pilots flip through the preflight, start engine, and taxi checklists with ease born of repetition. For my benefit, they explain the latest equipment. I understand a lot about the movements performed by Tyler and Gillis because, two days earlier, Major Charles Brown, 337th Bomb Squadron Operations Officer, instructed me on the procedures while I flew a mock-up of the B-52. He crammed a dozen years of experience into two hours of simulated flight—an experience similar to studying marine biology on water skis.

My ego took a hit when I crashed the B-52 flight simulator on landing approach. Just manhandled the hulk onto the rocks—KRUMPH. But, by then, Brown had me struggling along with three of the four right-hand engines inoperative. "Anybody can fly when everything goes right," Brown said happily. "It's when things come apart that we earn our money."

Tyler taxies the bomber to a holding position a hundred feet short of the active runway, and Rod Gillis asks tower for clearance to roll. "Wait," the navigator calls, "we're two minutes early." Because control times dot our route, the nav prefers to start even, so we sit and watch the long hand creep away the time. Then Gillis gets another clearance.

Tyler shoves the eight throttles forward to start the big bird rolling and veers left onto the runway. Every SAC takeoff mimics an Emergency War Order (EWO) "rolling takeoff" launch in which pilots gang-start engines, race for the runway, and take off with minimum interval between actions and airplanes.

A few minutes earlier, Tyler had hooked a $1200 pltz (pronounced "plizzit") to his camouflaged helmet. The pltz is a white face plate that makes him look like a storm trooper from *Star Wars*. With lenses made from 21 layers of polarized lead-lanthanum zirconate-titanate ceramic, the pltz avoids flash blindness by turning opaque so quickly under intense light that the light rays do not reach the eyeballs of the person wearing the device. When the threat dims, the lenses fade to transparent. Each Alert bomber provides the face plates for pilot and copilot, who don them before takeoff and air-to-air refueling—times when the flash curtains are down. A gee-whiz device such as the pltz was wishful thinking when

I was in SAC. Prior to hooking on the pltz, Tyler admitted, "I haven't flown with this before, but with you along, I thought today was as good as any to try it."

As the bomber rolls onto the runway, Tyler cautions Gillis, "Make sure you're on the yoke with me in case this thing blacks out." Gillis gives a thumb-up and the bomber accelerates rapidly.

The plane lifts off before I can say, "General Curtis E. LeMay." Half the runway is in front of us and we climb like a homesick angel. Far below EWO gross weight, which exceeds 500,000 pounds, the airframe barely challenges the eight turbofan engines, each generating 17,000-pounds of thrust. We aren't using 100 percent power, I notice (the old C-model engine provided only 7500 pounds of thrust, and most of the runway was behind the bomber when it broke ground). *Lady Sundown's* engines whisper of untapped strength, assure us that more power is available when desired.

With a pale-blue West-Texas morning in front of us and clearance from control, we beeline to the Gulf of Mexico and coast out near Houston. Newly formed cumulus clouds litter our path. In the distance a few approach cumulonimbus proportions, hinting of anvil heads, billowing ominously outward at the top.

Dramatizing the moment, I daydream that the clouds are mushroom-shaped, envision grim rising sculptures of nuclear finality. This is how it will appear outbound across the United States if SAC bombers launch under missile attack. I recognize my having seen this vision before, in veiled valleys of nighttime dreams. Despite my background, I am psychologically chilled by the role a SAC bomber crewman plays in America's defense. I recognize I once played an identical role, a role taken for granted, a role that no longer counts. Back then I was another man in another life. Like an innocent seeing this for the first time, I have a new and frightening respect for ranks of faceless bomber crewmen.

It dawns on me that, in a thermonuclear battle, bomber crewmen might be the only warriors to see Soviet soil, to fight on the enemy's home ground. By comparison, air force intercontinental ballistic missile (ICBM) launch crews that hide deep inside hardened command posts and navy nuclear submarine crews that cruise ocean bottoms are snipers, lurking shadows that push buttons to shatter a world from which they are exiled. Try to sell that image to ICBM and SLBM (submarine-launched ballistic missile) crews, I think. Yet, somewhere in my elementary reasoning, I finger an atom of truth: bomber crews are special. I know that B-52s contribute 45 percent of the total megatonnage of the strategic triad of ICBMs, SLBMs, and bombers.

We slip into a controlled area called Pelican Bravo. Oak Grove, an early warning/ground control intercept radar site near Houston, grabs our electronic echo and vectors a pair of F-4 Phantom jets toward us. At 30,000 feet altitude, in the imaginary cage of a controlled area, we are not in a favorable position. Against fighters a bomber wants to zigzag low, very low.

Despite our handicap, the war is joined.

Side by side at the aft end of the flight deck, Lieutenant Stu Shartzer and Airman First Class Frank Serra sit in front of a 12-foot-wide, black-face console that reminds me of a miniature recording studio. Shartzer faces stacks of at least two dozen transmitters and receivers, automatic as well as manual systems.

Both Shartzer and Serra are short and trim, as if designed to fit inside the cockpit as snugly as their electronic gear. Shartzer appears to be the cooler of the two, waiting with the patience of a professional athlete who reserves strength until competition begins. His compactness reminds me of a gymnast. To his right, Serra bounces with the nervous energy of a Golden Gloves lightweight who has just vaulted into the ring. I get two impressions: Shartzer is oblivious to my presence behind him; Serra wants to show me how good he is.

Shartzer stares at the world's largest oscilloscope, one with multiple traces, a device that reads the electromagnetic spectrum from pi to infinity. Every second or three, he puts a grease-pencil tick on the face of the scope, plays a game for which I have no training. Things on his console blink and Shartzer croons, "Got a lock, eleven o'clock." A black box recognizes that one of the fighter's radar has found us.

"Dump chaff, dump chaff," Serra shouts. Chaff is strips of metallic foil cut into various lengths. When dispensed into the air it confuses enemy radar by creating spurious images. Moments later, Serra calls, "Turn right, turn right, pilot."

Brooks Tyler sights the foe visually and reports, "I got a fighter, eleven high."

"Break left," Serra orders. Tyler rolls the plane into a 45-degree bank while Serra tells Shartzer, "Dump chaff, all you got."

The console starts blinking like a game of "Missile Command" gone amok.

Shartzer and Serra catch a mutual downbeat and begin to play the console with the skill and agility of two concert pianists performing a duet.

"Lock, seven o'clock," Shartzer says. His fingers fly across the console, shoot streams of chaff, double-clutch tiny black boxes that are no part of my world—actions designed to negate the fighter threat. At the same time, like a silent third partner to The Defense, auto-jammers kick in and out of gear, wink on and off, provide overlapping protection that kills threats still unborn. Their unpredictable tempo reminds me of a complicated missile-age metronome.

"Dump more, don't give him a chance to get position," Serra urges.

"Don't know where he's coming from," Shartzer says.

"Lock, pilot," Serra calls. Auto-jammers glow. Chaff twinkles. "Broke it."

Talking, pointing, waving, passing the lead back and forth, acquiescing to the other's demands, each man displays the consummate artistry of a maestro. Together, they conduct a soundless symphony of survival.

The fight continues for nearly an hour and, gradually, time between attacks grows shorter and shorter. Inside the bomber, the tempo increases, reaches frenzy when the fighters trap us against the invisible eastern wall of Pelican Bravo.

"Lock, nine. Start a left turn," Shartzer says.

Serra orders, "Break left."

"Chaff out."

"Broke lock."

"Lock again," Shartzer corrects. "Continue turn."

"Broke lock," Serra says.

"Eleven o'clock," Rod Gillis warns.

Tyler acknowledges the sighting and starts descending in the turn.

"Two locks, nine and six," Shartzer says.

"Broke one."

"Nine and six again."

"Closing at six," Serra sings out, like a chant of doom. Directly behind us, the heat of our engine exhausts forms an enormous target for a fighter's infrared-seeking weapons. An air-to-air missile up the tail is imminent.

The airframe hums. Tyler is pulling Gs, descending, tightening his turn into the enemy, sharpening the attack angle, straining to out-perform the fighter's computer's capacity.

"Closing, six o'clock, two miles," Serra says. If this struggle were real, the fighter would fire about now.

Over interplane radio frequency, a Phantom pilot carols, "That's it. Thanks, guys." After all his labor, he sounds as if he finally got a missile-launch indication. The electronic battle is ended. "Time to RTB" (return to base), he tells us with satisfaction in his tone.

"Quit while you're ahead," I think and ask Serra, "Did you get a shot at him?"

In its tail, the B-52H has a 20-mm Vulcan cannon capable of grinding out 3000 rounds per minute.

Serra shakes his head. With less disappointment in his face than I expect to see, he says, "They didn't come close enough."

Why doesn't the B-52 carry defensive missiles? I wonder. There isn't time for discussion while on a training mission, however. Coasting in from the Gulf, we head for our air refueling control point.

For me, air-to-air refueling had a space-age quality before man reached the space age, well before Sputnik attained its surprising orbit. The concept of pulling into position beneath an aluminum gas station drifting in the blue fit my Buck Rogers-bred vision of the future (SAC has been conducting aerial refueling operations since the KB-29 joined the command in 1948, but not until the operation involved purely jets did it take on an ethereal quality). The rendezvous maneuver alone has its own fascination and employs various patterns. Using the classic one, a tanker offsets from the refueling track and heads toward a receiver. At a set separation distance, the tanker executes a 180-degree turn and, if all is flown precisely, rolls out on course two miles in front of the receiver.

Now, inside *Lady Sundown*, six eyes eagerly scan the sky for first glimpse of a KC-135 Stratotanker. The navigators in both airplanes have been in electronic contact for many minutes. On radar, using beacon transmitters, the navs generally locate each other at 100–200 miles' separation. Once, by using radar sweep delay, I found a tanker beacon 400 miles away.

Tyler and Gillis spot the tanker at the same instant, point out a distant speck in the high, clear sky. We close rapidly. The tanker enters its turn and soars across our left windscreen like a silver bird, rolls level slightly right of track, then eases left and finishes directly in front of us. The bomber slowly closes the distance. The tanker grows in size until its wings overlap our center windshield.

At that point the tanker's boom operator normally takes charge, coaxes the bomber pilot forward until the two airplanes became one, linked with a winged silver shaft that pumps endurance, range, and survival. When the tanker boom thrusts home, it locks into the bomber's receptacle with a clanking thud, the solid sound of two metallic monsters touching in greeting.

Brooks Tyler needs no words from the boom operator. He drives into the linkup with fluid grace, holds position so effortlessly that both aircraft hang motionless in space. Time stops. The tanker floats an arm length away. The only noise is the subliminal race of jet engines, the flow of high-altitude slipstreams, the silvery silence of air-breathing weapon systems.

Tyler calls for a disconnect, backs off, and tells Gillis to do it. Copilots get little refueling practice, and so the routine becomes less routine. The difference in pilot technique is evident—like the difference between the graceful, gliding, major-league play of Ozzie Smith compared to that of a heavy-footed college shortstop. Gillis's movements are choppy, half a beat behind what is required. I relive my spastic reactions in the B-52 flight simulator and empathize with Gillis.

Like an infielder bolstering a nervous pitcher, Tyler speaks encouragement: "Stop the movement first. Stabilize." Gillis levels the airplane and Tyler says, "Now, move in." Gillis advances the throttles and approaches the tanker. "Don't forget to relax, Rod. Wiggle your toes. Breathe." And, as if the words are incantations—Contact.

Within moments Gillis is laboring over the throttles and yoke. We disconnect. The tanker climbs away from us. "Where the hell's he going?" Gillis asks.

"Nowhere," Tyler says quietly. "You're continuing to pull the power off." In reality the throttled-back bomber is dropping away from the tanker that holds a constant altitude, airspeed, and heading. The spatial disorientation fooled me as much as it fooled Gillis.

Tyler takes control, drives back into the tanker's envelope, says, "You almost have to fight to get out of position once you get inside here," and gives the bomber back to Gillis. "Half the energy," Tyler whispers. "Easy. Easy."

Gillis makes contact and holds it. He grasps the controls gently. "I'm more relaxed now," he says. "Don't have that death grip on the yoke."

"Gaze at the whole aircraft," says Tyler. "Look around. Check his lights." Located on the underside of the tanker's fuselage, two parallel rows of directional lights display the bomber's position relative to the boom's limits. Some pilots use them, some don't. Gillis apparently doesn't. After a few smooth minutes, Tyler warns him, "You're holding left."

Gillis jerks the yoke from side to side. We remain hooked up. In fact, despite Gillis's abrupt movements, the bomber hardly changes position relative to the tanker.

"Take it back in small increments," Tyler hints.

Gillis carefully tilts the yoke right, lines up nicely.

More minutes pass. I have been leaning forward, supplying body English. Now my legs and buttocks are numb. Sympathy cramps creep into my arm and neck muscles. "Don't forget to relax, Hank," I tell myself. "Wiggle your toes. Breathe."

The secret behind Tyler's coaching is its lack of rivalry. It contains no conflict of personalities. His goal is to communicate understanding, to share perfection. He teaches like a much older and experienced person, a man who is passing the torch. How did he get it together at such a young age?

Gillis slumps a bit and appears to be tiring. Tyler takes back control of the bomber and holds position so delicately that I stare up at the tanker and, again, time and motion stop. I experience the marvel of being enfolded in a protective cradle formed by the tanker's swept wings. In some unexplainable way I sense a regeneration of body and of spirit: I shed a quarter century in an instant. Around me the sky shines dazzling blue, shimmers crisply. I feel electricity in the air. I have rejoined the eagles, am once again a young vibrant warrior, if but for the moment. The majesty of the sensation is overpowering. The tanker blurs in my vision. I bow my head and wipe my nose. Impulsively, I punch Tyler's shoulder and hoarsely shout, "You got the best job in the whole world."

He frowns at me, questioningly.

We have reached the end of the refueling track. The boom operator initiates a breakaway. Tyler cuts throttles to idle. The tanker accelerates and climbs rapidly, making the bomber appear to drop like a shot bird. Again, it is an illusion, the opposite of what we experienced before. This time the bomber is holding altitude. Then Tyler leans on the yoke and we do drop like a shot bird.

In his poem "Invictus," Bill Henley could have been describing the B-52 navigators' milieu when he wrote "Black as the Pit from pole to pole." Below the flight deck, once the entrance hatch slams shut, the navigators' compartment becomes a tomb of absolute night, untouched by light from sun, moon, or stars. Lowering myself from the flight deck, I sink into this chamber, instantly recall that the navs are always cold, always asking the pilots for more heat. Here I spent nearly a thousand hours of my youth.

In dim red-lighted darkness broken by the thin orange sweeps of radar scopes and the brackish green glow of low-light-level television/ forward-looking infrared monitors, Radar-bombardier Captain Marv Chan and Navigator Lieutenant Ron Pacheco calculate endless time and distance problems. Until now, Chan and Pacheco have been quietly providing headings and times, keeping the airplane within the confines of Pelican Bravo, talking to the tanker navigator to accomplish the rendezvous, gaining a minute here or losing one there to hit control times smack on the nose. During such activities, good navigators go unnoticed by supplying the answers before others think of the questions.

Chan is quiet, introspective, perhaps mentally rehearsing what will come later. The same as most radarmen, he wears glasses. Scope-watching quickly defeats the eyes. Surprisingly, he gives great latitude to Pacheco who appears aggressively eager to control the game. In my days, the radarman–navigator relationship was a Captain Bligh-Mister Christian-type affair. Of course, back then, a wider age, rank, and experience gap existed between men filling the positions. Pacheco soon will be promoted to captain and upgraded to a radar slot. As if designed to match their defensive counterparts, the two men are dark haired and trimly built.

We enter phases of the mission that are the responsibility of The Offense: celestial navigation, low-level evasive maneuvers, and weapons delivery. From end refueling to the H-hour control point, we fly a celestial grid leg, practicing the type of navigation used in polar regions. On the flight deck, Shartzer uses a periscope sextant to shoot lines off a sun invisible to Pacheco. Pacheco compares the sun lines with computer calculations. Chan cross-checks.

Aided by the sophistication of banks of equipment that envelop them, Chan and Pacheco appear to have it too easy. By my ancient standards, they perform twice the work in half the time. However, something of quality is missing. Quicker than hand or eye, the electronic genius of their equipment makes machines equal to men, replaces reason with rote, abases the infinite lure of celestial toil.

When I was a crewman, celestial navigation was an art. A bomber was inherently an unthinking beast of burden. The navigator supplied its brain. In the manner of an old-time accountant bent over aged ledgers, a navigator painstakingly extracted numbers from the yellow pages of Air Almanac and HO-249 sun and star tables, meticulously compared the figures to celestial sightings, manually plotted the differences on a chart, and predicted the bomber's position in space for a future time, minutes ahead. The computations came alive but for an instant, that moment when the aircraft flashed through the predestined point. The death of each solution produced the conception of a new problem. The toil was minor mathematical logic, often performed in one's head with deliberate haste, and dependent upon intuition as much as upon scientific judgment. No computer provided counsel. Ghosts of Prince Henry, Magellan, and Drake flew with navigators back then. But nostalgia doesn't win wars.

Much thanks to computers, celestial accuracy today is indisputably superior to any period in history. Today's worst results match the past's best. For a long time, using pure celestial means, SAC's goal was to deliver a weapon with the accuracy of a radar-guided bomb run. Today it is possible. The same as the pltz, the goal was wishful thinking when I crewed.

We arrive at the H-hour control point exactly on time because Pacheco killed a minute by overflying the previous turn. This control point is critical: if we miss it by more than two minutes, we abort the remainder of the sortie. In combat, it is the point that resolves weapon conflicts.

If we were carrying air-launched cruise missiles (ALCM), we would simulate launching them now. ALCMs fly below the speed of sound, with a range of 1500 nautical miles. They are employed in what SAC originally called a "burn back" tactic but now refers to as "shoot-and-penetrate." ALCMs are fired before the bomber descends and penetrates enemy radar lines at low altitude. A B-52 can carry a dozen ALCMs in external pylons, along with up to eight in the bomb bay. In EWO scenarios, some B-52s act strictly as standoff ALCM-launching platforms.

Today, Tyler's crew is simulating delivery of short-range attack missiles (SRAM) and gravity bombs. At low altitude, the SRAM has supersonic speed and allows the bomber to hit heavily defended targets without overflying them. The SRAM's low-altitude range of 35 miles is greater than that of enemy surface-to-air missiles (SAM). In EWO configuration, the B-52 generally carries eight SRAMs in a rotary launcher, along with four gravity bombs.

Nuclear weapon loads of those sizes overstress my imagination. I had carried no more than four. In a weird sort of mental One-Upmanship, I recall that my four weapons were 2.2 megatons each; today's weapons are only 200 kilotons; and I flew with mine on Airborne Alert, which is no longer routine. Furthermore, I sat Alert with a single 19-megaton weapon. Bombs of that scale are obsolete because war planners have concluded smaller weapons in greater numbers produce more devastating effects. My ridiculous mental game is meaningless. How does anyone truly comprehend the nature-shattering force of any of the loads?

Twenty weapons. A dozen weapons. How do the navigators keep the targets straight in their heads? I understand why Marv Chan is closemouthed. I picture him sick to his stomach, throwing up millions of tiny radar images. Then I recall somebody mentioning that the circle size for an acceptable weapon delivery is now only half as large as the circle at which I used to aim. The logic is irrefutable: smaller weapons demand greater accuracy; greater accuracy allows reduction in weapon size. Conclusion? Today's crews are far more effective.

I haul my body back up to the flight deck and again squeeze in behind the pilots. My left shoulder is raw from the weight of a parachute. My left ear burns from the pressure of the flight helmet the specialists in personal equipment carefully fitted the previous day. However, it takes several flights to find and correct every hot spot in a helmet. We have been airborne four and a half hours. The mission is half over. I steel myself by recalling that I used to strap on this stuff and wear it for 14 hours at a stretch, but the hot spot on my ear doesn't go away.

Before reaching our target area, we must fly a low-altitude route over eastern Colorado. For training, low is defined as two wingspans above the ground—370 feet. For combat, the altitude is 200 feet. At altitudes below 300 feet, a bomber becomes immune to detection by ground-based radar sites that depend on line-of-sight vision. When searching low along the horizon, radar beams are usually interrupted by terrain and man-made structures. Therefore, continuous tracking of a low-flying plane is impossible, and firing problems for surface-to-air missiles or antiaircraft artillery cannot be resolved. By making random course changes in conjunction with low-altitude flying, the bomber crew also outwits computers that predicted an intercept point based on viewing fragmented sections of an aircraft's flight path.

The low-altitude route is navigated primarily by use of low-light-level television and forward-looking infrared. Both sensors see in the dark. They present pictures of the terrain ahead on video monitors located at the pilot, copilot, radar, and navigator positions. Steering, altitude, and timing data are superimposed on the pictures, allowing the pilots to watch the screen at all times. The B-52 pilots fly terrain avoidance rather than terrain following: that is, they manually steer the airplane around and over obstacles rather than relying on computers to hug contours for them.

Legend has it a bunch of veteran Boeing test hands once put up the flash curtains and flew an entire combat profile—from takeoff, through refueling and low-level and bombing, to landing—using only television and infrared guidance. I have heard the tale and, before Tyler or Gillis can tell it, I point to the monitors and ask, "You think you two could fly the entire mission, takeoff to landing, using just those?"

"The refueling will be a little difficult," Tyler says, and Gillis relates the legend of the old Boeing hands.

In descent to the low-altitude route entry point, white lines on the green forward-looking television and infrared monitor screens doodle rapidly, drawing contours of a big-city skyline and then the Rocky Mountains. Is it trying to tell us something? Tyler and Gillis ignore what I find entertaining. As we pass through 6000 feet altitude, the white traces level and skyscrapers and mountains recede, reforming into shapes that conform with terrain ahead.

Now comes the part of the mission that is more intense and exciting than a day at Disney World—low-altitude penetration in a B-52 Stratofortress. For three hours we race at 400 knots airspeed, only 300–400 feet above eastern Colorado. Our flight resembles speeding along the edge of a cliff on a road with no guardrail. Every detail of the ground looms up and appears exaggerated. The television and infrared monitors further light the already bright day. Crews fly these routes at night and at the same altitude, I have been told—a factual rather than boastful declaration. Down low the world flashes by, and moments are stamped into my memory.

The first time we whip through a turn in a 30-degree bank, I stretch forward and search for the downside wing tip. My mind reflexively asks, "How close is it to the ground?" Cognizant of the problem, SAC planners added a graph to the B-52 Flight Manual that shows the maximum bank angle at any altitude right down to ground level. Pilot teams are required to memorize the graph.

At eye-level, a herd of sun-bleached cows glances blindly toward us, staggers sideways out of our path. Do the animals recognize this giant bird from previous days?

A pickup truck on a dirt road spirals dust upward, races to intercept our oncoming nose. The driver leans out the window, watching us, obviously knowing we fly this route. Is he playing a jet-age game of Beat the Train to the Crossing?

A red hang glider appears to our right, at our altitude, motionless. "Hope he doesn't go behind us," Gillis says as we roar by the fragile craft. If the glider pilot flew into the vortex of our jets, he probably experienced the ride of his life, a thrill he perhaps sought.

Tyler, Gillis, Chan, and Pacheco converse briefly, act as one person in solving the problem of keeping the bomber on course. They engage in no idle interphone chatter, a mark of true professionals.

Ground-effect vibrations massage my stomach. The sensation goes unnoticed as long as one is busy performing duties but, with my mind unoccupied, I have time to think about the clamminess spreading over me, and about the ham sandwich and fruit juice I rammed down a short while ago. I am thankful I missed the pancakes. Never having yawned in Technicolor on board an airplane, I resolve not to break my streak today. I grit my teeth and, to neutralize the upset, clamp on my mask and snort 100 percent oxygen. It cools me, settles my stomach, peps me up. Laughing at my frailty also helps.

I acclimated to the altitude and think about pressing lower, wonder how dangerous the landscape would appear from 200 feet. From 100 feet? Even lower?

We make the final turn and line up for La Junta strategic combat range, a ground radar complex for scoring simulated weapon releases. We climb to 600 feet so that the site can find us.

The previous day Captain Ken Wilkerson, Chief of Domestic Target Study, briefed Tyler's crew on its target assignments. He used maps and hand drawn predictions of television and radar pictures. Afterward he told me, "We no longer spend hours—as you probably did—in studying radar scope photography. Today's planning parallels EWO activity. After all, we don't have rolls of footage on Soviet targets. And a lot of the

EWO targets are no-show on radar. Of course, the computers are more accurate today, automatically put the crosshairs on offset points that you had to search for." In the old days, computers accepted data for one target at a time, and navigators had to constantly update information. Today's computers bank practically an entire mission. When the navs want to locate or identify a landmark or target, they press a button and the computers find the spot.

Wilkerson took me into a viewing room and showed me radar photography of a recent run on La Junta. To the untrained eye, a city or man-made cluster of structures appears on radar as a glob of light, an illuminated Rorschach blot that blurs into pinwheels of flashing dots. To the eye of a radarman, each complex forms a distinctive pattern. Like a connoisseur of Persian rugs, a radarman sees patterns within a pattern and focuses on interior designs that lead to a street and to a specific building, that pinpoint a designated corner of that building. While Wilkerson briefed me, I stared at La Junta until it was etched into my brain, symbolized every target in the world. With cold, bitter, timeless vision, I recognized that I possessed an inescapable talent for finding and putting a weapon exactly on any target. For the first time, I wondered: Would I if I were ordered to do so today? I felt as if I accidentally had encountered a forgotten love that I no longer desired. Nothing remained to prove.

On our initial pass abeam La Junta, Rod Gillis makes the first release visually, simulates a gravity bomb drop on the northernmost intersections of dirt runways at an abandoned triangular-shaped airfield. Unfortunately, Gillis doesn't locate the overgrown target until we are a mile or two from it. We are right of course, and he is forced to bank sharply. When we fly directly over the runway, he shouts, "Hack," and Chan simulates a bomb drop with an electronic tone. The aerial swerve throws us far off heading for the second release point and, immediately after the first bomb drop, Brooks Tyler calls, "I have it," and banks the aircraft sharply in the opposite direction. The horizon tilts precariously.

Below deck, Ron Pacheco updates the coordinates in his SRAM present-position computer at the instant Gillis calls "Hack." The computer provides steering for the next three weapon releases—three

SRAM launches made by Pacheco with help from Marv Chan. The two navigators race through checklists, talking so rapidly that I recognize nothing they say. Their words and the duties associated with them are foreign to me.

The SRAM releases come one minute apart. As backup, in case the computer malfunctions, Gillis and Stu Shartzer hack and rehack stopwatches with the dexterity of old time Olympic track judges. Voices that I don't recognize are calling numbers that have no meaning. Between the first and second SRAM launches, Tyler swings the bomber 21 degrees right, still compensating for Gillis' large last-second correction on the visual release. From there, Tyler flies straight to the final SRAM drop. As if whirling in free fall, I experience twinges of anxiety and guilt for not understanding all that happens.

While the bombing takes place, Shartzer counterpunches his way through the electronic jabs of SAM and antiaircraft-artillery tracking radars. His fight is a non-stop series of rounds: detect, jam, counter, jam; detect, jam, counter, jam....

Wild, wild, wild, I think and rank the bomb run as the most aggressive peacetime flying in my experience.

We racetrack left, return to the initial point, and line up for another run on the strategic combat range. This time we depend on Chan to perform a triple synchronous radar release with SRAM. I laugh out loud. The program sounds more like Olympic diving than strategic bombing. We bomb the first target exactly on the desired axis of attack, turn right 11 degrees, drop on target two, alter left five degrees, drop on three; 30 seconds later Pacheco fires the SRAM. The interval from first to last release is 175 seconds. The radar site scores us reliable on all activity.

We climb back to altitude for the jog home to Dyess, and the 25 years I lost earlier now falls on me from nowhere, hits like a megaton of bricks. We have been airborne eight hours and my parachute hangs like the weight of another person on my back. My left ear is numb. Three days from now I will still have knots on my head from other helmet hot spots.

Eager as two boys heading for recess, Tyler and Gillis discuss the hour of low approaches they are about to begin—go-arounds, simulated engine-out patterns, various other pilot feats, the works.

I nose dive into my oxygen mask and steal precious minutes of sleep more refreshing than any post-coital nap. When I am jarred back to reality, the airplane is lined up with the Dyess runway for the third, fourth, or fifth (?) time. I crane my neck and check the clock on Gillis's instrument panel: 40 more minutes. I shift left, then right, attempt to wiggle life back into my cheeks. I recall Colonel John Puckropp, the Director of Operations, mentioning a three-cushion mission. I have three. They aren't enough.

Time passes and Tyler announces to the tower, "This will be a full stop." I cheer. In response, Tyler tells Gillis, "Or should we ask for a one-hour extension, shoot a few more go-arounds."

Gillis shakes a fist of approval.

"Let's find a tanker and fly all night," I say.

We land, taxi, park, and are practically dragged from the airplane and shoved off the flight line. Armed guards, refueling and maintenance crews, loading teams swarm over *Lady Sundown*. They are conducting practice regeneration, a simulated relaunch. Inert SRAMs in a rotary launcher and gravity bombs in cluster sit poised on hydraulic lifters to be jacked into the bomb bay so that the aircraft can theoretically fly away within the hour and head for another complex of targets.

A new crew would obviously fly the next mission, I think. But when I look around the bus and study the faces of the six men I just flew with, they look as fresh and alert as when we drove out to the bomber 11 hours earlier. Instinctively I know that, if it were war, they would be at some remote post-strike base and another crew would not be available. As soon as the plane was loaded, these six warriors would do it all again.

★ ★ ★

With the end of the Soviet Union, SAC's Alert plan went into mothballs. Since then America's bomber fleet has continually decreased in size and the threat of a nuclear-weapon exchange has significantly diminished. Today's worry is a rogue nation delivery of a thermonuclear weapon to one of our cities by way of a container ship or other crafty means. In their time, bomber crews on Alert served a distinct purpose matched by crewmen in missile silos and in nuclear submarines: they were men ready to make war instantly. The Alert program that started in 1957 continued until the dissolution of the Soviet Union in 1991. In 1992, the United States deactivated SAC and assigned its forces to the newly formed Air Combat Command (ACC). In 2010, all B-52s were transferred from the ACC to the new Air Force Global Strike Command. Based on my visit with the 96th Bomb Wing at Dyess AFB in 1985, the following is an account of how SAC crews lived in the latter stages of the Cold War.

★ ★ ★

As tense as sprinters poised in the blocks at a starting line, bomber and tanker crews waited with coiled fury in Alert bunkers alongside SAC runways. At a practice Start Engine scramble that I witnessed at Dyess AFB, the entire Alert Force—B-52H bombers and KC-135 tankers— were ready to taxi three minutes after klaxons alerted the crewmen. Crews did not know a practice scramble from the real things. "When we hit the plane, it's controlled chaos," a tanker crewman explained to me. "People are copying and exchanging information faster than buyers at the New York Stock Exchange. But everything's done with precision."

Under war conditions, bombers took off at 15-second intervals. Following the last bomber, the tankers paused for 30-seconds to allow the river of jet turbulence generated by the eight-engine monsters to subside, and then the tankers rolled, with 15-second spacing—or less.

In a 1981 no-notice exercise—the largest in SAC history—400 bombers and tankers conducted simultaneous "positive control" launches (meaning crews could not fly beyond a designated point unless they received a "go code" that authorized them to penetrate enemy airspace and expend weapons) from 70 locations in the continental United States. The entire fleet was airborne within minutes.

Advanced stages of world tension dictated activation of an Alert Aircraft Repositioning Plan (AARP) that reduced crew reaction time. In that configuration, bombers and tankers lined up adjacent to the runway and men lived inside them. Crews practiced AARP on *Global Shield* exercises. "Like practicing being buried alive" was how one navigator described the experience.

"I spent more than two whole days in an airplane," a bomber pilot told me.

"Did that build a little character?" I asked.

He rolled his eyes. "Usually, on exercises, we catch twelve-hour shifts. Two crews swap between a plane and the Alert bunker. You sleep in the bunker."

"You can't go home to sleep?" I said.

With another roll of his eyes, he let me know I wasn't seeing the Big Picture. "Nobody goes home until everything is over," he said.

Under normal Alert conditions for one week out of three, a SAC crewman ate and slept in a bunker 50 yards from his warplane. His schedule was composed three months in advance, printed in grease pencil on a wall-size Plexiglas board. The Alert dates could as well have been cut into stone. No excuse changed them. Alert duty was the primary task of bomber and tanker crews.

★ ★ ★

SAC crews believed in their mission and equipment. At a rap session in the Alert facility, I baited them about their task. They good-naturedly stood their ground. Well, almost good-naturedly.

"You guys are flying airplanes that are older than some of you," I said. That produced a few frowns (the first H-model B-52 was delivered to SAC on 9 May 1961 and the last on 26 October 1962; now, the youngest H-model was 22 years old). "You think you'll make it to your targets?" I said.

A pregnant pause seemed to increase the air pressure in the room.

"The H-model can penetrate defenses, and can deliver weapons on-target, and can survive for relaunch," said aircraft commander Captain Joe Culpepper. I got the impression Culpepper had been through the argument before, had exhausted his patience with ignorant people that started it.

"We can sneak in anywhere," copilot Lieutenant Mark Dibrell said. "Out at *Red Flag* [a no-holds-barred war game in Nevada], we beat fighters time after time, and they know when we're coming."

Navigator Lieutenant Julio Sotomayor backed him. "We fly right on the black line so they have a chance to find us. In the bar, after one mission, some fighter jock comes over and goes, 'We shot you down.' I told him the truth: 'You're right, but we were Number Three. And we were already rid of our weapons. We were a decoy. You didn't see One and Two. They got through and blew up everything you own.'"

Culpepper nodded. "All you need to ask a fighter pilot is how many hours of flying time he has within two wingspans of the ground."

"And at night. And in the mountains," Sotomayor added.

"That shuts them up," Dibrell said. "They don't want to play down where we live."

Where the bombers lived, or rather, survived—in that narrow band below radar coverage—was a different world.

★ ★ ★

The Alert facility was a different world, too. Living within an atmosphere ripe with the aura of imminent destruction had the potential to become psychologically debilitating. SAC planners recognized the stress and created programs to keep crewmen from falling into a mental abyss.

One program was a command-wide refurbishing of Alert living quarters, most of which were more than 20-years-old. The program started at Dyess. Alterations there made the rooms in the half-buried Alert bunker more spacious and brighter. A flashback struck me when I walked through the building. I recalled that, shortly after it opened in 1959, several crewmen complained that the windowless, underground rooms were overly confined. In answer, a staff type pasted panoramic scenes of mountains and lakes in the center of the largest wall in each room. He framed the scenes with drapes. A few crewmen went through the routine of closing the drapes at night and opening them in the morning. Although a sauna and weight room had been added, the cinder-block building remained austere by civilian standards. No Congressman would have lived in it for more than a day—if that long. The structure reminded me of a clean, low-scale motel, with the bathroom down the hall.

A Visitation Center stood adjacent to the Alert bunker, a place where a crewman could spend time with his family. The Center included a tiny swimming pool, a playground, outdoor barbecue and dining area, and a modest-sized building with a large central lounge and three individual television rooms that could be privately reserved for two hours at a time.

Sight of the Center filled my mind with a cool night in the early sixties outside the Bergstrom Air Force Base Alert facility. Gray-haired Major Jim Ready came trudging in from the parking lot beyond the fence and stopped beside me on an access ramp. Sharing my view of the bright Texas stars, he said, "When I got out of high school, I thought I was finished with doing it in a car." He shuffled off to his room. His words became my Quote of the Month.

Now, the visiting wife of a crewmember told me, "In a way, this is like being back in high school. You have a date, then at the end of the evening, each of you go to separate homes."

The Visitation Center had a curfew of 11 o'clock on weekdays, but extended it to midnight on weekends. Shades of Penn State.

★ ★ ★

Fliers and their wives were not far removed from school days and curfews. Youth pervaded the crew force. The 200 combat qualified fliers of the 96th Bomb Wing were primarily lieutenants and captains. The officer roster listed 18 majors, 65 captains, and 77 lieutenants. Among enlisted gunners and boom operators, 18 of 40 were staff sergeants, with 9 above that grade and 13 below.

"We balance the experience," Captain Eric Conrad, a KC-135 aircraft commander, explained to me. "I'm an instructor pilot and I was just assigned a second lieutenant navigator, a new man in the squadron. My former nav was assigned to a pilot who just upgraded to aircraft commander."

When I flew with Conrad's tanker crew, our receiver had a maintenance problem that delayed the pre-planned mission for four hours. Not many minutes later, we were scrambled to the tanker and launched on an alternate route.

Irked, I figured somebody had screwed up. Conrad cooled me by saying, "We're going to fly. That's what counts." The same as most of the guys I met, Conrad's positive attitude grew infectious. He told me, "An Air Force career just isn't long enough to do all the good things there are to do."

On board the tanker, Conrad provided encouragement and guidance while his copilot and navigator, Lieutenants Rich Galiata and Brian McGhee, replanned faster than Magellan could have done on his best day—before losing his head to Lapulapu. Boom operator Staff Sergeant Jim Hall, joined in the planning. I felt guilty for doing nothing.

The same as bomber crews who were expected to reach their targets even if they ran out of gas at bomb release, tanker crews were expected to give everything when the situation demanded. Tanker crewmen understood the fuel they carried belonged to the bombers they serviced. Tankers were expected to gas up a bomber to the maximum, even if it meant their airplane would be out of fuel and crash land after completing the offload.

★ ★ ★

The irrepressible vigor of youth provided its own touches of comic relief to a world-shattering occupation. Practical jokes were limitless among SAC crewmen as a B-52 copilot on his first Alert tour learned. His aircraft commander had him sign a hand receipt for a packet of "cyanide" pills disguised to look like candy. "In case you're captured…" and "If torture becomes more than you can stand…" was the aircraft commander's short, cryptic briefing. At the end of the week when the copilot handed back the pills, the aircraft commander unwrapped them, popped them into his mouth, chewed, and reported, "I think this batch has lost its strength."

Another Alert crewman returned to his room and found it bare. After a search, he located his furniture rearranged in the middle of the parking lot.

Water balloon booby traps were as common as car bombs in Beirut.

A popular trick took place at two in the afternoon when the klaxons sounded for the daily maintenance check. Anyone catnapping at that time was fair game. Men quietly gathered behind the sleeper and, at the klaxon's blare, stomped their feet to produce the sound of runners. Almost without exception, the sleeper reflexively leaped to his feet and raced for the door before recognizing the ruse. Walking back into a room filled with the pranksters took nearly as much guts as facing a SAM.

From the beginning, a klaxon has been Big Brother to Alert crewmen. It spoke, they jumped. Years ago in England, the Greenham Common klaxon emitted a faint electronic beep a second before blaring its "Ooooogah." Rooms emptied in that half-breath between whispered beep and dictatorial blare. A klaxon's electronic command overrode all others. If a man was taking a shower and lathered from head to toes when it sounded, he didn't pause to rinse or to turn off the water. Trailing suds, he leaped into flying suit and boots and dashed for his plane. I saw a copilot jump into a flying suit both legs at a time. On Guam, sunbathers caught by the klaxon taxied bombers to takeoff position while wearing bathing suits and boots. Those crewmembers kept extra clothes in the airplane, knowing they had plenty of time to dress after getting off the ground.

I suggested to Major Charles Brown, 337th Bomb Squadron Operations Officer, that inherent in the youthfulness of aircrews was a devil-may-care sense of immortality. Brown reflected and somberly said, "No. Our crews don't have that carefree attitude attributed to fliers. The typical SAC crewman knows he has a tough mission. He has been trained to approach it with deliberateness. His daring is premeditated, a necessary part of accomplishing the strike. Inside a bomber, there is nothing rash or wild or crazy in his behavior. His courage recognizes and squarely faces the challenge, which is the only realistic approach to war on any level."

★ ★ ★

I was permitted entry everywhere but inside the fenced area where the armed Alert aircraft waited. The sincerity with which the Strategic Air Command guards its weapon systems rang true in a minor incident the Sunday afternoon that I arrived at Dyess.

It was dark, cold, and misty. I hadn't been on the base for more than 20 years and my curiosity led me to drive around aimlessly. The place looked deserted except for security policemen patrolling the Alert area, which was fenced by razor-edged concertina wire.

In my eyes, a lone, armed guard walking with head held high a good distance from the Alert aircraft and bunker symbolized all the positive military traits I could image, especially in that weather. I drove as close to him as possible and, without leaving the car, asked to please take his photograph. He raised an eyebrow and whispered, "Sure, sir." I shot three frames.

He reported me as a suspicious person, and minutes later, two air policemen pulled me over to check my credentials.

★ ★ ★

A week with SAC set off a chain reaction of memories. Recollections from my past returned with so much force that waking hours weren't enough time to process them. Memories overlapped and flooded my mind with dreams, created imaginative recombinations of things I once knew or, perhaps, suspected. The dreams became convoluted and revelatory and I began keeping a pencil and tablet on my bed stand to record and better understand them. Come along and pick my brain with me.

My first dream of a series occurs on an enormous laterite red landscape, an endless set fit for a Beckett play, a foreign place surrounded by infinity. I am looking northward when a white flash fills the sky. Recognizing the brightness as a nuclear-weapon burst, I drop into a depression a foot or two lower than the surrounding terrain, curl face down, my head between my knees. A hot blast of rumbling wind pins me against the ground, then after long seconds rolls heavily onward. My only injury is a thermal burn that covers my upper back. Had the depression been deeper, would I have been uninjured? I sit and watch and wait for I know not what. My back throbs. Am I the last man on earth?

In another dream I walk alone on an identical landscape when my left cheek puckers. I touch the spot. A bony point like a rhinoceros horn has grown there. Stroking the horn's bristly surface fascinates me.

My condition is farcical. Is the growth punishment? It does not matter. Burdened with the same physical abnormality, I walk the endless landscape on following nights, believing I am the last man on earth.

Alone in another dream, I realize the world is dead. I hope the destruction is irreversible. There is no right or wrong, no life or death, no meaning to anything. My absolute knowledge is divine.

Less dramatic dreams stuck around for months until they became lucid and I learned to turn them off.

In one dream I am in uniform—blue suit with coat and necktie, not flight suit—alone in a planning room, and awaiting call to fly a B-47 nuclear weapon delivery mission. Puzzled by how I was chosen for the assignment, I know I'm retired but know I must do what is expected of me. I'm anxious about my ability to operate B-47 equipment after years away from it. I sit and wait for instructions that never come.

In the other dream I am walking in a city but meet no people. Deserted streets are parts of downtown Pittsburgh. Half the time I know where I am and then I turn a corner and am lost. I waste a great amount of energy in backtracking. Night after night through repeated mistakes, I learn more and more about the city's layout but reach no destination.

Are those dreams the story of my life?

★ ★ ★

Bear with me, please. The following history lesson is highly appropriate. It is 500 words. You and the world call it "NSC 68: Blueprint for the Cold War." I think of it as "The Script for My Generation."

> In April 1950, working through the United States National Security Council, the Department of State produced NSC 68, a top secret study that delineated America's role in the ongoing cold war with the Soviet Union. During the previous five years, the US had promoted the Truman Doctrine and the Marshall Plan, actions aimed at helping free people to resist communism. The Soviets responded by sealing off Eastern Europe, overthrowing the Czechoslovakian government, and temporarily blockading Berlin. In Asia, Mao Zedong turned China into a communist state. Shortly thereafter in 1949, the US signed the North Atlantic Treaty, pledging to react to an attack on Western Europe as an attack on itself.

Being the sole possessor of atomic weapons validated the US role in NATO; however, within a year, the Soviets successfully tested an atomic bomb and attained a degree of parity with the US. President Harry S. Truman then ordered the NSC to reexamine American objectives in peace and war and relate them to a strategic plan. Secretary of State Dean Acheson tasked Paul H. Nitze to conduct the study, which produced NSC 68. Nitze based much of his thinking on the writing of George F. Kennan and NSC 20/4, both of which supported a policy of "containment" toward the Soviet Union.

Basically, NSC 68 analyzed world conditions by dissecting the difference in fundamental values between the US and "the Kremlin," stressing "we must make ourselves strong" to affirm our values, while fostering a "change in the nature of the Soviet system." It warned that a resort to force was "a last resort for a free society" and that the true struggle was for "men's minds." Containing the expansion of communism became the US goal. NSC 68 viewed the role of military power as serving "the national purpose by deterring an attack upon us," a philosophy that led to the Strategic Air Command motto of "Peace is our profession."

NSC 68 also examined atomic armaments at length: capabilities, stockpiling and use, and international control of atomic energy. The study concluded that atomic weapons compensated for "our present situation of relative unpreparedness in conventional weapons" vis-à-vis the Soviet Union.

In reaching a conclusion, NSC 68 discussed four possible courses of action: continuation of current policies; isolation; war; and a more rapid building up of the political, economic, and military strength of the free world. It emphasized "a more rapid build-up" as the "only course…consistent with progress toward achieving our fundamental purpose." Identifying the "formidable power of the USSR" as "the gravest threat to the security of the United States," NSC 68 advocated a substantial increase in the United States' "general air, ground, and sea strength, atomic capabilities, and air and civilian defenses to deter war and to provide reasonable assurance in the event of war, that it could survive the blow and go on to the eventual attainment of its objectives." Its reasoning set the stage for SAC to pursue the strategy of massive nuclear retaliation, which led to mutual assured destruction, culminating in mutual deterrence between the two super powers.

That's how our baby was born and grew. A 1992 deactivating of the Strategic Air Command had its beginning in 1965 when B-52 bombers undertook tactical support strikes in South Vietnam, Laos, and Cambodia; and meanwhile F-105 and F-4 Tactical Air Command fighter-bombers flew strategic bombing missions against North Vietnam. Those role reversals persisted until December 1972 when President Richard Nixon executed Operation *Linebacker II*, the B-52 bombing of North Vietnam.

At that time, I was the Special Operations Forces liaison officer, working out of Tan Son Nhut for six months under orders that gave me unlimited travel throughout Southeast Asia. During *Linebacker II*, I split my time between Saigon and U-Tapao Royal Thai Air Force Base from where part of the B-52 fleet launched against the North.

At U-Tapao I met guys I knew from past assignments. My memory retains a picture of a dimly lit Officers' Club filled with seriously drinking men in flying suits. An atmosphere of doom prevailed. The men were frightened, stoic, and pissed off about mission demands and tactics. Their discontent paralleled that of fighter pilots who for years had followed the same entry and exit routes to northern targets. In other words, popular sentiment agreed that higher headquarters couldn't plan for shit. One night, word passed among the crowd that a damaged bomber had crashed on landing but only a small group of people left the club to see what was happening. Resignation reigned. Hardly anybody left the club until dawn. One guy of my age and rank said, "You know how it is. Up to now, life has been easy for us. Now we're paying our dues."

Linebacker II cost SAC 15 bombers in 11 nights.

In the midst of the operation, a captain pilot turned in his wings and quit flying rather than go up north.

At Tan Son Nhut, I attended a secret daily staff meeting and watched American generals gloat over photograph collections of the massive damage inflicted on the North Vietnam industrial and transportation infrastructures by the B-52s. One asshole two star who showed up freshly starched at four in the afternoon actually danced with joy.

The generals had less interest or concern for the bombings of Kham Thien shopping district that killed 250 civilians and the destruction of the Bach Mai hospital that killed 28 staff members. Collateral damage was an acceptable accident.

Conjecture suggested that if President Lyndon Johnson had used the B-52 in a strategic role earlier, the war might have ended sooner. However, fearful of losing a B-52, Johnson and Secretary of Defense Robert McNamara—fearful also of losing face—had chosen less costly fighters to strike North Vietnam targets. Their decision altered the philosophy behind our air force structure.

The pulse of the Vietnam War caused SAC's aggressive thermonuclear assured-destruction philosophy to devolve to contentment with deterrence. Simultaneously, fighter jocks' deep-penetration attacks of North Vietnamese strategic targets performed a bomber's job. The jocks paid a heavy and disproportionate toll in losses but gained heroic superiority. Meanwhile, B-52s laboriously obliterated tactical targets such as remote NVA outposts in Laos with few tangible results beyond terrorizing people hiding in the jungle.

My closest experience with a B-52 strike, code named *Arc Light*, happened late in the 1970–1971 dry season in Laos when I filled in on the Night Observation Device (NOD) with a crew of Spectre new guys. Their rookie navigator locked his head up his ass and failed to copy and plot coordinates of an *Arc Light* mission that premeditatedly delivered its load where we casually cruised to hunt trucks. Standing behind the NOD and unblinkingly watching the explosions of an endless stream of bombs that rained through our altitude, I roared for a breakaway maneuver. Death by friendly fire was the ultimate bullshit. I will tell you this: That helplessness experience ate a chunk out of my soul.

Bluntly stated, operations in Vietnam ended separation between "strategic" and "tactical" uses of air power. In *The Air Force Way of War*, Brian D. Laslie examines the decisive final changes relative to the air war over Iraq and Kuwait in the 1990–1991 *Desert Storm* operation. He says *Desert Storm* overturned everything about the way in which air power was traditionally conceived and the 1992 merging of TAC and SAC into the Air Combat Command (ACC) commenced the onset of "theater air war." It was determined that SAC had no role "outside the nuclear realm" and former SAC members seamlessly moved into ACC and reorganized bomber doctrine to fit with the mission the tactical community had been performing for years.

Nowadays a wave of cynicism engulfs me when the United States flies a B-52 over a foreign hot spot as a show of force.

★ ★ ★

One month after the final mission of *Linebacker II*, at four minutes before six o'clock on the sunny morning of 28 January 1973, I awoke in a Tan Son Nhut BOQ room when four mortar rounds impacted on base. We were six hours ahead of Greenwich, where it was nearly midnight and the start of the Vietnam War cease-fire designated by the Paris Peace Agreement. No further rounds followed, but Big Voice kept ordering people to shelters. I rolled over in bed. The North Vietnamese were telling us they hadn't quit, I thought, with a touch of admiration. Two years and three months later, the North completed its conquest of the South.

CHAPTER 13

From Russia, Without Love

Over 1987–1988, Jan and I swapped homes with an English economist who contracted to teach at the University of Texas for a year. He, his wife, and his two sons moved into our humble Austin residence while Jan and I lost ourselves in their three-story home—with a large and fertile garden—in Salisbury. The year taught me why the Brits fell so deeply in love with India and South Africa: those places were warm. I froze my ass in Salisbury, which had four seasons every day. For me, the year's highlight was a trip to the Soviet Union for the 70th anniversary of the Revolution.

★ ★ ★

As if fleeing from the sun, the tiny Aeroflot tri-jet speeds Jan and me from London's brash sunlight to Moscow's stolid darkness. We see nothing on our path across Russia. Thick clouds conceal the terrain, exactly as I anticipated, a strictly radar day. On descending, the only light is reflection of the plane's rotating beacon off clouds that extend nearly to the ground. The jetliner breaks into the clear and its wheels touch down a moment later. Through ground fog, the terminal appears as a blur. Darkened commercial aircraft with Soviet markings dot the icy apron. The airfield looks deserted.

When our plane taxis off the runway, I have a schizophrenic reaction, a duality of mind and soul new to me. I am in a place I know in my bones, far from home yet born of home in that it long had been the target of ruthless calculation. After decades of dreams I have entered the enemy camp, except that I have come as friend, not foe. Is my arrival a form of betrayal? Tears fill my eyes. I am swept by the glow of arrival that a defector must experience when escaping from one life to another, openly surrendering an old allegiance for a new. Do I fleetingly share the emotions of Philby and Burgess and Maclean? Is this the reaction of a traitor? At the same time, I know my melodramatic tears are the product of false pride. As a young man, regardless of the years spent planning to do it, I had not destroyed this city. The Moscow terminal's counters and offices are tightly shut on this Saturday evening. The empty corridors tease my imagination: I think about neutron bombs and vacant cities.

Passport control jerks me back to reality. Unlike passports of the British tourists ahead of me, my American passport stops the line, necessitates a telephone inquiry. A hyper-active ego makes me wonder if my background has caught up with me. I recall writing an article about making war against the Soviets that a zealous editor titled "Eat Death, Comrades." From inside his glass booth, a young passport official listens on the phone and coldly studies me. I rock on my heels until he puts down the phone and without a word returns my passport and visa. Then comes Jan's turn and he stares at her with equal seriousness until she leans forward and they are practically nose-to-nose against the glass. Jan tips her head and grins. Her vivacity is irresistible and the man's mouth curls upward. He ducks his head below a wood partition and a disembodied hand slides Jan's paperwork to her.

The Soviet Union does not stamp foreign passports. It transacts business with a three-part visa collected prior to departing the USSR, leaving a visitor with no official record of the journey. When I phoned the Soviet Embassy in London and questioned the procedure, I was referred to the Consulate from where a woman told me, "It could be that certain countries do not want their nationals to have the stamp in their passport." I asked which countries. She said, "I do not know. We do not keep a list."

For the ride into Moscow, Jan and I sit near the front of the bus and the Russian driver turns, smiles, and greets us with 100 decibels of Bruce

Springsteen being born in the USA. What do the British passengers think? Driving along a six-lane highway through what appears to be a forest on the outskirts of Moscow, we see an automobile perhaps every quarter mile. Traffic increases slightly when we reach the built-up area. I ask the bus driver why most cars use nothing but parking lights, and he says, "Only automobiles of high-ranking officials are permitted to turn on headlights."

Our hotel is the Rossia, an enormous structure with, we are told, 1000 rooms. Bordering the Moscow River, it sits across a broad avenue from the Kremlin. The idea of sleeping a hop, skip, and jump from ground zero momentarily unsettles me. Such a thought never fazed me in an American city. Having studied our War Orders, do I too fully understand my nation's violence?

By the time we eat dinner it is midnight and snowing.

Jan's eyelids droop. "I'm ready for bed," she says.

I ask Peter, an Englishman we had met at dinner, if he cares to take a walk. "Think we're free to?" he says. A jolly, dapper man, four years from retiring, he eagerly anticipates the day when he can call it quits.

We bundle up and set off at a vigorous pace through thick snowflakes, walking down the middle of empty boulevards. Looking over our shoulders to study the psychedelic paint job on Saint Basil's and the gold domes of the Kremlin cathedrals, we jostle each other.

"Think they're real gold?"

"Not solid."

I explain to him how Thais coat statues of Buddha by pressing on small squares of 22 karat gold foil. "It's like lighting a candle in a catholic church. The gold square is to remember someone who's dead. Or for making a wish."

We reach Lenin's Tomb. Under floodlights it appears squat, lacks the enhancing perspective of a low-angle camera, the view I know from newspaper photographs and television cameras.

"You sure this is Red Square?"

In the dark it, too, looks smaller, narrower than expected. We compare landmarks with what our memories have stored from second-hand views and agree we are in the right place.

Peter and I circle the Kremlin, a long walk on a cold, wet night. A large illuminated red star tops a spire on each corner of the old fortress. We pass pairs of patrolling soldiers and solitary stationary sentries dressed in fur hats, belted greatcoats, and glistening boots. All stare but none speak. No other civilians are on the street. Snow piles up on our hats and shoulders. Peter relates his experiences as a seaman in the Royal Navy. We discuss the merits of squash racquets. And then we find ourselves back at the Rossia, home again, as safe as if we had circled Buckingham Palace. This definitely is *glasnost*.

In our room, Jan has already fallen into a deep sleep. In the middle of what remains of the night, a large group of drinkers serenades our side of the hotel, singing *Yesterday* in broken English. The hotel is primarily occupied by East Germans and Soviets. What do they think of the singing?

A few days later, when passing the Red Army Museum, our guide says, "On display are many World War Two weapons that were used for fighting between the Soviet Union and West Germany."

In the queue to view Lenin, I end up among a crowd of East Germans. Only tour groups are permitted into the tomb on this day. However, an Intourist official has granted me written permission to enter as an individual. Jan had called my visit "corpse cruising" and made her own arrangements elsewhere. Except for me, everyone in the queue has a partner.

I am half a mile from the tomb entrance, and the queue stretches another half mile behind me, when a stocky woman marches swiftly from the end of the line, passing hundreds of people, and halts alongside me. She greets me with a burst of words that sound like Russian and pairs up with me. Dressed in a black babushka, a black cloth coat frayed at the collar and cuffs, and thin-soled black shoes, she carries a knitted red handbag. She reminds me of Khrushchev's wife. In my new clothes—tweed hat, heavy tweed jacket, wool sweater and pants, leather gloves, and stout English walking shoes—I smile and shrug. Has the woman mistaken me for someone who speaks her language?

A guard leaves his post and sternly addresses the old woman in Russian. She responds in kind, matching his tone of authority. The guard glares, talks low and menacingly to her. Impetuously I put an arm around the woman's shoulders and say, "My mommy." The guard gives me an expressionless glance and fires a clip of words at both of us before returning to his post. The woman studies me. I wink and she soothingly pats my arm like a real mother. We are more than likely the same age.

A bride appears at a gate of the small park near which we wait. Her wedding dress is a spotlight of white against the noon grayness. Holding the arm of her new husband, the bride walks to the memorial to the Soviet Union's unknown hero, places her wedding bouquet beside the memorial's eternal flame, and pauses for a long moment. Is she wishing, perhaps praying, that her children never will know war?

The predicament of being trapped between a grandmother and a bride makes me happy. Are these the enemies I dreamed of vaporizing?

In addition to walking abreast of a partner, a visitor to Lenin's tomb has to button his coat, remove his hat, and keep his hands out of his pockets. A hundred yards from the entrance, soldiers search women's handbags and, if they choose, frisk men. No cameras are permitted. Inside the squat but massive building, sentries enforce silence, condone not a whisper.

Lenin's body rests underground. After passing between a pair of armed guards who stand as rigid as temple dogs at the tomb's entrance, a visitor walks down two shallow flights of stairs. Tight-jawed soldiers in brown greatcoats line the walls along the visitor's route, give directions with sharp gestures and reserved shoves. Everything in the tomb is constructed from black granite. Somber lighting fades as the visitor descends. The shadows deepen and the guards grow invisible, but they materialize when a visitor lags a step behind or drifts mere inches out of line. The visitor enters the viewing chamber from behind and to the right of the embalmed body.

Bathed in a celestial light, Lenin lies with his right hand closed in a worker's salute. His high-domed head is preternaturally clean, glows saintly white. His neatly trimmed beard is golden red, more like the shadow of a beard than a beard itself. His face is set in a relaxed expression. I imagine his last words: "It is accomplished." He rests in peace.

Visitors shuffle in a U-shape path, gazing trancelike into the crystal box that holds Lenin. The only sounds are a pulse of breathing, the rubbing together of thick winter clothes, and the rasps of shoe soles on stone. My Catholic boyhood training pops out of somewhere long past and I momentarily await those ahead of me to genuflect when they pass before Lenin's closed eyes. Lasting less than a minute, the viewing ends too soon. The visitor is directed up broad steps toward daylight, is waved outside into an overcast afternoon.

Passage through the tomb has altered my vision: I see everything in shades of gray, as if life has been drained from the people and the city. I feel an unfocused anger. I feel tricked, too. The colorless world appears fake. Turning in a circle, I search for the living golden domes of the Kremlin. Instead I see a gigantic red flag streaming arrogantly in the wind. I feel enraged, cheated by the solemn but artificial pilgrimage just completed.

After leaving SAC, I instructed at Air University, the only ivory tower within the USAF subculture. For four years, part of my job was leading seminars on ideologies—comparing democracy and communism. I developed a fondness for communism. In the classroom, historical dia-lectical materialism and its logic of thesis-antithesis-synthesis transcended the reality of "us against them." Comparing forms of government was a purely intellectual transaction, a series of evolutions from point A to point Z. In theory, communism became more appealing to me than any religion. Utopia offered heaven on earth. When I verbosely championed communism in its purest form to my students, I was championing the philosophical possibility of eternal happiness for mankind.

Now in the gray and red Moscow afternoon, I stumble and find myself speechless. The idolatry of Lenin's tomb has choked my lungs, made my eyes burn, hangs stagnant in my mind like tobacco smoke in a den of thieves. Did I actually view the man whose goal was to make all men equal? Wasn't Lenin the one person who supposedly had no vanity? Would he approve of the use made of his body? Hatred for the Soviet rulers who followed Lenin pounds like a hammer in my chest. Empathy for the millions of working class citizens that had been betrayed by the apparatchiks wells inside me, dissolves my fragile intellectual innocence.

Guards call out and gesture, direct me to close ranks along the sidewalk that leads behind Lenin's Tomb. There I pass busts and graves of boss comrades who came after Lenin. This plot is out of bounds to visitors except when they are departing the tomb. Now is my only chance to see this area, but guards do not permit loitering. Viewing must be accomplished on the move. I grow irritated by the procedure, want to stop, to study, to learn exactly who is buried here. Seeing Stalin's face among the busts disappoints me: he allowed no man to be happy. Then I feel greater disappointment, a sense of defeat, because no memorial to Khrushchev is in sight. The omission represents a final insult to the peasant class, I think, and shake my head at my simplification of complex issues.

Khrushchev's boasts and threats live in my memory. Had he been motivated by Soviet power or by fear of superior American strength? If the latter, then was it only now that the Soviets considered themselves equally armed and therefore able to negotiate disarmament? And if that were true, then was the history of Western intelligence networks nothing more than a history of overestimating Soviet strength?

I pass more gravestones embedded in the Kremlin wall, with names written in Cyrillic. One of the East Germans says, "Gagarin." For some men a single name is enough. Another voice says, "John Reed." I stop looking and move forward as if finishing a forced march. In the near distance I see the brightly painted domes of Saint Basil's and colors beyond gray and red return to my world.

Crossing the square near GUM (the famous department store), I overhear a young man in a "Penn" sweatshirt say to two companions, "Did you see the bayonets those guards were carrying? They were sharp! Man, they were scary." The others nod in wide-eyed agreement.

I want to shout, "Can't you see beyond the tip of the sword?" Instead, in a final burst of cynicism I ask myself, "Am I searching too deeply?" Does no synthesis to my anguish exist?

My musing leads to the confession of a terrible fact, something that an astute reader has already acknowledged: I played the Cold War game in SAC and later flew more than 900 assorted sorties in the Vietnam War without a political orientation. I filled a warrior role to gratify my ego, to thrill to the power and the glory of destroying, to become omnipotent, to grow god-like in a godless world. I knew that if SAC ever played the game for real to its unquantifiable conclusion, a few thousand men would kill millions upon millions of people, and I wanted to be among the few thousand. Why did peace-loving citizens provide arms for men like me? In the moment after the sun touched the earth at Hiroshima, why didn't national boundaries evaporate? Why didn't sane men of all nations unite for their own survival?

In Vietnam, and especially in Laos where we were shot at every night, I didn't hate my enemy. He was too necessary. Without him I was nothing. At that time I discerned that opponents on a battlefield had more in common with each other than with any groups from their own societies—particularly their political leaders, but I was too firmly hooked by the excitement of destruction to change my behavior.

My social enlightenment had evolved over the past dozen years, since I stripped off my uniform. In that time, while writing three novels about the military as I experienced it, I learned that growing from a boy into a man was only half of life's cycle. A man next had to become a human being. There was much to learn, and it was not easy to become sane.

Each day in Moscow offers another step toward enlightenment, a lesson in group dynamics. While part of Air University sensitivity training as an observer who was not permitted to speak, I often spent five emotion-filled days in a room with a dozen junior officers who interacted by discussing each other's personalities. The Moscow days become equally draining as I, unable to speak the language and committed merely to reading body language, wander about the city. In the midst of the 70th anniversary of the glorious Bolshevik revolution, people appear to be going nowhere, doing little, sharing nothing. It happens in slow motion. It seems as if in the next moment the entire city will stop and go into hibernation. The plodding pace becomes infectious, creeps into my bones and permeates my spirit. The comrades' clothes are functional, fashionless, funereal in color. I see a solitary woman dressed in matching fur hat and coat and boots with patterns blending so perfectly they appear to be a single garment. Her fur is as light and soft as angel's hair. I follow her at a distance. She strides purposefully, imperially. Others lower their eyes when she passes them. She radiates authority.

Amid the crowd each day, I find it more difficult to generate enthusiasm. I am not alone. Without prompting, Jan says, "I couldn't live here. Nobody smiles."

At the Moscow Circus, Jan grows fascinated by the audience. She watches the spectators rather than the performers. She whispers, "They're deadpan. Are they afraid to warm up? Shouldn't there be at least a flicker of smiles? I mean, this is fun."

I have no time for the audience. The circus dazzles me with its simplicity. No wild animals, but lots of clever acts: human feats of strength and balance, surprising humor. Much credit for the show's success belongs to a multi-talented ringmaster-clown who makes three hours pass like 30 minutes. The show's epic finale nearly unravels all that came before, however. A group of dancing women are balancing a large globe of the world overhead when the houselights dim and hooded aggressors riding motorcycles equipped with missile warheads roar into the arena amid clouds of smoke, flashing searchlights, whooping sirens, scattering and falling bodies. Chaos is boss until the aggressors disappear in puffs of smoke, as if vaporized; triumphal music plays and the lights come up. I say, "The good guys won," laughing at the blatancy of the finale's message.

The audience stifles a yawn.

"They've seen it before," Jan says. "A hundred times."

In the market place, the principal product is resignation.

For example, a group of women wordlessly hip-check and shoulder each other, jockey for position rather than queue to buy fresh flowers at a kiosk across the square from KGB Headquarters. Making it to the narrow kiosk window demands no small feat of strength, resembles a task such as pushing through the Chicago Bears' defensive line. However, when the women emerge from the scrimmage clutching their purchases, they display, as Jan says, "Not a flicker of satisfaction." Their expressions remind me of a club prize-fighter who has won another tough but insignificant battle, a fighter who knows the same wage-earning struggle awaits him every time he steps into the ring.

Prices are high with little to buy. Grocery stores that were formerly mansions intrigue Jan. Overhead crystal chandeliers, carved friezes, paintings on the ceiling are lusterless with grime. Marble counters contain messy piles of salted fish, tins of fish, bread, cheese, butter, or margarine. Bread is inexpensive: 13 kopecks for a large loaf, perhaps a kilo. A token amount of fresh fruit is on display: desiccated apples, wrinkled oranges, and pomegranates costing three rubles each—about five dollars. In the butcher shops, red meat is in short supply. What looks like rib cuts of beef are topped by three-inch slabs of fat. The counters display some fowl. Chickens are blue-skinned, breastless, bony. Strewn helter-skelter, scrawny ducks are casualties of a cartoon collision: head, beak, wings, and webbed feet intact, but featherless.

Queues are shorter than I expected, but denser. The waiting people close ranks tightly. The longest lines stretch outside the liquor stores, which now remain closed until two in the afternoon, after people have put in a day's work.

Sidewalk vendors appear haphazardly throughout the central area. Taking up half the sidewalk, women stand silently, wait patiently for someone to buy their wares: potatoes, ground meat, Soviet-made blue jeans. Potatoes sell quickly. In half-kilo packages, the ground meat moves slower. People mill around the blue jean vendor, but while I watch he makes no sale. A pair of jeans costs 70 rubles—$125, based on the official exchange rate. A block from Red Square, a young man sells unadorned copper bracelets on the same corner every day, drawing good crowds. He crouches over his small display stand, exhibits his stock with quick movements, eyes his customers with shifty glances. His hyper-furtive manner makes me feel that each time I see him will be the last.

The state tolerates freelance vendors.

The intensity of the policeman role played by soldiers appears whimsical away from Lenin's Tomb. When they want to be, however, the soldiers become world-class harassers. Seeing a pedestrian place one foot outside a crosswalk, they whistle the transgressor back into line. When a sidewalk becomes crowded, they stand in the gutter to make sure pedestrian traffic doesn't overflow into the street. Their actions are pure hassle because there are practically no cars.

Sightseeing, I turn into a path used by other civilians. Two soldiers curtly stop me before my second step. In my mind I outrank them and I wave a hand in the direction of those who have gone before me. The soldiers shake their heads, point in the direction from which I came. We repeat our messages in more emphatic sign language before I accept there is no recourse. After walking a block out of the way, I catch up with the civilians I had been following.

I think back to a time in Washington, D.C., when a plain-clothed security agent appeared from nowhere and scolded me because two children and I were flying a kite along the National Mall. "Reel that in and get out of here," he said. I ignored him and he got into my face. "I told you, 'Reel that in and get out of here.'"

"Why?" I said.

"This is the flight path for his helicopter."

I scanned the empty sky and pointed out that no helicopter was anywhere in sight. "The sky belongs to all of us," I said.

"Not this part. This is the flight path for his helicopter."

"Who's 'his'?" I said.

"You know who," he said. "Now do what I say or I'll arrest you."

I slowly reeled in the kite but couldn't resist muttering, "Jesus, for a minute I thought we were in the United States—land of the free."

Who was I to complain? I had played the guardian policeman role in a duty called *Chrome Dome*. Provocatively patrolling an international beat two or three times a month, my six-man B-52 crew took off from Texas with four nuclear weapons and flew for twenty-four and a half hours, waiting for a message that would unleash us against Soviet targets. We had a single purpose—a single goal—and all the logic in the world could not have altered our behavior. Power made fools of us.

In the USSR, tourists have rank predicated on money. They are permitted into Beriozka shops where prices are lower and goods available in greater quantity, primarily luxury items such as furs and brandy not found in public stores. In a Beriozka, buyers must pay with foreign currency—American dollars and British pounds preferred. Soviet citizens are not permitted to possess foreign currency, which presents no problem to Soviet citizens because they are not permitted inside a Beriozka either.

However, a black market operates based on foreign currencies.

Rubles cannot be brought into or taken out of the Soviet Union.

In an evening outside our hotel, young men approach tourists in hopes of exchanging money. They offer two rubles for one pound sterling or three rubles for two American dollars. The official exchange rate is a few kopecks more than one ruble for one pound sterling. Jan and I are approached by a clean-cut group of men who look to be in their late teens, whose clothing would have made them indistinguishable as foreigners on a Big Ten college campus. The leader says, "You want to exchange money?"

"All right," I say. "Eighteen for one."

"What?" The young man leans backward. "Sterling? Dollars? What?"

"Green American dollars. One for eighteen rubles. That sounds fair to me."

The man grins broadly. "How about seventeen?"

"Seventeen fifty," I offer.

"It's a deal." He reaches into a pocket. "How much you change?"

"Three thousand."

His eyes sparkle. "A deal. Right now." He shakes the hand inside the pocket. "Let's do it."

Off to the side, one of his friends translates for the slower three. They laugh.

"I'll give you a credit card number, you give me a check," I say.

"It's a deal." He raises his eyebrows. "But my bank is not open for a few years."

His friends hoot.

"Where did you learn to speak English so well?" Jan asks.

"From Bruce Springsteen records," he says and breaks into a gravel-throated rendition of "Born in the USA," throwing in hip bumps, rejoining his group that is drifting away but singing along with him.

"Wait," I call. "Does one of you want to guide us on a tour of the Metro stations?"

A voice says, "Hey, I already been there."

Several shout advice.

"You don't need a guide."

"Take the Circle Line."

"Follow the signs."

"But we don't read Russian," I say.

"Look at the map."

"Match the letters."

"Hey, it's easy."

The Metro proves everything while proving nothing. On our last night in Moscow, we await a train to return to our hotel when a Red Army major in uniform greets us with both hands held palms up in front of him. He asks, "Americans?" He is my size, a middleweight. He has a thin scar on his left cheek, a ruddy Slavic face not unlike mine.

I reach out and grasp his empty right hand. Jan later tells me, "I thought he was going to offer directions. It surprised me I was so wrong. Then I thought he knew you. Why did I think that?" Earlier in the week, while waiting to cross an intersection near Gorky Park, a woman spoke to me, said what sounded like, "You Polish?" I said, "My grandfather was." The woman spoke rapidly in Russian to her companion. He addressed me in English. "I apologize. She thought you were our friend. We haven't seen him for long."

Am I Everyman?

The major says, "When were you born?"

"Nineteen-thirty-three," I tell him.

Jan says, "Forty-seven."

"Where?"

"Texas," Jan answers.

"Pittsburgh," I say.

The major focuses on me. "Oh, Pittsburgh. Good. A busy city." He moves closer. "We all are young." He exhales deeply and a sweet odor of alcohol surrounds us. He stands tall and announces, "I am a military man."

Responding to the challenge, I say, "So was I. I flew for the Strategic Air Command. In B-47s and B-52s."

Buried underground in the subway, we face each other like life-long comrades. The major has questions about our hotel, people on tour with us, our itinerary. He urges us to visit cities in the south, concluding, "It's best."

And now comes a man that smacks of fiction. One expects to find such a character in parody. In reality, however, he is there. From the moment the major approached us, a gaunt man in a black leather trench coat trailed him. When the major and I shook hands, the shadowy figure reached out and touched the major's arm as if to restrain it. When I mentioned SAC, the shadow's angular face showed contempt.

I invite the major to our hotel for a nightcap, and the shadow says, "Nyet," adding a string of advice. The major waves a hand as if to make the shadow disappear. Then we shove aboard a train. Jan finds a seat. We three men stand. The major and I chat. The man in black scowls, turns his back on us, then edges closer to listen. A young soldier watches the interplay, barely keeping a straight face.

I inform the major Jan and I had spent a few days in London before flying to Moscow, that we live in Salisbury, and that we would soon be visiting Spain. With a wistful smile he says, "London."

We reach our stop, but the major does not get off with us.

I walk backward from the train. "Wait," my mind shouts, "we have not spoken of Afghanistan, Vietnam, peace in our time."

From the platform, I see the man in black lecturing the tight-lipped major.

The young soldier is grinning.

★ ★ ★

Visiting the Soviet Union—particularly Moscow—was an experience Jan did not want to live through again. She did not recommend going there to anyone. She saw Moscow as a city with eight million citizens and one smile, and you couldn't take a number for the smile. Each person got it for two and a half seconds on his or her birthday, unless some bureaucrat wanted it first. My thought on the subject related back to Vietnam where strangers smiled at me; on the darkest days somebody could be found laughing in public.

A guidebook claimed Moscow had two million visitors every day. Despite knowing this, Jan claimed we were targeted everywhere we went, that people in the street looked first at our shoes, and then they stared, some curious and some hostile. "But what did you expect?" I asked her, knowing it was an unanswerable question.

Every English couple we met had no desire to return to the USSR. But everyone was pleased to have made the trip once. On the far side, a lone Scotsman was on his ninth tour. Was Scotland actually that fucking bad?

For eight days in the Soviet Union, Jan and I heard the word "No" more times than in the rest of our lives combined. And we had to take "No" for an answer every time. For example, the Moscow hotel's food was so inferior that two fish meals went untouched by the people on our tour. I complained to the guides and was told that we were getting "fair ration" and that "the menu is set" by a higher authority and "cannot be changed." The quality of food was not an item for discussion.

We were free to roam the city unescorted.

A view along the Moscow River reminded us of a section of downtown Chicago. It disappointed Jan that older buildings were allowed to deteriorate. Large chunks were missing from walls and every structure needed a fresh coat of paint or a healthy cleaning. For the most part, churches were empty or being used as museums. A guide explained it was difficult (too expensive?) to repair the old mansions and buildings, virtually impossible to restore the interiors, and therefore the government planned to preserve only the facades. Were government administrators satisfied by creating another Village Potemkin? Churches used for religious purposes were not permitted to carry out repairs, and no new churches could be built.

To Jan's way of thinking, the facades with nothing behind them symbolized the USSR. However, to me, the Moscow Space Center was more representative of the nation's progress. Super-tech satellites were displayed inside a large, unheated building, more like an enormous tin barn with an uneven concrete floor. And it was standing room only. The master plan: Keeping up with the Americans.

On the other hand, Moscow's Metro was cleaner than the average kitchen. We toured the dozen main stations ringing the city and did not see one piece of litter, not the tiniest scrap of paper. Babushkas drifted through the Metro corridors, endlessly sweeping invisible dust. The Metro charged one fare—five kopecks for any destination. The stations were beautifully decorated, except for the newest where the money obviously had run short. The Metro's art—murals and friezes—was heroic social realism.

To Jan's eyes, the art, particularly the statues in the squares and parks, was too aggressive, too forward thrusting, nearing life threatening.

On our tour were two long-haired and bearded male nurses from Glasgow. They were about 25 years old and worked in a ward for terminally ill cancer patients. Their keynote was total irreverence. Their patter kept things in perspective, let in large shafts of light from the West. At the summer palace in Pushkin, when the tour group entered an enormous, breathtakingly ornate room, one of the nurses spotted scaffolding in a far corner and said, "Ah, I see they have a Henry Moore, too." In another delicately painted room, I noticed the two nurses silently counting the ceiling art of women and angels; as we left the room, one of them reported to me, "For sure, that was a forty-two-tit room." The lilt in their voices made anything they said humorous, even their constant use of "fook."

We traveled from Moscow to Leningrad by overnight train, in a compartment shared with a British couple. The accommodations were crowded, but the cramped quarters produced the good-natured air of a slumber party. In general, conditions improved upon reaching Leningrad, which strongly resembled a Western city. Compared to Moscow, the streets had no soldiers. Heavy motor traffic created rush-hour jams. The people dressed better, moved livelier, and appeared to enjoy life. The shops offered far more goods.

Jan and I played "Wow" and "Gee whiz" for a whole day in the Hermitage and Catherine's Palace. At the same time, we were saddened to see that modern paintings hanging in the Hermitage were not preserved and were exposed to direct sunlight. Van Gogh's works were cracking and chipping. We wondered why the Soviets didn't sell them. Were they not truly thought of as "art?" On the other hand, the French Impressionist paintings the Soviets own were neatly displayed in the comfortable Pushkin Fine Arts Museum in Moscow, a facility much like a Western gallery.

Wandering through the Hermitage, Jan kept whispering, "Murderous bastards." I was too amused to ask whether she meant the czars or the communists.

The Leningrad Circus was more artistic than the Moscow Circus but not as entertaining. We decided that dancers who failed to make the ballet ended up in the circus.

In Leningrad, our hotel housed large groups of Finns who drank all day and all night. Finland practiced prohibition, but Soviet booze was nearby and inexpensive—not by our standards but by theirs. In the mornings, Finns could be found sleeping (passed out?) in the hotel hallways, even in the elevators. Basically, Finns came to Leningrad and seldom left the hotel, which had five bars that stayed open around the clock. Other than staggering and falling down a lot, the Finns didn't bother anyone.

In retrospect, I would return to the Soviet Union. I would focus on people, rather than on places and things. I've read Koestler and Kafka, Zamyatin and Orwell, Solzhenitsyn and the lot. I long ago recognized no answer satisfied everyone. I would have liked to meet the men who were planning to kill me at the same time I was intent on destroying them. The joke was on us: we more than likely were going to die of old age.

★ ★ ★

Four years after our visit, in December 1991, the 15 members of the Union of Soviet Socialist Republics dissolved into the Commonwealth of Independent States. Damn. It looks like all of those nuclear weapons will go to waste.

CHAPTER 14

Way Out of Step

Operation *Desert Storm* in 1991 changed me into a turncoat. Writing under the pen name Dan Forgan, I produced "Out of Step," a weekly anti-war editorial for the left-leaning *Austin Chronicle*. Unrestrained by Editor Louis Black, I ranted against America's making war. My initial column—"Ready for War"—opened with overwrought finger pointing:

> It's a bright cold day in January, the clocks are striking thirteen, and Saddam Hussein is an "insane motherfucker who snacks on unborn babies at teatime." The enemy boss is always a beast. Ask Winston Smith.

From there I preached against how our government portrayed enemy leaders or other opponents as immoral beasts. I supported my thesis by telling about classified briefings I had attended from the fifties through the seventies, wherein intelligence officers had sneeringly detailed the sexual weaknesses of Mao, Fidel, Che, Tito, and whatever other foreigners threatened democracy. They unabashedly reported on the private habits of Martin Luther King the Younger as if sex was the decisive criterion for approval. Their nifty secret tidbits came from the CIA and FBI. Where else? Listening to them, I had an urge to ask, "Are you jealous? Guys in this room have more in common with the enemy than with our supposedly pure leaders." As we have repeatedly learned, our pure leaders were not pure. The intelligence officers had paid special attention to Nasser, an Arab. They told us:

> Nasser is a syphilitic. Almost all Arab males of his age have syphilis. They acquire it either congenitally or, as young men, contract it from prostitutes. National

poverty prevents proper treatment. Usually there is no treatment. Therefore, five to thirty years later, the syphilis reemerges in an advanced stage. Nasser, who is forty, now shows signs of tertiary syphilis. As a result, his political activity runs in cycles. When he's well he works constantly, feels he must get ahead or make up for lost time; when he suffers attacks he is incapacitated by lack of concentration and impaired judgment.

The briefing drill was nothing less than Orwell's *1984* Two-Minute Hate, government-approved 100 percent character assassination. I vividly recall it because the stories were a first in real life, at least for me. I wrapped up my initial diatribe in a fever nearing insanity.

If you've been reading between the lines, you've probably guessed what happened to me. I failed to learn to hate my enemies. Instead, for example, Khrushchev delighted me. When he banged his shoe on the table at the United Nations I rocked in tempo to his "fuck-you-world" attitude. He responded to threats like a muzjik (Russian peasant), a man with whom I could identify. Hadn't I been told he was a drunkard and vain? Therefore, didn't I have more in common with him than I did with the overly wealthy, saintly Catholic icon JFK? Sure, I balanced megatons of firepower on my fingertips, but in reality I was a lowly lieutenant living in a two-bedroom, thousand-square-foot duplex, and still wearing suits from my college days.

Was it then I developed a subliminal warped psycho-polisci-economic philosophy and began to recognize that the battle isn't between democrats and communists? Nor is it between Christians, Muslims, Jews, and Buddhists. The honest core of conflict is between the haves and the have-nots. Permit me an aside. Years before the Soviets let down their Wall, their eight-foot-tall infantryman had already been replaced as the American poster enemy of choice. At least that's the way our Marines were taught to view the world. Their universal foe had become the wild-eyed Arab shortly after 200-plus Marines were blown up in their Beirut barracks.

It took me a long time to complete my adult education, including close to three years as a player in the Vietnam theater of the absurd. How does one get across the simple lesson I learned? In war the people who are most similar to each other are the people standing face to face on the battlefield. When will those opponents wise up and throw down their weapons? The common enemy is the leadership from both sides that sends those poor ignorant bastards off to war.

If history is a book of dreams, the latest chapters have been nightmares.

In their daily briefings, had our intelligence officers been cleverly looking ahead? To clarify the thought for *Chronicle* readers, I characterized our new poster enemy the following week by writing:

The Ruler of This Game
Let's pretend...
1. You're the leader of a nation that's half the size of Texas.
2. Vastly superior enemy forces surround your nation, so much so that you could say the whole world is against you.
3. Your supply lines are cut. Barely a trickle gets through. However, your population is inured to living on short rations.
4. Your political allies have abandoned you, at least temporarily.
    Ready to surrender?
    Before you answer, hear this...
5. The majority of the people who surround you are infidels. Surrendering to them is equal to surrendering to the devil.
6. Although your enemies will bomb you relentlessly, odds are better than even that they will not invade your nation. They want neither a protracted ground war nor the headache of administering your population.
7. Your principal enemy is deeply concerned with world opinion and strongly desires to appear humane. So who are you?
    Of course, you figured it out: You're Saddam Hussein.
8. And the rules are...?
    None. There are no rules except for the ones you make up.
    Months ago, before the shooting began, speaking theoretically, I told my friends, "If it comes to war, I'd rather be on the Iraqi battle staff. Think of it. Think of the freedom. No limit to how many men you can lose. No rules of engagement. No rules at all. Anything goes."
    Today my thinking has become reality.
    Saddam Hussein has shown that he is above international law. If you don't believe me, ask him. He'll tell you that his actions are justified. If you were in his place, wouldn't you act the same?
    The causalities will come. They're inevitable. They're the one certainty of war.

★ ★ ★

I read and read and anything a touch beyond the ordinary sufficed to trigger my outrage. The next week a short newspaper blurb sent me into the following orbit:

Toys for Boys.
On the stairs of a gallows, a Fascist sore loser supposedly said, "One day the Bolsheviks will hang you Capitalists with the ropes you sold them." After a barrel roll of the brain, his words align nicely with the Knight-Ridder News Service lead: "In the Persian Gulf war as in no other war, arms sold by the allied manufacturers are aimed at allied troops."

The 1991 list of Iraqi Toys for Boys runs on and on:

Tanks: British Chieftain. Soviet T-72. Soviet T-62.

Missiles: Soviet Scud-B. French Exocet. French/German HOT. French Milan. Soviet SA-3. Soviet SA-6. Soviet SA-7. French Roland. U.S. Hawk.

Airplanes: Soviet MiG-29. Soviet SU-25. Soviet SU-24. Soviet MiG-21. Soviet MiG-23. French Mirage F-1.

Bunkers: British designed. German built.

Assorted gasses by Germany.

Assorted mines, shells, bombs, bullets, barbed wire, and bayonets from a host of nations.

That much firepower adds up to big business. The business requires no conscience. What man can read the trademark on shrapnel that's ripping through his guts?

Around '87–'88, there was a day when Mikhail Gorbachev paused to chat with Margaret Thatcher while flying west for a conference with Ronald Reagan. I was living in England then and, reading the prevailing winds of peace, I persuaded myself that Maggie would announce her nation's unilateral nuclear disarmament, thereby setting a positive tone for the Gorby-Ron conference. I imagined a Nobel for Maggie. After all, I told myself, the United Kingdom had no need for nuclear weapons. Nobody wanted to sink its anthills. The weight of immigrants would do that soon enough. I was convinced that if death threatened to rain from the sky, John Bull could comfortably hunker under Uncle Sam's umbrella.

My hopes had been vestiges of earlier dreams that had longed for the United States to unilaterally scrap its thermonuclear stockpile. It wouldn't have mattered if the Soviets fried us the next day. I wanted to bask in the purity of doing the right thing—to stand before the world totally free.

Not long ago, the US and USSR agreed to dismantle a few dozen IRBMs [intermediate-range ballistic missiles]. The timetable for taking the things apart (mobile launchers included) stretched to nearly four years. Explain to me how a four-man team of high school dropouts can turn a stolen car into an empty tin can in the time it takes to watch a Toyota commercial, while the world's greatest engineers need a month or two per machine.

It takes a long time to do whatever you don't want to do.

I have a friend who designs warheads for cruise missiles. He has worked at the task for more than a decade. He is the gentlest man I know. He is divorced and remarried; he has been my friend since 1970 and in all that time I never heard him speak one unkind word about his first wife. That fact alone qualified him for sainthood. His children love him. My wife thinks he is a prince.

Did I mention that he designs warheads?

He learned the trade in the Air Force, was hired by industry the minute he retired. Design is his fascination: how to best penetrate six, twelve, eighteen feet of concrete, or six, twelve, eighteen inches of steel? What's the biggest possible bang from the smallest possible payload? Conventional or nuclear, he comes up with answers. He's the gentlest guy I know.

My friend has more intelligence that the University of Texas student body, and he can't see what he does. But he has 20/20 vision for his paycheck.

Anyone here know how to educate people to stop the proliferation of arms, conventional and nuclear?

The same as any enthusiastic reader, I know that Reagan missed a blockbuster opportunity to begin significant arms reduction because his henchmen, I mean advisors, failed to anticipate such possibilities prior to his Reykjavik meeting with Gorbachev. Furthermore, Commander-in-Chief Bush refuses to sign an agreement to end nuclear testing. He reasons that as long as the world has thermonuclear weapons, the US must continue to improve its stockpile.

Is it possible that the buck stops at the top?

It took me half a lifetime to clean up my Toys-for-Boys thinking. I recognize that, like a member of Alcoholics Anonymous, I'll never be totally cured. Sometimes I still lapse and display a killer-elite mentality.

One recent night, while talking to an engineer who had been out of college for about a year, I asked, "So why don't we take the money for weapons and spend it on old people who are alone and freezing in fire traps? How many old ladies would one ICBM [inter-continental ballistic missile] keep warm?"

The young engineer shrugged. Wasn't his problem.

Like a guided missile, my mind streaked back two decades. The infra-red and low-light-level television channels of my brain glowed with convoys of trucks ablaze along the Ho Chi Minh Trail, boats sinking in the Mekong River, two-thousand-pound-laser-guided bombs flashing downward like thumb smears, obliterating anti-aircraft gun emplacements. The Nintendo function overrode the logic channels of my brain and my mouth played the inane background noise of the Warrior Game while I said, "Who gives a shit, right? Fuck those poor old ladies. The weapons are too much fun to give up."

The young engineer laughed at my heartlessness.

Or was he laughing at Man's eternal folly?

One of the Menningers from Topeka wrote a book in which he preached, "If man cannot create, then he can destroy. In that manner he gains a feeling of omnipotence."

Let's remember that today's war is largely about reducing the Iraqi weapons stockpile to a heap of junk. Call our action a war of checks and balances.

By the way, has anyone checked Syria's stockpile lately? Could our present friend Hafez al-Assad be the next domino pusher? Is he another "Hitler" who's waiting for the right moment in history to turn on us? He still has 40,000 troops in Lebanon. Will the US—with our all-volunteer Rent-an-Army for protecting Germany, Japan, et al.—end up having to defend an unarmed Iraq against his aggression?

The war ended. We won and broke megatons of other people's property in the process. Did lives matter? I strove to elevate our nation's success with an upbeat critique.

After the Ball.

Hip! Hip! Hooray! Victory is total for the USA. We won the Gulf War. US consumers still pay only a dollar a gallon for gasoline. Hang those freshly won streamers from the battle flags, boys. And hear this, world: Our president is no wimp.

By the age of fifty every man gets the face he deserves, an adage tells us. Eventually, every nation gets the government it deserves, according to my daily journal.

My history profs taught that a nation's fundamental objectives are supposed to be the security and welfare of its citizens. Now that the US has provided for the security of the citizens of Kuwait (not to mention Grenada and Panama) can it finally turn its thoughts to home? Does anyone find it amusing that the US peace dividend was squandered on a war?

A few days ago on National Public Radio, South Bronx mothers were complaining that drug dealers had taken control of their neighborhood and were hawking drugs of choice on every street corner. How come we can't send a few troops from the Big Red One (Motto: If you're going to be one, be a Big Red One!) to kick ass there?

I believe our all-volunteer army would be adequate for the task. Staying busy justifies its existence. They are World Class Warriors, and in my mind a World Class Warrior possesses the following attributes:

- A desire to be in combat after experiencing combat.
- An ability to ignore personal safety, a feeling of immortality after witnessing the mortality of others.
- Knowledge of one's equipment to the point that it becomes an extension of one's body, or one's body becomes a part of the machine.
- Being young at heart.
- An overpowering will to win, an almost certain belief that one will win, that one cannot be defeated.

Undoubtedly the coalitions force possessed such attributes, particularly the last three. The fighting wasn't intense or prolonged enough to fulfill the first two completely. Coalition forces also had virtually limitless technological superiority and absolute control of the air. In a set piece battle against such a force, an opponent is playing only with pawns.

Iraq's soldiers recognized that they faced such a dilemma. I admired them for surrendering often bloodlessly, usually without a fight. Perhaps they knew how the US operates. Within six months, the clever ones expect to have either small business loans or big contracts for writing their life stories.

Was Iraq a rerun of *The Mouse that Roared*?

From watching the North Vietnamese play the peace role wrong, Iraq's leaders at least should have learned that all they now have to do is say "We're sorry" (they don't have to mean it) and the US will guiltily rebuild their nation. Given time, the West will re-arm them.

Because everyone saw that superior toys work exactly as described in the catalog, international arms marketers should become richer than ever. At a lower level, good guys appreciate that the toys worked as designed and helped them to do the good stuff they did in the face of danger.

The real winners of the Gulf War are the soldiers who are still alive, regardless of their allegiance. For most men who've been in combat, life gradually returns to its normal patterns, but the victory of survival is a continually amazing personal realization.

Sixteen years after I last returned from Vietnam, I was contentedly cruising down the interstate in a 300Z when "Yellow River" unexpectedly poured forth from the car stereo. I hadn't heard the song for a long, long time. It delivered such an overpowering flood of overseas memories that, before it ended, I had to pull off the highway to cry without wrecking the car. You see, I once again was just so fucking unbelievably happy to be alive.

★ ★ ★

Securely implanted in my *Chronicle* editorial pulpit, I expanded my victory celebration with finger pointing stabs to find criminals among the war survivors. My ardor blanketed combatants in general and failed to identify specific crimes perpetrated by either side before or during the war. I wrote:

FYI

For crimes committed in the Gulf War, persons can be tried under the articles of Geneva Convention Relative to the Protection of Civilian Persons in Time of War, 12 August 1949. Traditionally, war crimes have had an international character, having been committed by a member of the armed forces of one nation-state against either the armed forces or the civilian population of another nation-state.

The ultimate responsibility for war crimes lies with a nation's leaders. Geneva Convention Article 144 states: "The High Contracting Parties undertake, in time of peace as in time of war, to disseminate the text of the present Convention as widely as possible in their respective countries, and in particular, to include the study thereof in their programmes of military and, if possible, civil instruction, so that the principles thereof may become known to the entire population. Any... authorities, who in time of war assume responsibilities in respect of protected persons, must possess the text of the Convention and be specifically instructed as to its provision."

Article 4 defines protected persons as "those who, at a given moment and in any manner whatsoever, find themselves, in case of a conflict or occupation, in the hands of a Party to the conflict or Occupying Power of which they are not nationals."

The Convention has sharp teeth.

"Article 27. Protected persons...shall at all times be humanely treated, and shall be protected especially against all acts of violence or threats thereof... Women shall be especially protected against any attack on their honour, in particular against rape, enforced prostitution, or any form of indecent assault.

"Article 32. The High Contracting Parties specifically agree that each of them is prohibited from taking any measure of such a character as to cause the physical suffering or extermination of protected persons in their hands. This prohibition applies not only to murder, torture, corporal punishment, mutilation and medical or scientific experiments... but also to any other measures of brutality whether applied by civilian or military agents."

Article 33 prohibits pillage.

Article 34 prohibits the taking of hostages.

Article 146 puts the bite into the convention. It obligates a "search for persons alleged to have committed, or to have ordered to be committed, grave breaches, and shall bring such persons, regardless of their nationality, before its own courts." Article 147 describes grave breaches as "willful killing, torture or inhuman treatment, including biological experiments, willfully causing great suffering or serious injury to body or health, unlawful deportation or transfer or unlawful confinement of a protected person...."

Will a valid authority please take control here.

★ ★ ★

My concern for mankind took a twisted journey through the pros and cons of killing and the pain involved in the process. The journey offered a history lesson that harks back to the opening chapters of this book. Enthralled with attempting to identify parties responsible for international chaos and death, I neglected to point a finger at myself for causing pain and destruction through warfare. Is it too late for me to say "I'm sorry" and, if not, would my expression of sorrow be sincere? Otherwise, I am nothing more than a predictable product of our militaristic environment whose mind is not his own, a malady that grows more prevalent as reflected in the behavior of our citizenry and our leaders, both elected and self-appointed. Perhaps that psychology has evolved into a world-wide epidemic. Whichever the case, I disgorged this argument for my *Chronicle* fans.

Unnecessary Suffering

Recently a woman complained to me about the cruelty of western nations, their impulse to make war. She was a tiny woman, beautiful, fragile. Although she looked sorely offended, her words were tentative. She was American-bred enough not to indict Commander-in-Chief Bush or his henchmen with her charges.

Carrying a full dose of insensitivity, I gave her a knee-jerk, machine-gun response. "Hey, why limit it to the west? Look at the eastern nations. Japan and China haven't had a historical honeymoon. Mongolia goes way back. Thailand and Burma, India and Pakistan. All the Arab states. The whole bunch has a history of not getting along."

As if searching for an escape route, her eyes looked everywhere but at me.

I rethought her plea, then asked, "Do you dislike the western nations for making war or for the way they make war? I can see how you'd be upset by the sophistication of weapons, the intensity of firepower, the totality of it all."

Her eyes focused on mine.

"The humorous part is that after western minds developed more efficient weapons to expedite the killing process..."

She winced at my word choice.

"...then those western minds turned around and wrote international laws to regulate the killing."

"It's not funny," she said. Her face was a mask of resignation. "Why did they have to make the weapons in the first place?

"To rule the world. To make money," I thought, but my mind was on the laws.

I returned home, dived into my books, snorkeled straight down to the Hague Convention No. IV, Respecting the Laws and Customs of War on Land, dated 18 October, 1907. These rules still govern today's plan.

A footnote to the full English text warns that "...the only official text...is the French text which must be consulted and accepted as controlling in the event of a dispute as to the means of any provision of these particular conventions." Can you picture it? A guy in the crosshairs shouting, "Stop. Hold it. Wait, wait, wait. Before you shoot me with whatever-the-fuck-that-is, does anyone here read French?"

A cynic might delightedly point out that among the Sovereigns and Heads of State who sent Plenipotentiaries to the Convention were the President of the United States and His Imperial Majesty the Shah of Persia.

"Regulations Respecting the Laws and Customs of War on Land" contain fifty-six Articles broken into chapters such as The Qualifications of Belligerents, Prisoners of War, The Sick and Wounded, Spies, Parlementaires, Capitulations, Armistices, and Military Authority over the Territory of the Hostile State.

My favorite passages come from the chapter titled "Means of Injuring an Enemy, Sieges, and Bombardments." Therein, Article 22 states, "The right of belligerents to adopt means of injuring the enemy is *not unlimited*." Article 23 tells us "...it is *especially forbidden*... a. to employ poison or poisoned weapons; b. to kill or wound *treacherously* individuals belonging to the hostile nation or army... e. To employ arms, projectiles, or material calculated to cause *unnecessary* suffering...." (italics mine).

As you see, Article 23 expands 22. For example, "means of injuring the enemy is not unlimited" indicates that you can kill the bastards all day long, but it is "especially forbidden" to poison them. Does "*especially* forbidden" have the connotation of "*very* dead?" Is it like telling a delinquent teenager that if he keeps using that shit, he's going to get into *real* trouble? We must remember that grown and supposedly sane men wrote and signed these laws. Not a mother, sister, or daughter was in the crowd.

Let's review the history of gas in warfare since World War I, when about fifty different chemical agents were used by the French (who started it), British, and Germans (who escalated from tear gas to chlorine, a choking agent).

In 1925, along with 129 other nations, the United States signed a Geneva Protocol "for the prohibition of the use in war of asphyxiating, poisonous, or other gases, and of bacteriological methods of warfare." Following that agreement, Spain used poison gas on Moroccan rebels (1925), the Soviet Union used chemical weapons on Muslim insurgents in China (1934), and Italy used poison gas on Ethiopian soldiers and civilians (1935-36). Except for Japan's use of poison gas and biological weapons (bubonic plague) against the Chinese (1937-45), World War II was free of the use of gas. The Eisenhower Administration stressed the use of incapacitating rather than lethal qualities to the US chemical arsenal. In other words, tear gas was acceptable; nerve gas and anthrax were to be used only at the discretion of the president. Gas was not used in the Korean War. In Vietnam the US used tear gas-type agents to clear tunnels and underground bunkers; it also used herbicide sprays. In 1969, President Richard Nixon ceased the production of biological weapons while reserving the right to "retaliatory use by the US of chemical weapons and agents." On an international level, the Biological Toxin Weapons Convention forbade the production or stockpiling of biological weapons in 1972. In 1975 the US Senate got around to giving its advice and consent to the 1925 Geneva Protocol. For the invasion of Panama the use of tear gas was approved by the Pentagon; its use also has been approved in the Persian Gulf. Since 1975, US production of deadly gases has fluctuated in accordance with the nation's perception of Soviet capabilities in the field. During that period, according to intelligence reports, the Soviets have employed poison gas in Laos—through communist intermediaries—and in Afghanistan. In the '80s, Iraq used chemical weapons against Iran and against its own Kurdish minority, and Libya reportedly used chemical weapons on Chad. In 1990, Bush and Mikhail Gorbachev agreed to the progressing destruction of chemical weapons. By 2002 the US and USSR will reduce their stockpiles to only ten million pounds of deadly gases each.

Do you get the idea that the applicable paperwork regarding poison gas is a joke? I'd like to know the last time that one of the men who negotiate the treaties suffered a whiff of gas.

The beauty of Hague IV can't be fully appreciated without US Army Field Manual 27-10, the Law of Land Warfare, which elucidates the Articles. I'll allow the Manual to speak for itself as follows.

"What weapons cause 'unnecessary injury' can only be determined in light of the practice of States in refraining from the use of a given weapons because it is believed to have that effect. The prohibition certainly does not extend to the use of explosives contained in artillery projectiles, mines, rockets, or hand grenades. Usage has, however, established the illegality of the use of lances with barbed heads, irregular-shaped bullets, and projectiles filled with glass, the use of any substance on bullets that would tend unnecessarily to inflame a wound inflicted by them, and the scoring of the surface or the filing off of the ends of the hard cases of bullets.

"The use of explosive 'atomic weapons,' whether by air, sea, or land forces, cannot as such be regarded as violative of international law in the absence of any customary rule of international law or international convention restricting their employment.

"The use of weapons which may employ fire, such as tracer ammunition, flamethrowers, napalm and other incendiary agents, against targets *requiring their use* is not violative of international law. They should not, however, be employed in such a way as to cause *unnecessary suffering* to individuals." (Again, the italics are mine).

It appears to me that there are usually *people* among the targets "requiring their use." I've never been hit by a flamethrower or by napalm—or a fuel bomb—but I can't image not feeling "unnecessary suffering." In fact, being struck with a most regular shaped bullet probably hurts like hell. A paper cut takes my breath away.

Have you noticed that the weapons sanctified by FM 27-10 are the type that mainly the US uses on opponents? I'll tell you, seeing my thatch hut fried in napalm would sure make me want to rub shit on my barbed-headed lance before I next ran it through an enemy.

Is it possible that these international laws and their interpretations are designed to keep the warrior caste enslaved? With rules and a quasi-humaneness, national leaders provide the hope (or in the case of virgins to combat, an almost blind belief) that the individual will somehow live through the battle, will survive the worst.

What if nations tossed out all the rules? What if nothing were forbidden? What if conflicts were permitted to grow to an intensity in which agonizing death was inevitable? What if they have a war in which everybody got killed? Then, finally, might nobody come to the next one?

★ ★ ★

In "Unnecessary Suffering" I mentioned that "in Vietnam the US used tear gas-type agents to clear tunnels and underground bunkers; it also used herbicide sprays." I was remiss for not expounding on the destructiveness of the sprays, particularly *Agent Orange*, which caused more long-lasting pain and suffering than any weapon employed in the war. With it, America damaged enemy troops, innocent civilians, its own soldiers, and the environment in horrific numbers and manners at the time and for future generations. The majority of *Agent Orange* victims have already died without adequate recognition or compensation and the remainder are close behind them. The absurdity of the program is that it was as destructive to ourselves as to those we opposed. When people cannot find recourse within a government that is killing them, and it is their own government, then any inkling of democracy as we know it has disappeared. When the same victimization extends to the world at large, mankind grows perishable and the perpetrators must be punished. None of that has happened. America's debt in this regard is incalculable and unpaid.

The *Chronicle* column that made me proudest linked my generation with a young man that could have been my grandchild. I wrote:

Death and Duty

The afternoon of 16 January, the day that Commander-in-Chief Bush attacked Iraq, my neighbor's son came to my door. Let's call him Michael. I've known him since he was in Third Grade. His reserve Marine company had been activated. "I thought you could give me some advice about what to expect," he said. Looking into the distance, he lowered his voice. "You know, I mean about combat. You've been there, done that."

I should have told him, "Don't go." Since the Vietnam War, I've repeatedly thought through events of my lifetime and have concluded that the bravest men from that conflict were those whose convictions allowed them to be sent to prison rather than to serve in the military. In my mind, that act took the most courage, violated the greatest number of our society's taboos.

I knew that tall, blond, muscular Michael wouldn't accept that advice, wouldn't begin to understand how to live such a life.

We drove to the Broken Spoke saloon and dance hall. I bought him a beer. We settled into a booth. "I've been thinking about it a lot," Michael said, "what it's like to come under fire."

"It's not so bad," I told him. "The first time's the toughest. You get used to it in a hurry." What more could I say? Didn't each man have to learn it on his own? Time had reduced the private winds of war to puffs of ego in my memory.

"It's going to be—I don't know—if we invade Kuwait," Michael said, "I mean, there'll be frontal assaults..." His voice trailed off. He sipped his beer, then said, "Going into Kuwait'll mean house-to-house fighting. I don't want..." He left his wish adrift on the beery air. "So what do I need to know?"

"Remember all of your training," I said.

As if I'd asked him to recite the periodic tables from high school chemistry, he frowned. I practically read his mind: "But that was stuff that was taught years ago. You expect me to know that now?"

I ignored his expression. "Believe me, if you remember all your training, you're not going to encounter a situation that is totally unfamiliar. Training's the starting point. Based on what you see once you get over there, use your imagination, think yourself into the worst possible situation, then work out what you're going to do, how you're going to act in that situation. Always think ahead."

It dawned on me that if Michael was worrying about frontal assaults and house-to-house fighting, he already was doing what I suggested. I reinforced the idea. "Talk to the guys around you. Work out situations with them, before they happen. Figure out the best way to meet a challenge before you come face to face with it. And, afterward, after you've been in action, talk over what happened, figure out ways to do things better. You have to work like a team. You have to talk to each other." Was he listening? I wondered. Was he hearing? Did I sound too much like a football coach?

My deepest thoughts centered on survival. "Michael, once you get over there, you have to concentrate. Think about what you're doing all the time. And make sure the guys around you are just as focused. Look, think of yourself as on another planet. When you're there, nothing else matters. Forget about the world back here. Don't worry about whether someone's taking care of your dog. Don't think about what your girlfriend's doing. Forget you have parents and friends. If they're worried about you, that's their problem. Put those distractions out of your mind. There's nothing you can do about them anyway. When you get back everything will sort itself out."

I hesitated. How, in a minute, could I explain a philosophy of survival, a value for life that I had been refining since before Michael was born? I tried. I said, "There will be impossible situations." I know that the Marines teach their troops to fight for each other. Read the records: It's Marines who get the Medal of Honor for falling on grenades to shield their buddies. "There'll be times when you can't do anything," I said. My mind warned, "Don't get killed trying to save somebody who's already dead," but my mouth didn't speak the words. Instead, I told Michael, "It's not the movies. There's not always something clever you can do."

"I know it's going to be tough," Michael said. Then he stammered a string of clichés. He recited the litany about fighting men not wanting war, about their knowing how terrible war is. He mouthed the "However..." He spoke of being tested, confronting the enemy, proving oneself. It was more than I could listen to because all I heard him saying was "I want to kill somebody." I can hear between the fucking lines.

Why didn't I scream in his childish face what I truly believe? When I was your age I thought that killing was power, that a warrior's death was the only death. I was insane. If otherwise, then why did I go back to Southeast Asia a second and third and fourth time? Now I know, regardless of which side you're on, the only winners in a war are those who are alive in one piece when the fighting ends.

Instead I said, "I know what you're going through." I stared into his eyes. "All I can say is that I hope you don't have to go into battle." It wasn't the message he sought.

While writing this, I wonder if my advice is outdated. Today's military forces are all-volunteer. Doesn't that automatically mean total personal commitment to the cause, right or wrong? I was a lifer, an officer. I never expected anyone to mourn my death for long. I knew a few guys like me who were killed in action; at the time, I didn't mourn for them. We were professionals. Death was part of our duty. Back then, I mentally wept for only the short-time grunts who didn't make it. They were so young, so vulnerable, so unprepared for the grimness of it all. Who feels sorry for mercenaries?

The concept of an all-volunteer machine lights the question lamp in my head: Would Commander-in-Chief Bush have dared to send draftees to fight the war?

★ ★ ★

Despite my ranting, and much to his credit, Louis Black did not censor a word of mine. In fairness, he published Letters to the Editor that challenged the logic and emotions of what other people and I wrote in protesting the war. But then, by March, the war ended. Afghanistan grabbed our attention and too soon we forgot.

CHAPTER 15

& More

The American invasions of Afghanistan and Iraq defeated me. I changed into an apolitical bystander to America's relations with foreign nations. Our leaders desired to rule the world to make themselves rich, and my voice was a shout into the abyss. My metamorphosis was uncomplicated because, from September 1991 to September 2011, as a contract laborer with no benefits, I tutored rhetoric to University of Texas student-athletes, with the final 10 years devoted to football players.

The best feature of the tutor walk-in program was that each student determined how much of my time he needed for an assignment. Within my tenure, individual sessions lasted from 10 minutes to four hours. Yes, a senior brought me a 40-page term paper at 10 pm and we argued about it until 2 am. He turned it in six hours later.

I had no authority over the students and limited responsibility beyond the moment. Therefore, I chose to play the role of friendly older person, a semi-hipster grandfather, who wanted to help them. Along the way, the players hung the title of "The Hankster" on me. A lot of the all-stars were children at heart, and maybe I was, too.

★ ★ ★

My favorite student was quarterback Major Applewhite with his irreverent attitude. In 1999, Major was named the Big XII offensive player of the year. He accomplished the feat with brains as much as brawn. No matter what hour I finished tutoring (I worked the six-to-whenever—often midnight—shift), as I walked out of Moncrief-Neuhaus Athletics Center, I invariably saw Major studying game films alone in the quarterback room. Major had a nimble mind and for that reason I was disappointed when he gave stock answers to sports reporters' questions. "Goddamn it, all the clichés make you sound like Nuke LaLoosh," I told him. "You're clever enough to give answers that show the shallowness of sports writers' questions. Man, liven up that bullshit." Major said, "I've thought about it. Funny remarks pop into my mind, but I can't say them. If I do, it's too easy to get a reputation as a wiseass, and that's a problem I don't want. It's easier to play the fucking game."

I told Applewhite, "You got your title at birth, like royalty. I had to put twelve years into the air force before anybody called me 'Major.'" Later he found a copy of one of my novels that contained a list of my medals. As a result, he told me, "In World War Two, my grandfather flew B-24s and was awarded a Distinguished Flying Cross. For the rest of his life, every member of my family looked up to him for winning that medal. He was the warrior hero of our family. So how do you think I feel when I find out my fucking tutor has eight DFCs? Jesus…!" I patted his shoulder and said, "Hey, your grandfather was in a real war. Whatever he did to win his medal more than likely took more courage than everything I did combined."

★ ★ ★

Talking about quarterbacks… Arguably, the two most successful that ever played for Texas were Vincent Young and Colt McCoy.

At Texas, Vince was a class act. He had a smile for most people. He continued to exude that friendliness when he visited campus after turning pro. He once hugged me when we met by accident in the middle of campus and passersby looked at me as if asking, "Just who the fuck are you?" To the best of my knowledge, Vince was the only Texas player to make it to the National Football League (NFL) and still remember his former teammates enough to send them a big boxful of souvenir Tennessee Titans apparel. I got a cap.

Vince definitely ran the Longhorns—especially in the 2005 national championship season. When he walked through a door, all eyes turned toward him, instantly recognized him as the Alpha Dawg. His smile lit up his entire face and, in turn, lit up an entire room. At the same time, Vince had, and enforced, his own standards. If a player failed to meet his team responsibilities, Vince corrected him, occasionally with a physical confrontation. At least one guy opted to leave school after Vince "talked" to him. Vince's leadership and his skill on the field made the 2005 team run tick-tock. In my opinion, that season's team did not need offensive coaches—Head Coach Mack Brown could have just let Vince do his thang.

From the opening game, the 2005 players seemed to take for granted they would go undefeated. By then, I had watched and sensed the moods of more than a dozen teams—under three different head coaches. Without a hint of anxiety, the 2005 squad squarely focused on each upcoming game—like the book says—one at a time. In victory, the players showed a quiet and confident smugness rather than a blatant joy. The team had a wealth of talented players supporting Vince, yet they all recognized and appreciated that he added the extra touch of magic that made them unbeatable.

Colt McCoy resembled Applewhite more than Vince. Foremost, like Applewhite, Colt painstakingly studied game film, a labor that Vincent barely found time for—or needed. Did Samson waste time by pumping iron at the Zorah YMHA (Young Men's Hebrew Association)? Along with studying film, Colt was conscientious about his class work and we spent a goodly amount of time together. One semester, he started having his dates meet him in the study facility. The women played with email or chased around on the Internet while he finished his study chores. One night, two women showed up together for Colt (his idea of a double date?), flashing hair styles and clothes like models from *W* magazine. Trend setters that would have stopped traffic in any decade from the Roaring Twenties to today, they jokingly vamped with a sophistication that awed me. I found it difficult to believe that two ladies barely out of their teens could be so knowledgeable and satirical about life. Colt seemed agitated by their humor. Now you have to understand that the night following a date, Colt asked me what I thought about his latest woman. I scored those two ladies as an 11 and a 12, which made them a 23 date. Even in New York City, I doubt that fucking Derek Jeter ever did that well.

★ ★ ★

Girlfriends attended night study hall when it was held downstairs at Moncrief-Neuhaus, located at the south end of Darrell K Royal-Texas Memorial Stadium. In 2009 the tutoring and mentoring programs moved from the cramped downstairs position rooms to an expansive academic center in a newly built upstairs wing. While we worked downstairs, along with girlfriends, women athletes dropped in occasionally to check email or to put finishing touches to a writing assignment. The occasional short invasions by a couple of long-limbed, table-grade volleyball beauties that studied strictly independently dazzled me. As the gulf between football and the rest of the world widened, women athletes were less welcome to the study area; a few months after we moved upstairs, they were banned from the football academic center. Girlfriends also disappeared after we moved upstairs.

The downstairs study area had a family atmosphere when coeds were present. Having a girlfriend sitting alongside a player accelerated the pace of his work. Girlfriends pushed players to concentrate and not waste time. They filled the roles of teachers and secretaries, assisting not just their boyfriends but other players as well. All of their effort was voluntary. This approach reflected the desire by everyone for the best learning experience in the shortest time. And then we all go home and party? Student-athletes had a good time while learning. What more can any educator want? In comparison, the new upstairs academic center—as modernistic as possible—became more like a concentration camp, with rules to enforce rules and punishments to enforce them, during my final two years on the job.

★ ★ ★

Teaching student-athletes how to improve their writing generally boiled down to teaching them how to improve their thinking, and part of teaching students how to think included teaching them how to win their teachers' attention. Humor helps, I preached and emphasized opening sentences that grabbed a reader's imagination. Tien Van Nguyen, a walk-on linebacker and cousin of Texas A&M and Dallas Cowboy star Dat Nguyen, took my advice to the limit. He began an essay with "I never owned a dog of my own, but I've eaten several." His instructor loved it.

★ ★ ★

From a purely academic perspective, the most capable student-athletes were those who had a parent that taught school. They had had basic grammar skills drummed into them and recognized a coherent argument, but they were not necessarily overly motivated to perform to the maximum of their academic ability. Tight end Dave Thomas perfectly exemplified that group. I ragged him for not busting his ass in class like he did on the field. He told me, "You sound like my mother [a teacher]. All I need is a C." I continued to pursue him and, almost reflexively, David made the academic honor roll every semester.

Plain hard work helped, too. I ranked Jamaal Charles as the Longhorn most determined to succeed academically based on my 20 years of teaching student-athletes. Although he turned pro after three seasons, in his first two years on campus, Jamaal met with tutors every—yes, every—study hall night and put in three or four hours of book work. Limas Sweed ranked a close second behind Jamaal. The two of them took the maximum advantage of everything the program had to offer and both earned academic honors, which required a 3.0 GPA.

Cory Redding got the last laugh when it came to being bitched at for not putting enough effort into writing. "You can't play football forever," I said. "What if you end up owning a business that requires you to write letters, or directions, or policy papers?"

"I'll hire somebody like you to put it all together for me," Cory said.

The ability not to study and still pass was a badge of honor among players. At the end of one semester, a couple of linebackers scoffingly turned in still-shrink-wrapped textbooks and boasted that they scored a

2.0 GPA. When I suggested they could have done better, they stared at me as if to say, "Who needs it?"

Swimmers—who I saw only the first half of my tutoring career—took a different slant with me. They brought in A-quality papers with the intention of turning a 90 into a 98. Swimmer Brett Stone—God rest his soul—sought 100s, and he occasionally got them. Tennis players and golfers were close behind in a quest for perfection, often visiting me more than once for the same essay. I believe that athletes in non-team sports—meaning that their performances are independent of support from a teammate—possessed a greater desire for perfection in academics compared to football, basketball, and baseball players.

Track Olympian Leo Manzano also sought to over-achieve academically. For hours he labored over essays before discussing them for more hours with me. Along the way, he encountered a teaching assistant (TA) prone to making mistakes as simple as confusing further and farther. The TA took points from essays based on his own ignorance. Lee's near-perfect essays received low Bs and high Cs. I convinced Lee to copy pages from grammar guides to educate the TA, but the TA ignored what Lee offered him. After the third essay, we bundled his semester's work and his advice to the TA with the TA's critiques, and Lee presented the package to the department head. For the semester, Lee got the A he merited.

★ ★ ★

Because tutoring was a walk-in program conducted one-on-one with no time or frequency of visits limits, I had opportunities to offer students the benefit of learning from failures I had brought upon myself throughout life. In other words, we talked about issues related to problems with parents, girlfriends, coaches, teachers, or life in general. Sidetracks usually happened when a writing assignment touched on aspects of life that students puzzled over. I couched my advice, derived from my mistakes, in the form of an experience I had watched another person go through. My advice began with "Let me tell you about a friend of mine who…"

I cut no corners on one topic: I personalized drinking booze. I have told numerous students, "If I had one thing to do over in life, it would be to never take a drink of alcohol." If they asked why, I gave them chapter and verse. Believe me, I have a history filled with personal fuckups unsuitable for all occasions.

Students presented problems that reflected suffering outside of my sphere of knowledge. For example, while discussing police corruption in New Orleans with Derek Lewis, I said, "Your paper would have greater impact if you could describe an encounter when cops screwed you or somebody close to you." Derek said, "Like when I watched the police shoot my uncle dead in our front yard because he didn't go in the house like they told him?" That fact triggered a series of heart-to-heart talks.

I had no association with professors and minimal interaction with coaches. Therefore, a player who confided in me was assured his problem was safe from exposure. Talking to me did not put him at risk academically, athletically, or socially. A wall of the cubbyhole where I taught held a poster with a silhouette of a squatting bull dumping a load inside a red circle with a slash that graphically announced, "No bullshit in this room."

Academics could have benefitted from more involvement by coaches. The only football coaches that showed interest in study hall were Duane Akina and Bobby Kennedy who occasionally dropped in to give encouragement to defensive backs and wide receivers. Otherwise, bouncer-size mentors like Ty Williams and Octavious Bishop filled a first sergeant role in controlling student-athlete attendance and behavior, but their limited authority had nothing to do with grades.

★ ★ ★

No matter how tall or heavy, a player shrunk to my size when we sat shoulder to shoulder for a study session (I confess that, in my first year of tutoring, Blake Brockermeyer and Dominic Bustamante—six-five and carrying 300 pounds each—staggered my imagination when they arrived at study hall side-by-side: the door simply wasn't wide enough).

A classic encounter with a big guy took place when Casey Hampton sought help for a freshman essay. Studying his bulk, I said, "You're not as big as people say." At the time his weight was an issue and the coaches were happy because he recently had brought it down to 320. "I'll bet you don't weight twice as much as I do."

He looked me over. "Bet I do. How much you go?"

I carried exactly 160, which would have made the bet a draw if I had admitted it, so I said, "One sixty two."

Casey winced. "I had you beat when I got here. Now I'm 320. You win."

I told him the truth—that we tied—and he shook his head. "You lied? Man, teachers aren't allowed to lie."

He was wearing a sweatshirt that had the sleeves cut off at the shoulders, and his right deltoid had a tattoo of a bulldog wearing a derby and spiked collar, chomping a cigar, and holding a smoking Thompson machinegun in each hand.

I pointed at the tattoo. "My dad used to say, 'When I go, I want to go with a gun in each hand, a cigarette between my lips, and all three smoking.'"

Casey showed no reaction.

"Nice picture," I said. "Where'd you get it?"

"Around home. I don't want to talk about it."

"You get it all done at the same time?"

"Yeah. I don't want to talk about it."

"How old were you?"

"Fifteen. Listen, I don't want to talk about it."

"When your mother saw it, what did she say?"

Casey winced again. "Now that's what I don't want to talk about."

I seldom worked with Casey after his freshman year. He was one of the people obviously destined for a National Football League (NFL) career. Guys with his personality type quickly got their shit together in ways that gave them maximum independence. In other words, they identified the critical academic requirements and fulfilled them as quickly as possible with minimum effort, thereby allowing themselves to concentrate the remainder of their time and energy on football.

Leonard Davis exemplified this approach to school work. He showed up at study hall around 11 o'clock at night, about the time when everyone else had finished studying, and quietly did his homework alone. I suspected he took a nap following practice and dinner, giving him the advantage of attacking schoolwork with a refreshed mind.

Leonard ranked among the biggest of the big. I was a guest coach on the field for the 1996 Texas-Notre Dame game—which the Irish won on a last-play-of-the-game field goal—when Leonard walked out along the sidelines in street clothes as a high school recruit. The Notre Dame players paused in their warm-ups and nudged each other in awe. Granted, teenage Leonard was only six-five and 350, but he carried his size like a much larger man.

Leonard seldom spoke. But when he was on a computer and things developed not to his liking, he burst out with over-the-shoulder comments concerning what must be done to satisfy him. The difficulty inherent in Leonard's pronouncements was that his deep voice rumbled—like a diesel idling—and muffled his words. Rather than repeat himself, he seemingly lost interest in his complaint and ended up ignoring the situation. Major Applewhite told me a story related to Leonard and diction.

Against Baylor, Major called a "Menu-seven," a pass play that required Leonard to block straight ahead. The playbook also contained a play called "Seventy" that required Leonard to pull and lead a run to the left. On executing the Menu-seven under discussion, Leonard pulled, leaving his hole open, and a linebacker charged through the gap and flattened Major. Texas gave up the ball on downs.

Trotting off the field, Major looked up at Leonard and said, "I called a Menu-seven on that play where I almost got killed."

Leonard looked down and said, "Sounded like you said 'Seventy.' You want to be successful in the huddle, you better learn to speak more distinctly and coherently."

Reconsidering the incident, Major said, "Who gives a shit, right? It's only one play. And I'm still alive."

Another big guy that amused me was a classmate of Casey—Shaun Rogers. He conducted himself as if he were the Sultan of Brunei. Women flocked to serve his needs. For his rare study hall appearances, three or four petite packages of sweetness surrounded him, performing chores such as summarizing required reading, searching the internet, typing, or fetching soft drinks. Shaun preferred the easiest path. For example, if a game's outcome wasn't on the line and a play didn't come his way, Shaun would not chase after it—an approach he altered in the NFL.

The study hall night I am least proud of involved another big guy, Roy Miller. During his sophomore year, after I had given all the help I judged necessary for him, Roy asked another tutor for advice. You see, Roy and I had collaborated on all of his writing assignments in his freshman year, and I thought he now was capable of doing everything on his own. I told the other tutor, "Roy's being lazy. Don't help him." Roy and maybe a dozen other people overheard me. He took a deep breath before turning his back to me. The next day I apologized to him until my eyes bled. That happened in 2006 and it still bothers me because Roy ranks among the most sincere and socially conscious players to come through the program. He has performed uncounted days of voluntary work with soldiers from Fort Hood.

Let's finish our talk about size with a poem. An otherwise forgotten walk-on expressed his reaction to big guys with the following observation for an English class.

FLIT
Streamlined Leonard Davis is truly Goliath.
But bulky Marcel, Octavious, Casey, Shaun, Antwan
Any of a dozen others
Could play that killer Philistine, too.
Reaching seven feet in helmets and cleats,
With padded armor each tips the scales
At a fifth of a ton,
Sprints his mass fourteen miles an hour.
Even getting backed over by a truck at that speed hurts.
These mammoths teach my freshman mind new views of
High school physics: Mass x Velocity = Pain.
Their wide-load jerseys display high numbers.
Sixties and Seventies proclaim strength.
Me? I wear a single digit—1.
Last season, I was 4. Am I fading away?
At 150, 5-8, I flit among this army of giants like a gnat.
Like David's flimsy slingshot, speed is my only weapon.
A tenth of a second difference lets me live in their war zone.

I shit you not, the kid came up with Goliath and Philistine and the formula for pain on his own.

★ ★ ★

How about them running backs? I never tutored 1998 Heisman Trophy winner Ricky Williams—John Mackovic recruited Ricky, Mack Brown gobbled up the coaching accolades connected with Ricky's senior year of glory—but I frequently watched Ricky enter the Belmont Learning Center, sit down and type what he needed, and then go on his way, all without talking to anyone. He was contented with an entourage of two friends.

After four years of Ricky's record-breaking performances, Texas relied on Hodges Mitchell for running duties in 1999 and 2000. Mitchell weighed 190 and stood five-seven—a Barry Sanders look-alike with a few of the great one's moves. In Hodges's first two years on campus, I worked with him and learned he was a conscientious and humble person with a low-key sense of humor. He had sat anxiously on the bench for two years, watching Ricky do his thing, which pretty much humbled anybody who longed to carry the ball.

In his junior year as a starter, Hodges gained over 1300 yards rushing and nearly 350 receiving, establishing a new level of achievement among Longhorns. Against Oklahoma, he carried 30 times for 204 yards and a touchdown. Texas won 38-28. Hook 'em!

Nearing the end of his senior year, with another thousand yard performance in the book, Hodges dropped by to talk over an essay. We were alone in study hall and, out of nowhere, I said, "You're my wife's favorite player. She thinks you're Superman."

"Tell her 'Thanks,'" Hodges said and asked, "What about you? Am I your favorite player?"

I hesitated too long as other stars flickered through my mind.

Looking at me from the corner of an eye, Hodges said, "You didn't expect me to be as good as I am, right?" He lowered his head, looked embarrassed. "Forget that remark," he said.

"Why? You spoke the truth. I admire you for it. I'm honored that you shared your feelings with me."

"So I'm not your favorite?" he said, and we laughed.

Hodges graduated on time with a degree in business. He stayed away for 10 years. On his first trip back to campus in 2011, he told me, "It's too hard to watch a Texas game and not be able to play—to contribute."

Cedric Benson—I hope he's hearing the angels sing—impressed me because of the way he shifted gears his junior year. I had watched him play in high school, and he had been devastating. In the three consecutive state championship games his Midland Lee High team won, he scored 15 touchdowns. His senior year, he could have beaten Westlake with just a center to snap the ball to him.

Cedric arrived at Texas and rode the bench for his first four games, which I considered an insult to his talent. He did too. He asserted his independence by signing a contract with the Los Angeles Dodgers and playing A-level baseball over the summers. After two years, he focused solely on football. Before his final season with a Dodgers farm club, he told me, "I'm getting the rhythm of hitting. Learning what to look for. I expect a great year." At the end of the season, having batted 200, he said, "Fast balls weren't a problem. I hit them. But curves ate me up." He started training twice as hard for football, stepped up his academic efforts. At mid-season of his junior year, he again stepped up the pace of his workouts and studies, brought greater energy to everything he did.

Cedric and I had several heart-to-heart talks in his junior and senior years. I told him a story running back Juan Kemp had told to me in 1992, a time when a few Texas fans still bragged that their 1969 squad was the last "all-white" collegiate national championship team. John Mackovic arrived as the first Texas head coach that didn't have a previous affiliation with Texas or at least a Southern background. Juan told me that Mackovic scheduled a team meeting to introduce himself to his players, but when he walked onto the stage in the Longhorn meeting hall and looked at the players, he said, "Something's wrong here. Fix it and I'll be back." He walked off the stage. The players looked at each other, trying to figure out what he meant, until one of them said, "Maybe we should mix it up," meaning that the team was sitting divided—blacks on one side of the center aisle and whites on the opposite side. The players shuffled around and integrated the room. Mackovic returned, looked over the players, and introduced himself.

The story brought tears to Cedric's eyes. He said, "That's the kind of coach I want to play for."

* * *

I am not a psychologist, but based on 20 years of quiet conversations with athletes, I have decided that no matter how famous they become, black players still do not feel they are appreciated as human beings. They believe the dimension of their stature is defined by their athletic skills alone. And that is not enough. Cedric Benson was a poster child to validate my thinking. His problems were based on what he viewed as disrespect from whites, especially white authority figures. He rebelled in self-destructive ways. The great light-heavyweight boxing champion Bernard Hopkins feels the same as me. "It's what you have and what you represent, not who you are," he said.

Again, based on 20 years of quiet conversations with football players, I believe the problem begins with the recruiting process. Texas players unanimously agreed Mack Brown was a masterful salesman. Repeatedly, players have described to me how Brown smoothly blended into their families on recruiting visits, focused on the parents, convinced them their sons would become part of a caring family if they sent them to Texas. Assistant coaches made similar promises to the players themselves. Pictures painted by the recruiting promises began to fade when players arrived on campus and recognized they had become scholarship slaves—less of an individual and totally beholden to the program at large. Players have told me that what most disturbed them was how coaches violated the most basic family concept: true parents do not abandon their children ever. The players had been led to believe that no problem on their part was too extreme for their new fathers to confront and solve. It did not happen that way.

A football team is not a democracy in regard to what takes place on the field, but it could be run democratically off the field. In 2008, a few days after the nation elected Barack Obama as President of the United States, a white Texas football letterman lost his scholarship for forwarding a racially insensitive e-mail.

University administrators deemed the disgraced player's apology as insufficient. He confessed to his own stupidity and immaturity.

What might have happened if Texas' senior players had had the option to decide his fate? What if the seniors had accepted his apology and had allowed him to remain on the squad, facing teammates he had insulted? He and they could have been challenged to examine their values in depth every day. The practicality of learning regarding racial attitudes might have transcended anything he and his teammates would have heard in a lecture or read in a book.

The unpublished truth of the entire episode is that on the night of the 2007 election, white players in study hall were unhappy when it became obvious that Barack Obama would win the presidency. Before that, many were disappointed Obama had received the nomination. Of course, blacks were delighted by the election's outcome but avoided boasting. Austin may be the liberal heart of Texas, but that feeling does not necessarily penetrate the core of sons that come here to play football from outlying communities.

The stories about Mackovic and the wayward player might sound like they are off topic, but they illustrate how responsibility could be taught. I believe Mackovic would have handled the wayward player's situation differently. When a player behaved improperly off the field, Mackovic's policy was to send the player before a court comprised of the team's seniors, according to Juan Kemp. "Players are tougher on each other than coaches," Kemp told me. In other words, Mackovic delegated authority, expecting his players to apply their own form of ethics in controlling each other; his wayward players paid a heavy price but got a second chance. In this way, the players themselves established the team's mores, became involved in determining the repercussions from life's endless confrontations: Choices—Decisions—Consequences.

★ ★ ★

Just as much as I liked Applewhite for his irreverence, I applauded Lovell Pinkney's careless approach to life. The baby of 12 children, Lovell grew up in D.C., dropped out of school in tenth grade to run his own street corner, then was dragged back to school and graduated under the daily supervision of his high school coach. At Texas from 1992 to 1994, Lovell was definitely his own man as a wide receiver. Teammates that were defensive backs described him as "a man among boys," a label they gave to Roy Williams in 2000 and Jermichael Finley in 2006.

Now is the time to discuss idiosyncrasies of receivers. Although most players looked forward to renting their own downtown apartment after a year on campus, Roy continued dormitory life as a sophomore. Everything he needed was right there on a daily basis, including a rotating roster of lady visitors. One evening, when study hall business was slow, Roy brought in a girlfriend and, at his request, I helped her to write an essay that was due the next day. Say what? No. No violation. I went off the clock. For a few years, I helped coeds who were not in the athletic program with writing assignments, often free of charge. Working with Roy delighted me because he saw the positive aspects of practically everything. Furthermore, he influenced academically needy players to seek my help.

Jermichael amused me. He set a record for the number of receptions by a Texas tight end, yet I preached to him: "They don't throw to you enough. If I were coach, I'd throw to you on every down until they double- or triple-team you, leaving somebody else wide open." My message sank in, and Jermichael delivered it to a sports writer who printed it. Mack Brown called Jermichael to his office and chewed him out for daring to challenge coaching strategy, finishing the reprimand by saying, "From now on, keep your damn mouth shut." When the sports writer heard that Jermichael had been counseled by Brown, he asked for details, and Jermichael said, "Coach Brown told me to keep my damn mouth shut." The sports writer printed that, too. I applauded Jermichael's honesty.

Back to Lovell Pinkney. Height, strength, and speed made him a superhero, but self-discipline wasn't part of the package. Under Mackovic, as a freshman Lovell was benched for missing classes. As a sophomore, a prank got Lovell barred from living in the dorm for a year along with a one-game suspension. In his junior year, Lovell was suspended for three games for a variety of missteps. Mackovic had to conclude that punishment that worked for others did not apply to Lovell. He tried an intellectual approach and ordered Lovell to write a thousand word essay on what football meant to him. Lovell brought the assignment to me. "For real?" I said. I helped him to produce the smarmiest piece of prose imaginable. In it, Lovell declared an unrestrained love for everything and everyone that had anything to do with football, the Longhorn 11, the University of Texas, the State of Texas, and the United States of America. Yeah, he drifted off topic, but who could criticize boundless declarations of "love?" Mackovic read the essay in Lovell's presence and told him to go away.

Despite multiple second chances at Texas, Lovell continued down the path of irresponsibility in his brief NFL career. Sometimes the magic works and sometimes it doesn't.

★ ★ ★

The football academic program is generous. Players who turn pro before earning a diploma are welcomed back to finish their studies because getting their degrees helps Texas' National Collegiate Athletic Association (NCAA) academic standing. Returnees receive full use of tutors and study hall facilities. In the late 1990s, I simultaneously tutored Peter Gardere, Spike Owens, and the Cash brothers—Keith and Kerry. After walking the stage, Keith telephoned me at home for assistance in writing material for his private business, which was not covered by my contract with the University. He still owes me lunches.

★ ★ ★

The same as anyone with half a brain, I evaluated plenty of NCAA rules as wrong—and still do. Question: How much help should a tutor provide for a student? My answer: As much as a student needs. A teacher should push a student to learn until the student says "Enough," and then the teacher should push a little harder. Too much help is not possible.

Demonstration-performance is a favorite teaching technique of the military services. The technique mainly pertains to manual activities but it can be adapted to teaching the skills of thinking and writing. For example, when working with a clueless student, for starters an instructor should be permitted the latitude of drafting topic sentences and then watching the student fill in the paragraphs.

Good writing requires good research; therefore, I helped students with finding information, which NCAA rules discourage. For example, I encouraged students to write about the collapse of Detroit as a viable city or the Deepwater Horizon oil spill, major problems of the time. I filled a shelf with book, magazine, and newspaper accounts of both topics and made them available to students. What I did was borderline improper, but I considered it a waste of time for students to scour the Internet for reams of information that already existed in every publication in America. While reading the entire Deepwater Horizon file, David Ash wrote three essays about British Petroleum that I considered worthy of publication.

A large NCAA problem is its refusal to permit unconventional teaching techniques in student-athlete study halls. To me, hard-core academicians miss the point. Student-athletes (particularly football and basketball players—the money earners) comprise the lowest SAT scores on campus and should be recognized accordingly. Methods for teaching them should have far greater exceptions than what is acceptable. Granted, a handful of football players, and fewer basketball players, possess remarkable academic skills and maintain close to 4.0 GPAs in difficult studies such as engineering or pre-med. They are the rare exception and even they seek help.

Student-athletes who need extra help certainly are not going to get it from the faculty. Faculty members tend to promote high ideals of learning that do not apply to ill-prepared students, and correcting major learning deficiencies is not the responsibility of faculty members, which they will tell you. I doubt any NCAA administrator has watched a student crouch over a computer keyboard and, concentrating as hard as possible, take an hour to write one paragraph—for a five-page essay. As you can see, the onus for teaching thus falls on athletic advisors to find and support people willing to spend hours and hours to drum knowledge into academically weak student-athletes.

I had daily study hall responsibility for Royal Ivy, Brian Boddicker, and James Thomas when they were basketball freshmen. We met in a private room after basketball practices in which Coach Rick Barnes worked them to exhaustion. After watching the three suffer whiplash from trying to stay awake, I began our two-hour study sessions with a 30-minute nap. When you teach, you do what you have to do.

Education is a team effort. Engrossed, and sometimes stymied by individual problems, players seldom helped each other through difficult personal situations. Playing football and partying together was near the limit of their interpersonal relationships. Center Chris Hall was an exception to the norm. In high school on his own, Chris developed strong Christian ethics that he did not hesitate to share at appropriate times.

One afternoon I saw three players who had been involved in grossly counterproductive off-campus activities waiting outside of Counselor Brian Davis's office, in line for an ass chewing. Chris sat down near them and gathered them around him. Few secrets existed between players, so Chris obviously had heard about the trio's transgressions.

Shortly thereafter, Davis came out of his office, saw the four players huddled together, walked by me, and said, "He'll reach them better than I would."

Quite a while later, after the four players had joined hands in silent prayer and Chris had finished talking, Davis stared down the troublemakers and told them, "Don't do any of that again. Get out of here."

Yes, sometimes the magic works.

Epilogue: Witnesses

Since 2014, I have reviewed more than 300 books for the *Air Power History* quarterly and the Vietnam Veterans of America *Books in Review II* (https://vvabooks.wordpress.com). The majority of the VVA books are memoirs, with a significant percentage self-published. They began as short stories used in counseling for post traumatic stress disorder. The stories contain overdoses of guilt and anxiety felt by the authors for having survived battles that killed friends.

Frequently the primary message of a book about the Vietnam War is uncomplicated: "Your job is to stay alive. This war is unwinnable and not worth your life." This often-unspoken message edges the sentiments of the most courageous men. At the same time, people who saw combat have a high degree of pride in their involvement in the war, and rightfully so.

I approach each book as if it is the first I have read about the Vietnam War. I try to ignore what I experienced in more than 800 days in-theater. I find enlightenment in reading about how people came of age in Vietnam—or long afterward—despite the fact that the horror and the humor do not balance out.

My greatest satisfaction in reading these books is that truths emerge. They pop up as innocent remarks filled with emotion. From tens of thousands of pages of reading, the following observations grabbed my attention regarding such moments for fellow veterans.

In *Content With My Wages*, Gregory Murry said, "I spent the night of my 21st birthday on ambush patrol, and I remember being pretty proud of myself for living so long."

In *The Court Martial of Corporal John Nutting*, the man himself introduced me to "battlefield gratitude": the term for watching a medevac disappear over the tree line, sorry for the guys in the bags but so grateful it wasn't me.

On one mission, he and his buddies were issued their own body bags to carry with them. "Now that was a real morale booster," David Duchesneau wrote in *Uniforms*.

Each book about Vietnam offers something new. In *The Blades Carry Me*, it was Jim Weatherill's "worry line": "the crossing point into battle—which draws itself across a person's path. Sometimes it's at the hooch door, sometimes at the operation briefing and sometimes it's attached to bullets coming up from the jungle. It's a soldier's early warning system."

Sparkles of wisdom periodically flash out of Tom Messenger's *Looking for Flyboys*, to wit: "Some guys could take a lot of trauma, which is another name for combat."

Many of Richard Udden's missions started with a helicopter assault. In *21 Months, 24 Days*, he describes them as "like hunting a mountain lion that was lying in wait for you."

Speaking from within a barricade of loneliness in *The Other Side of Me*, D.L. "Tex" Swafford said: "Madness is when the weight of the world is on your shoulders and your only escape is not to care; not to give a fuck. I could say this again and again, but at war there is no other choice but to stomach the inevitable. And the terrible reality of the whole thing is that deep down you do care."

"We were always exhausted going around in kind of a stupor twenty-four hours a day," Spec 4 Brian Richard Esher wrote in *Rolling Coffins*.

"The previous sickness in my belly turned to adrenalin and before I realized it, the firefight was over," said Richard "Doc" Kraft in *Now I Lay Me Down to Weep*.

Dr. William Zoesch said: "His brain was not going to tolerate an insult like this I thought, having seen enough head wounds of all types to last me for the next fricking millennium. His CT scan showed the bullet track through his brain, bone fragments lay where his personality once was, and then exited out through his right motor sensory strip." Zoesch wrote *The Man Who Walked 3,500 Miles to Kill Me*.

Loring M. Bailey, Jr. in *Calm Frenzy* times three:

"Just a dreary way to spend a hot, moist night, sitting, listening to your rifle rust."

"I have a new fantasy—I pretend that I'm a Belgian mercenary and this isn't my war, I just work here."

After he adopted a duckling: "When he made his pitiful little squeaks, I agreed with him."

In 1970, a booby trap killed Bailey.

"There was no time to be frightened; only to shoot well," Bob Andretta wrote in *Brown Water Runs Red*.

As part of describing a helicopter combat assault in *Walk Through the Valley*, Bruce I. McDaniel wrote: "With a rush of wind that almost knocked us over the nine choppers rose together into the air; they turned and were gone. Everything was quiet."

In *The Adventures of a Helicopter Pilot*, after checking out as an AC, Captain Bill Collier thought: "I could now live or die by my own bad decisions." And… "I don't know why we landed at that isolated airstrip, but everything was still. Still was always spooky."

Speaking of Xom Bo in *June 17, 1967*, David Hearne remembered: "When the killing started, it was slow and deliberate. They were killing us…and we didn't even know it." Hearne quoted David Aldridge: "I have never seen blood look so bright in my life. It practically glowed."

Quoting other people is an author's prerogative to make a point. In *US Navy F-4 Phantom II Units of the Vietnam War 1963–73*, Peter E. Davies cites Lieutenant Commander Ronald "Mugs" McKeown's description of a Phantom-MiG *Fresco* duel: "It's like a knife fight in a phone booth."

In *My Confessions from Vietnam*, Mark Miller wrote, "I never talked about my year in Vietnam. How could I explain to people what it was like? This was not a war I had chosen. I felt I had been a disgrace as a soldier: I had disobeyed orders, given false reports, gotten malaria on purpose, gotten a rear-area job because a friend found a way around the system, and had gotten a medal for killing a woman and a child. I would feel guilt for the rest of my life."

In *Grunts Don't Cry*, Richard Charles Martinez says, "I have laughed and cried the hardest in my life while in Vietnam. I have been so scared I could hardly move. I have done things that I can't believe I was capable of doing. War changes the person you are. I've asked my sister and anyone else that knew me before Vietnam, how much have I changed? I don't know. I hope I changed for the better."

Titles can be enough to strike a gong, to wit: *Fear Was My Only Weapon* by J. Dennis Papp, *I Came Home But It Wasn't Me* by Bruce Wm. Taneski, and *Please Enjoy Your Happiness* by Paul Brinkley-Rogers.

Everyday events were wondrous to these former soldiers most of whom were still in, or barely out of, their teens while in Vietnam. Their youthful exuberance was tempered by the realities of combat. Now they wanted people to understand the importance of survival. Their words represent a small sample of emotions Vietnam veterans share after the facts.

Dare I say: "God hates us all forever?"